AF569593

Art of Power Masterpieces from the Bute Collection at Mount Stuart

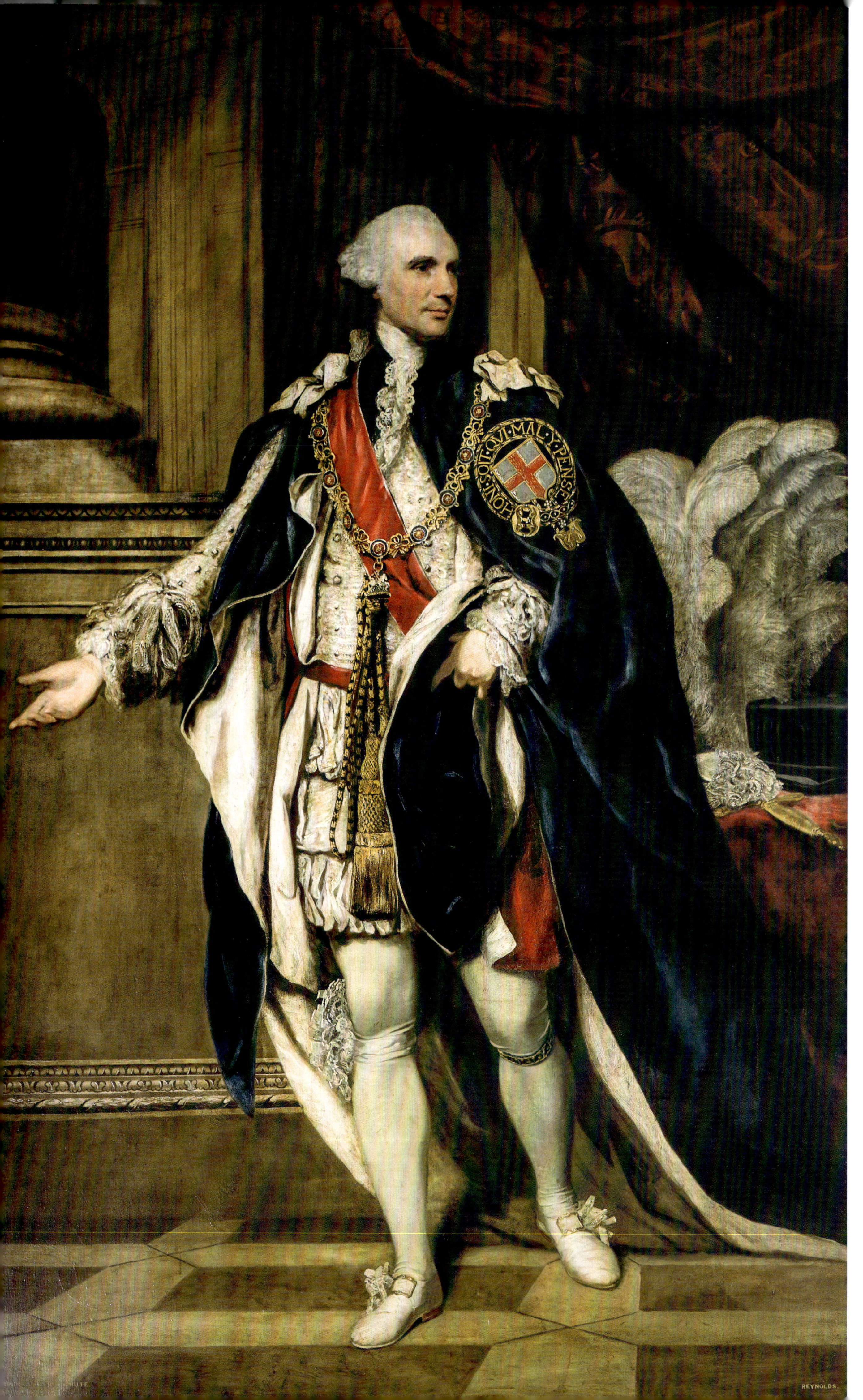
HONI SOIT QVI MAL Y PENSE
REYNOLDS.

Art of Power

Masterpieces from the Bute Collection at Mount Stuart

Caitlin Blackwell

With contributions by

Peter Black

and Oliver Cox

PRESTEL

Munich London New York

This catalogue has been published in conjunction with the exhibition
Art of Power. Masterpieces from the Bute Collection at Mount Stuart,
held at Mount Stuart and The Hunterian, 31 March 2017–14 January 2018.

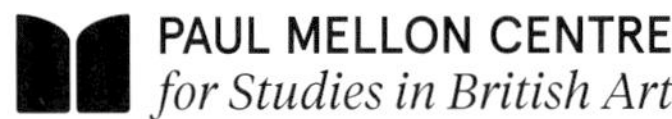

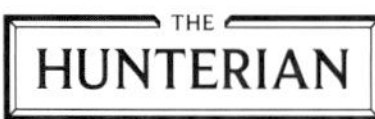

THE HUNTERIAN

Front cover Sir Joshua Reynolds (1723–1792), *John Stuart, Third Earl of Bute* (cat. 23, detail), 1773, oil on canvas, 233.7 × 144.8 cm, The Bute Collection, Mount Stuart
Back cover Joos de Momper II (1564–1635) and Jan Brueghel I (1568–1625), *Summer* (cat. 20), ca. 1620, oil on panel, 54.6 × 81.3 cm, The Bute Collection, Mount Stuart
Frontispiece Sir Joshua Reynolds (1723–1792), *John Stuart, Third Earl of Bute*, 1773, oil on canvas, 233.7 × 144.8 cm, The Bute Collection, Mount Stuart

A member of Verlagsgruppe Random House GmbH · Neumarkter Strasse 28 · 81673 Munich

Prestel Publishing Ltd.
14-17 Wells Street
London W1T 3PD

Prestel Publishing
900 Broadway, Suite 603
New York, NY 10003

A CIP catalogue record for this book is available from the British Library.
Library of Congress Control Number 2017932362

Project management, design, page layout, and colour separation Reschke, Steffens & Kruse, Berlin/Cologne
Copyediting and proofreading José Enrique Macián
Production management Andrea Cobré, Matthias Korff

Printing and binding Firmengruppe Appl, aprinta druck GmbH, Wemding
Typeface Janson
Paper 150 g/m² Condat Périgord

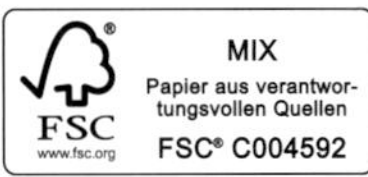

Verlagsgruppe Random House FSC® N001967
Printed in Germany
ISBN 978-3-7913-5663-1

www.prestel.com

CONTENTS

MUNGO CAMPBELL

DEPUTY DIRECTOR, THE HUNTERIAN

FOREWORD

It should come as no surprise that two of Scotland's greatest Enlightenment collections were assembled in the south of England by Scots who made their mark on British public life through their close association with the Hanoverian court in London. Evidence is scant surrounding the nature and extent of the relationship between John Stuart, Third Earl of Bute (1713–1792), and Dr William Hunter (1718–1783). Beyond their involvement in the life of the court, particularly during the early 1760s, the two men did share close associates in the worlds represented by the collections now respectively at Mount Stuart on Bute and at The Hunterian, at the University of Glasgow, perhaps most notably in their association with their fellow Scot, the portrait painter Allan Ramsay. Both men studied at Leiden, in the Netherlands. Bute, some five years older than Hunter, graduated in law; a decade later, Hunter was briefly there for medical research. The practice of science, particularly botany in Bute's case, anatomy in Hunter's, drove their collecting to their mutual interests in art. Both gathered impressive libraries which served to support the knowledge pursued in their other collections.

Hunter's art collection was never on the scale of that assembled by Bute, and it was intended to serve very different ends. Both collections are remarkable in the twenty-first century for the extent to which their respective provenances, extending over some two centuries, reflect the specific intentions of their respective collectors; in one, the continuity of lineal family descent; in the other, the continuity of purpose embodied in the public institution for which the collection was gathered. If both collections reflect the material fruits of the exercise of power in Enlightenment London, their subsequent histories both equally reflect the challenges faced by Scots exercising power within orbits of public life current in Hanoverian Britain. While Hunter had every intention that his collection function as a fully public institution after his death, that was not its purpose during his lifetime. By the same token, the astonishing pictures which are at the centre of this exhibition were not intended to act as an overt projection of Bute's public role. They were, and have remained for some two centuries, a reflection of personal taste and a source of private pleasure.

The generosity with which the Bute Collection and the Mount Stuart Trust have approached the prospect of sharing some twenty-five Dutch and Flemish masterpieces with The Hunterian and our visitors is remarkable. Thanks are particularly due to Alice Martin for her indefatigably creative and pragmatic energy as this project has advanced over the last couple of years. Along with Peter Black at The Hunterian, Alice has offered generously of her experience in supporting and advising Caitlin Blackwell, whose project this has been over the last eighteen months and whose singular abilities are reflected in both exhibition and this publication.

It is almost inevitable that objects become separated from even the greatest and most coherent collections over the course of a couple of centuries. Thanks are due particularly to Tate Britain for agreeing to lend Zoffany's portrait of the Ladies Anne, Caroline and Louisa Stuart, shown in the gardens of Bute's great rural retreat, Luton Hoo, for which many of the pictures in this exhibition were acquired.

This publication has been supported through a generous grant from the Paul Mellon Centre for Studies in British Art. We are grateful to the Scottish Government and the Government Indemnity Scheme for their assistance with our loans.

Both Mount Stuart and The Hunterian are embarking on an exciting period of rediscovery of their Enlightenment collections, encouraging important new scholarship and learning to engage twenty-first-century audiences with our uniquely significant collections. *Art of Power* represents a stimulating collaboration between two collections with strong connections reflected in their mutual histories. We hope that future projects will bring many new visitors, engaged by innovative and compelling displays and exhibitions to Glasgow and to the Isle of Bute.

ACKNOWLEDGEMENTS

The texts in this publication have depended heavily on the work of Francis Russell, whose *John, 3rd Earl of Bute: Patron and Collector* (Merrion Press, 2004) remains the standard work for the study of Bute. We are very grateful to Francis for his help in various ways during the preparation of exhibition and publication. Many other people have helped us with our research, and we would like to express our thanks to Richard Bapty, Rhea Sylvia Blok, Elise Boutsen, John Bute, Mungo Campbell, An van Camp, Anthony Crichton-Stuart, Anne Dulau, Samuel Dyer, Gail Egan, Adam Ellis-Jones, Klaus Ertz, Jonathan Franklin, Everhard Korthals Altes, Maud Guichané, Andrew Hansen, Thorsten Heese, Martin Hopkinson, Véronique van de Kerckhof, Elenor Ling, Ger Luijten, Henry Matthews, Alice Martin, Lynda McLeod, Lynsey Nairn, Michiel Plomp, Maggie Reilly, Helen Rosslyn, Frances Sands, F. Carlo Schmid, Laurens Schoemaker, Christian Tico Seifert, Kim Sloan, Sabine van Sprang, Isabelle van Tichelen, Sally Tuckett, Robert Wenley and Aidan Weston-Lewis.

CAITLIN BLACKWELL

INTRODUCTION: BUTE'S IMAGE

On 12 October 1773, John Stuart, Third Earl of Bute called in at an artist's studio at a fashionable London address in Leicester Fields to sit for his portrait. This would be the first of nearly a dozen sittings for a monumental, eight-foot likeness of the earl, designed to preside over his recently refurbished Bedfordshire estate, Luton Hoo.[1] Mirroring the grandeur of its intended setting, the full-length portrait (cat. 23) depicts the earl sumptuously draped in royal blue velvet Garter robes – a sartorial marker signifying his membership of the ancient Order of the Garter, a rare honour bestowed upon him by his old friend, George III.[2] The garter itself is prominently displayed on his left calf, emphasising both his elite status and his famously shapely legs of which he was rumoured to have been excessively proud.[3] At the advanced age of sixty, in spite of ill health, the earl appears virile, graceful and confident, perhaps even haughty. He would seem to be a man very much at the height of his power.

The artist responsible for this august image was none other than Sir Joshua Reynolds, the president of the newly formed Royal Academy and the most celebrated portraitist of the day. Reynolds was renowned not only for championing a style of art aptly known as the "Grand Manner" (a lofty, idealised aesthetic inspired by classical art) but also for his ability effectively to capture the essence of his subjects. However, it was Reynolds's assistant, James Northcote, who captured a rather different, yet equally evocative image of Bute. This was not in the copy of the portrait that Northcote was tasked with producing for the client's London townhouse, but rather, in a letter written to his brother in December of that year.[5] He wrote:

"[Lord Bute's] picture by no means gives me an idea of his character; if it be as the world says. He is a very tall genteel figure with a mean Scotch face; his skin very yellow and small blue

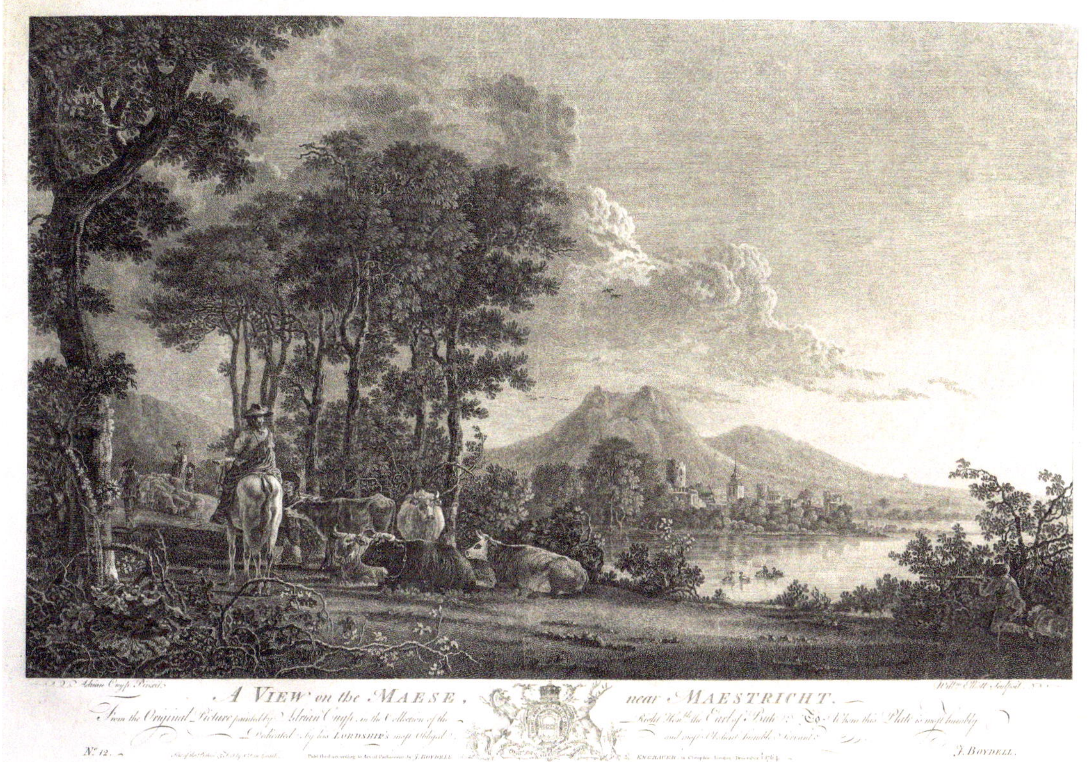

1 William Elliott (1727–1766) after Aelbert Cuyp (1620–1691), *A View on the Maese near Maestricht*, 1764, engraving, 41.0 × 60.0 cm, British Museum, 1877,0609.1559. John Boydell's print album, *The Most Capital Paintings in England*, reproduced five paintings from the Bute collection including his magnificent Cuyp, now in the National Gallery, London (fig. 35).

eyes, with a smile on his face which gives a look of vast good humour and humility. Sir Joshua has made a most extraordinary fine head of him. He must have found it very different from the time when he was forced to have bruisers behind his coach to protect him, for now he comes in a chair without any servants and often walks on foot on his surtout without any state."[6]

Here, Northcote attests to the fact that the sitter's life had changed dramatically since the last time he sat for the artist over a decade earlier – a time when Lord Bute held the dubious distinction of being the most hated man in Britain.

Today, the Third Earl of Bute is best remembered (if he is remembered at all) as being the first Scottish-born Prime Minister and the widely reviled "favourite" of George III. His lasting reputation has hinged on the brief but dramatic period, from 1760 to 1763, in which he rapidly rose in the ranks of political power following the accession of his former pupil George III, only to quickly fall from grace after less than a year in office. During this period, the earl suffered intense scrutiny and criticism, largely stemming from the widespread belief that Bute possessed inordinate powers and wielded a Machiavellian influence over Court and Parliament. He became the target of rampant xenophobic abuse, scurrilous rumours and charges of general corruption, all of which reached a fever pitch in early 1763 at the close of the Seven Years' War.[6] Political opponents, the press and the public united in their hatred of this smug Scottish upstart, who was blamed for everything from the unfavourable terms of peace with France to the suspicious influx of Scots in positions of power. As Northcote alludes, he was even followed by angry mobs wherever he went.[7] Indeed, Bute was arguably the most notorious figure in Britain, his image known to all, though not necessarily through the flattering state portraits that were produced by

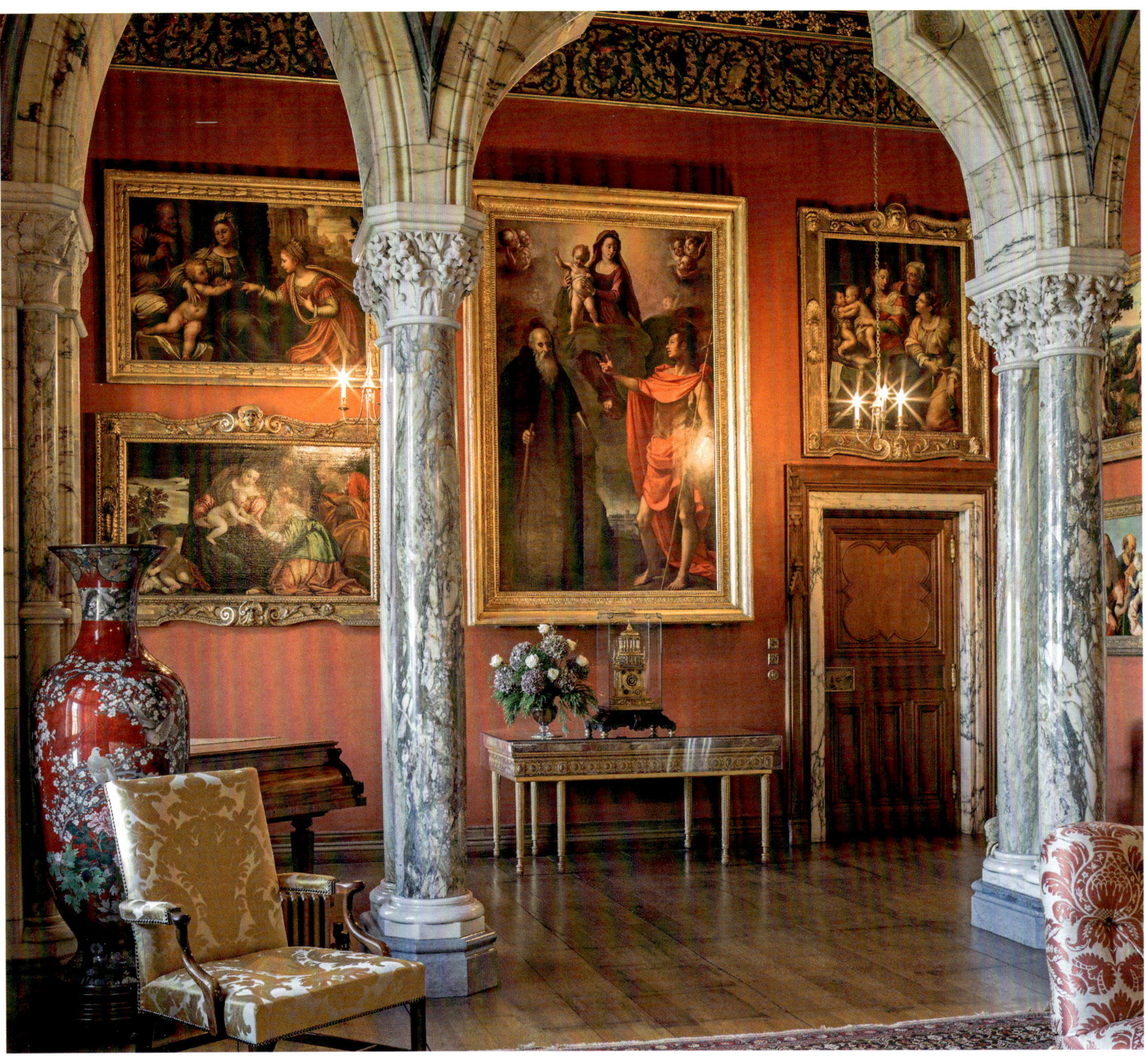

2 The Drawing Room at Mount Stuart with paintings acquired by the Third Earl.

Reynolds and Allan Ramsay but in the scores of scathing satirical prints (fig. 9, 24) that were churned out regularly.[8] According to his contemporary, Horace Walpole, there were enough "satiric prints to tapestry Westminster-hall."[9] In many of these, Bute could be quickly identified not in human form but in the form of a Jack-Boot, a crude visual pun on his name that was, at the time, recognised and understood by virtually all of British society.

But there is still another image of Bute. A less familiar one that was not captured by the scurrilous press, nor even by the skilled and sensitive portraitist, Reynolds, whose stately 1773 portrait of Bute completely belies the fact that, by this point, the sitter had long since retired from political office to pursue a quiet life of studying and collecting. That Reynolds depicted his subject not as a private man of learning but as a public statesman is confounding given that Bute no longer wielded power in such a role. Indeed, the earl had long been *persona non grata* in political spheres, having been forced to flee London and distance himself from the king a decade earlier, effectively making Reynolds's canvas a rather hollow pictorial statement based on a highly conventional mode of aristocratic portraiture. Yet, Bute's power was now manifest in a different way. Thanks to his immense wealth and new found freedom from the pressures of public life, Bute had both the time and resources to focus his attention on a number of ambitious cultural projects, including amassing one of the largest art collections in Georgian Britain. Years later, the history painter and second president of the Royal Academy, Benjamin West would associate Bute with a rather different sort of image – not a portrait of the earl but rather a particular picture from his illustrious collection (fig. 35) that was widely known through an engraved copy (fig. 1) included in John Boydell's *A Collection of Prints, Engraved after the Most Capital Paintings in England*, which was dedicated to George III in 1769. Ironically, given its benign pastoral subject matter, this Italianate landscape by the Dutch Golden Age master, Aelbert Cuyp, captures the essence of the earl's power much more effectively. According to West, "Lord Bute's picture by Cuyp ... was the first picture by that master known in England. Having been seen, pictures by Cuyp were eagerly sought for and many were introduced and sold to advantage."[10] Apparently, even after his political power was negligible, the earl continued to exercise some form of cultural influence.

The Third Earl of Bute's keen interests in art, literature and natural science were, in fact, lifelong pursuits which preoccupied him even during his hectic time in office. Yet, his identity as a patron and collector has been almost entirely overlooked, obscured by his infamously disastrous political career. As the essays in this volume demonstrate, however, Bute was actually in the vanguard of eighteenth-century cultural life, serving as a significant patron to some of the greatest names in Georgian art, architecture and literature. He provided support for painters like Reynolds and the German expatriate, Johan Zoffany. He introduced his talented countryman, Allan Ramsay to the Royal Family. He set up a government pension for the celebrated man-of-letters, Samuel Johnson. He commissioned homes with the most modern facilities, replete with highly fashionable Neoclassical interiors by Scottish architect, Robert Adam. He even seems to have set trends in taste for previously out-of-fashion Dutch Masters, such as Cuyp. Moreover, in his role as confidant to George III, Bute nurtured the king's interest in art and helped him to acquire some of the world-renowned masterpieces that are still held in the Royal Collection today. Meanwhile, the fruits of Bute's own collecting efforts are preserved in the Bute Collection. His once unrivalled assemblage of art and artefacts has survived even the depredations of substantial sales in the nineteenth and twentieth centuries, and a remarkable collection remains housed at the family's ancestral home of Mount Stuart on the western Scottish Isle of Bute.

The Third Earl's cultural contributions have gone woefully under-appreciated. In the more than two hundred years since his death, there has been only one serious attempt to recover his forgotten role as a connoisseur – Francis Russell's 2004 biography, *John, 3rd Earl of Bute: Patron and Collector*.[11] This oversight can, of course, be partly blamed on the heavily biased sources from the period which have served as the primary witnesses of the traditional Whig narrative of British history.[12] It seems that Bute's contemporaries were reluctant to give him much credit for anything – political, cultural or otherwise. Lord Shelburne, for example, a former political ally turned foe, was dismissive of Bute's intellectual pursuits in spite of the fact that the two men ostensibly shared similar tastes and interests.[13] He declared that Bute was:

"[like] any Scotch nobleman, proud, aristocratical, pompous, imposing, with a great deal of superficial knowledge such as is commonly to be met with in France and Scotland, chiefly upon matters of Natural Philosophy, Mines, Fossils, a smattering of Mechanicks, a little Metaphysicks [sic], and a very false taste in everything ..."[14]

Shelburne's statement not only encapsulates the prevailing negative attitude towards Bute but also reflects popular anti-Scotch (and French) sentiments, as well as serving as a critique of the stereotypical aristocratic connoisseur. These powerful prejudices have worked heavily against the Third Earl and his cultural legacy.

The present volume offers a fresh perspective on Bute's life, career and times in order to restore his central role in eighteenth-century culture. Here, an attempt is made to reconcile Bute's dual identities as a reviled public statesman and a thoughtful private patron of the arts and sciences. Moreover, a closer look at the contents of his collection reveals both prevalent trends in eighteenth-century art collecting as well as the unique personal preferences of an individual collector. The first essay, "Beyond expectation, beyond hope," explores the particular biographical and historical circumstances which may have impacted the earl's activities as a collector and patron, and will present his collection as both a reflection of and reaction to his own position of power. Oliver Cox's essay, "Creating a King," shows how Bute's special relationship with George III contributed to political instability and change. Yet the two men were equally closely involved in artistic patronage and collecting. Peter Black's essay, "Quality *and* Quanity," provides an account of Bute's interest in Dutch and Flemish art, relating his taste to that of other collectors of the period such as the Duc de Choiseul, Sir Lawrence Dundas and Joshua Reynolds.

While the primary focus of this study is Bute's remarkable painting collection, it also briefly touches on some of his other intellectual activities. Most significantly, the Third Earl was an avid amateur botanist. He accumulated a vast collection of plant specimens, patronised several natural scientists and served as the first director of Kew Gardens. Bute even published his own multi-volume treatise which laid out an alternative taxonomical system to Carl Linnaeus's now standard scheme. Bute's combined interests in art and science, collecting and taxonomy, were at once typical of Enlightenment connoisseurship and specific to a man who was desperately seeking to secure order in an often chaotic existence. The Third Earl of Bute, like many other eighteenth-century connoisseurs, used collecting as a means of ordering, understanding and controlling the world around him.

Notes

1 Joshua Reynolds scheduled eleven appointments with Bute from October–December 1773 (one of which was cancelled). There may have been more sittings documented in the artist's now lost pocket books from 1774–1778. There is one further appointment recorded on 24 October 1780, which was presumably when Bute made the payments recorded in the artist's ledger the following day (150 guineas each for two copies of the portrait). See Mannings, 2000, p. 437.
2 The painting is listed in the 1799 inventory of pictures at Luton, p. 6, as hanging in the saloon.
3 Allan Ramsay reported that while painting his 1758 portrait of Bute (MS no. B00203), the sitter held his robes above the knee so that his leg could be seen and maintained this position for an hour. Ramsay's portrait seems to have inspired Reynolds, not only in his own portrait of Bute but in his 1759 portrait of the Earl of Lauderdale (Art Gallery of New South Wales, no. 8.1977). Reynolds is alleged to have said, "I wish to show a leg with Ramsay's Lord Bute." See Smart, 1952, pp. 105–106.
4 In a letter to his brother on 15 December 1773, Northcote writes, "I have the honour to copy Lord Bute's face as there is to be two whole-lengths made of him." This second copy, now in the National Portrait Gallery (NPG no. 3938), likely hung in Bute's house on South Audley Street. See Mannings, 2000, p. 437; Whitley, 1928, p. 295.
5 Whitley, ibid.
6 For more in-depth discussions of Bute's negative public image, see Brewer, 1972; Brewer, 1973; Schweizer, 1997.
7 In a letter to the Duke of Bedford, Richard Rigby describes one instance of mob violence outside of the House of Lords on 25 November 1762: "Lord Bute to avoid the like treatment he had met in going, returned in a hackney chair, but the mob discovered him, followed him, broke the glasses of his chair, and, in short, by threats and menaces, put him very reasonably in great fear ..." See Bedford, 1846, p. 160.
8 Brewer estimates that there are more than 400 satirical prints which include references to Bute. The majority of these have been preserved in the British Museum. See Brewer, 1972, p. 103; Stephens, 1883.
9 Walpole, 1937–1983, vol. 38, p. 180.
10 West as quoted in Joseph Farington's diary (18 May 1818), see Farington, 1928, p. 178.
11 The present volume is indebted to this invaluable work, see Russell, 2004.
12 For discussion of the "Whig case" against Bute, see Brewer, 1972.
13 Early in his political career, William Petty, Second Earl of Shelburne and First Marquess of Lansdowne was closely associated with Bute, who employed him as a broker to negotiate the support of Henry Fox. However, Shelburne later quarreled with both Bute and Fox, and his bitter sentiments are captured in his memoirs written in the early 1800s; see Fitzmaurice, 1912, p. 110. Prior to this falling out, Bute sold his unfinished Robert-Adam-designed London house, Bute House (later Lansdowne House) to Shelburne in 1765. Shelburne retained the services of Adam until 1771.
14 Fitzmaurice, ibid.

CAITLIN BLACKWELL

"BEYOND EXPECTATION, BEYOND HOPE":

THE THIRD EARL OF BUTE'S PICTURE COLLECTION AT LUTON HOO

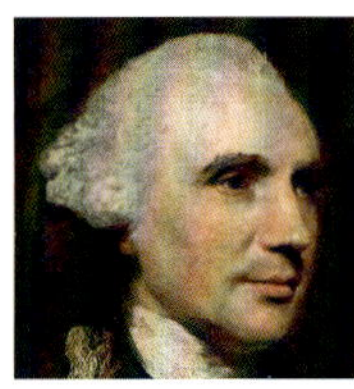

In September 1763, John Stuart, Third Earl of Bute resigned from his post as Keeper of the Privy Purse and retired from political office. This marked the conclusion of a relatively brief, yet tumultuous, chapter in the earl's life, which had witnessed his meteoric rise from an obscure Scottish nobleman to the most powerful man in British politics.[1] The story of Bute's rapid ascent to power had started little more than a decade earlier, when a chance encounter with the then heir to the throne changed the trajectory of his life forever. A casual introduction to Frederick, Prince of Wales at a horserace in 1747 – just a year after Bute had arrived in England from his native Scotland – led to a close friendship and a central role in the prince's court. Shortly after Frederick's untimely death in 1751, his widow Augusta appointed Bute as tutor to her teenage son, the future George III. On his accession in 1760, the king ensured that his "dear friend" and respected mentor remained by his side. Within two days of the succession, Bute was sworn in as a member of the Privy Council; and in the following year, he was made Secretary of State for the Northern Department. In May 1762, he succeeded the Duke of Newcastle as First Lord of the Treasury. Unsurprisingly, this rapid elevation inspired bitter jealousy and suspicion amongst Bute's political rivals, who made quick work of taking him down. Fanning the flames of public hostility, his opponents cast Bute as a villain to British liberty and valour, blaming him for the purportedly poor terms of peace that ended war with France, as well as the hated Cider Tax of 1763, which was widely feared to be a harbinger of a general excise. By spring of that year, Bute was the most hated man in the nation, insulted and mobbed wherever he went. Mentally exhausted, physically ill and fearful for his personal safety, Bute stepped down from his position as head of government in April, and five months later, withdrew from public life, more or less, for good.

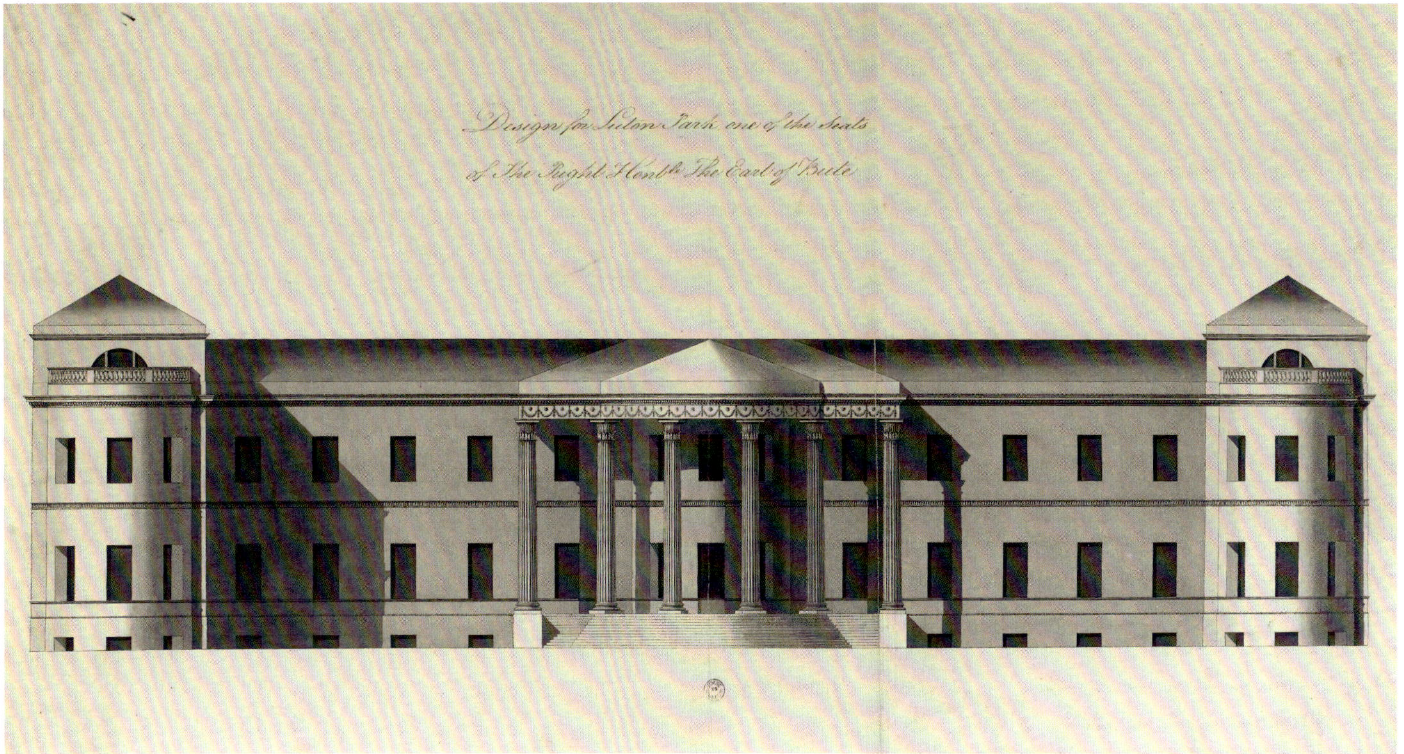

3 Robert Adam (1728–1792), *The East Front of Luton Hoo*, ca. 1773, pen and ink wash, Sir John Soane's Museum, SM Adam Volume 39/23.

Needing a refuge from the constant threats of attack from the London mob, Bute had recently purchased Luton Hoo, an estate in rural Bedfordshire, to which he retreated that autumn. In Luton, the earl found both a safe haven and a worthy retirement project that would preoccupy him for the next decade of his life. Here, he enlisted the aid of leading designers to undertake major renovations of the estate.[2] The grounds were overseen by Lancelot "Capability" Brown, who was to convert the parkland into one of his trademark "natural" landscapes – an idealised vista consisting of smooth, sloping lawns, ornamented with copses of carefully placed trees and serpentine lakes. Meanwhile, the original seventeenth-century house – believed to be the building depicted in the background of a portrait of Bute's daughters (cat. 34) painted by Johan Zoffany in that year, 1763 – was to be completely overhauled by fellow Scot, Robert Adam, the father of Georgian Neoclassicism, and the most fashionable architect of the moment. With Bute's considerable input, Adam was tasked with transforming this outdated and ill-suited old pile into a modern architectural masterpiece (fig. 3) that would serve as a suitable repository for the earl's expansive library and collections. It was here that the earl would install the bulk of his painting collection, which would grow to be one of the largest and most valuable in Britain.

In his role as mentor to the young George III, Bute had been active and interested in art collecting and patronage since the 1750s, primarily acting on behalf of the future king. Now, thanks to his freedom from responsibility to King and Country, combined with a substantial inheritance from his late father-in-law, the wealthy Yorkshire landowner Edward Wortley-Montagu, Bute had the time and resources to collect art for himself on a significant scale. With the help of his respected advisor, William Baillie[3] (cat. 1), an Irish engraver and art dealer, Bute eventually

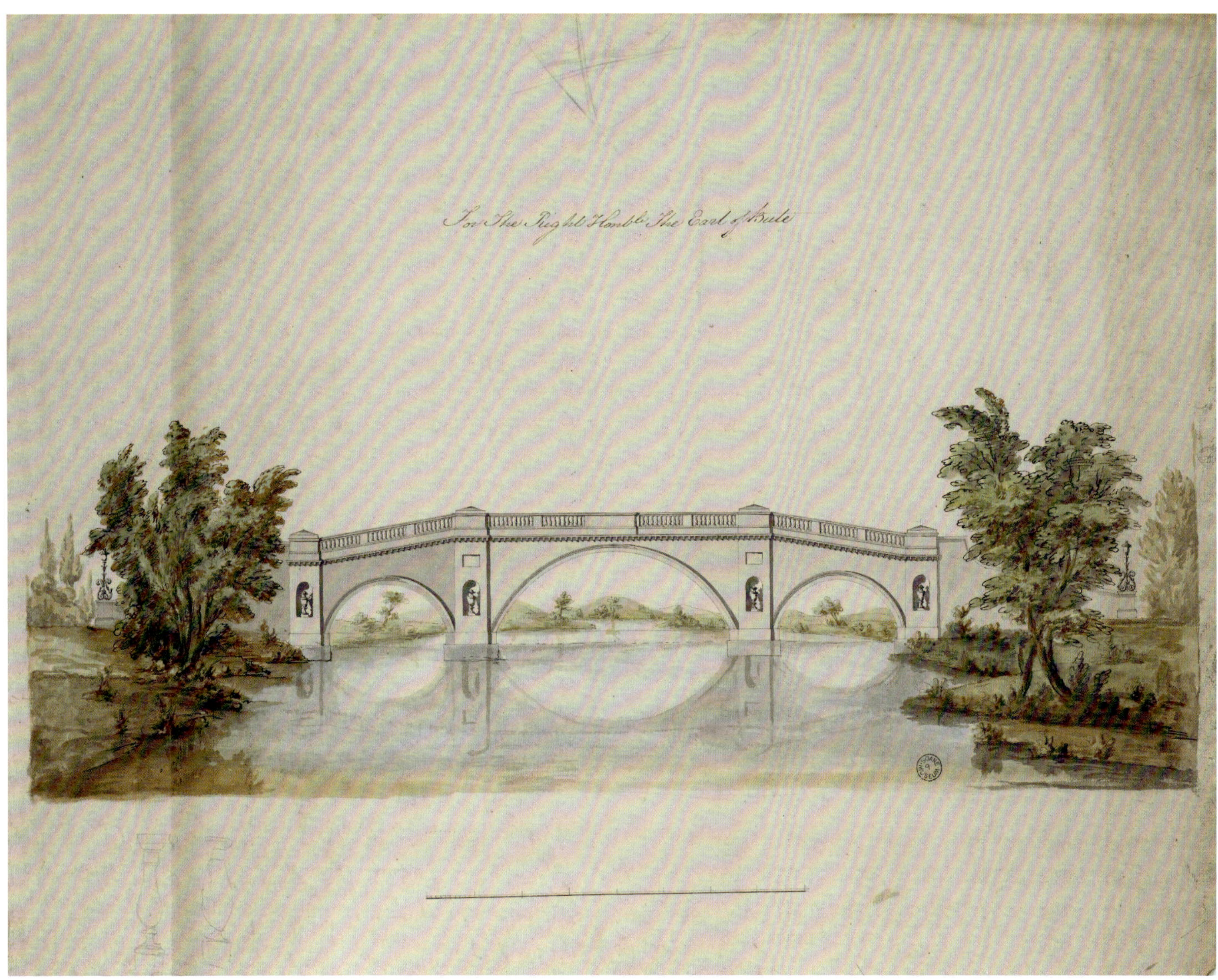

4 Robert Adam (1728–1792), *Bridge Across the Lake at Luton Hoo*, 1767, pen and watercolour, Sir John Soane's Museum, Trustees of the Soane Museum, SM Adam Volume 51/9.

amassed at Luton some five hundred paintings, ranging from monumental "Grand Manner" portraits by modern British masters, to imposing Italian Renaissance religious subjects, to domestic-scale, meticulously painted Dutch genre scenes. As impressive as the sheer quantity and variety of the paintings was their notable quality. Indeed, he owned examples of work by many of the most familiar and cherished names in the canon of Western European art. Describing the Luton picture collection in the *General Evening Post* in 1783, an anonymous visitor provided an impressive checklist of the earl's numerous masterpieces:

"The pictures ... are many of them undoubted originals, and some of them by masters who are in England not often met with, so that, added to *chefs d'œuvre* of Guido [Reni], Caravaggio, the two Poussins, Caracci, Rubens, Cuyp, Swannivelt, Vandevelde, Claude, Bassan[o], Titian, and Zuccarelli, you meet with wonderful performances by Velasquez, Libari, Griffier, Tempesta, Vecchio, and Busiri [sic]."[4]

At first glance, the Luton picture collection appears to be a highly conventional and conspicuous display of wealth (Bute was by now one of the richest men in Britain), and an index of the tastes and trends of the day. In many ways, it was a predictable product of the Georgian art market which was then dominated by contemporary portraiture, the nation's most ubiquitous art form, as well as a thriving secondary market for European Old Masters – that is, Italian, Dutch, Flemish and French paintings attributable to revered artists who were active in the seventeenth century or earlier. Much to the consternation of English artists like William Hogarth, who complained bitterly of the regularly imported "ship-loads of dead Christs, Holy Families, Madonnas, and dismal, dark subjects," European Old Masters were a mainstay of the British art collection, and ownership of them served as a statement of the collector's affluence and good taste.[5] Indeed, many of the distinguished Continental artists listed at Luton could likewise be found in the comparably illustrious collections of the Dukes of Marlborough and Devonshire, the Earl of Exeter and Sir Lawrence Dundas.

Yet, a closer inspection of Bute's collection reveals small idiosyncrasies, obvious preferences and notable absences which might subtly distinguish it from other art collections of the period. These differences are perhaps suggestive of the fact that the house and collection at Luton were designed to serve two separate and seemingly contradictory functions. Luton was conceived as an opulent noble seat, the ultimate advertisement of wealth, taste and fashionability, but also as a private sanctuary for the beleaguered owner, who could now find peace of mind surrounded by the art, books and other objects of intellectual interest that brought him genuine pleasure. Luton was at once a bold statement of economic and cultural power, and a reaction against the consequences of political power gone wrong. The art collection housed within it, though not uncharacteristic of its wider cultural milieu, was formed along personal lines for the enjoyment of its near-reclusive owner. We can therefore view the picture collection at Luton as a unique reflection of the tastes, experiences and exigencies of an individual collector.

Unfortunately, the full story behind the Third Earl's art collection will forever remain a mystery. While contemporary connoisseurs such as Horace Walpole and William Hamilton published descriptive accounts of their collections, Bute has left no surviving document which captures, in his own words, his opinions on painting, his ambitions as a collector or his plans for the display at Luton. Moreover, there is no definitive record of his purchases nor is there an inventory produced within his lifetime. We must therefore rely on other forms of evidence, such as contemporary descriptions like the one appearing in the *Post* or the comprehensive *Catalogue of Pictures at Luton Park*,[6] produced not long after his death, and some engravings from the period which are inscribed as being made "from the original picture, in the collection of The Right Honourable Earl of Bute, at Luton, Bedfordshire."[7] Additionally, there is extensive correspondence from the earl's art agents, much of which dates to the period when Luton was under construction, indicating that the impetus for Bute's painting collection was at least partially the practical requirement of needing to adorn the walls of a very large house. Nevertheless, the earl's pictures were clearly an integral component of his grand retirement project at Luton.

I

On the first floor at Luton, in the North Blue Dressing Room, a surprisingly intimate and informal space for the profusion of priceless pictures displayed within it, hung a landscape painting by the seventeenth-century, Haarlem-born artist, Jacob van Ruisdael (cat. 25).[18] This expansive view of the flat, fertile countryside surrounding Ruisdael's home town was a particularly fine and characteristic example of a work by a highly regarded Dutch artist. It was just one of over two hundred and thirty Netherlandish paintings at Luton by the late eighteenth century, representing nearly half of the Third Earl's collection. In an account of paintings in British country houses published in the 1830s, the German art historian, Gustav Waagen declared that Luton's "greatest treasure is a number of excellent pictures of the Dutch and Flemish schools. Of all the collections formed in England before the Revolution, it is the most important in works of this class."[9] Indeed, Bute's impressive assemblage of Dutch and Flemish pictures has come to be seen as the defining characteristic and highest achievement of his collection. As Peter Black will demonstrate in his essay, however, an interest and appreciation in Dutch art hardly made the Third Earl unique amongst eighteenth-century art collectors. Despite the objections of native-born artists and erudite connoisseurs, Dutch paintings and prints were in demand in Britain throughout the eighteenth century and could be found on the walls of princely palaces and public houses alike. Yet, the notably high quality and prodigious quantity of such works at Luton suggests that Netherlandish painting had a particular significance for the earl. Surprisingly, however, this connection to the Low Countries actually points to Bute's Scottishness. For as we will see, his early exposure to Dutch culture was, in fact, reflective of a typically Scottish intellectual upbringing that would have a significant impact on his later activities as a collector and connoisseur.

Born in Edinburgh on 23 May 1713, the Third Earl of Bute entered the world the scion of an illustrious Scottish family, descended from Robert the Bruce, the fourteenth-century King of the Scots.[10] Over the centuries, the Stuarts (or the Stewarts), whose name derived from the ancient office of High Steward of Scotland, acquired great swathes of land both on the Isle of Bute and the mainland, and wielded considerable influence through positions in civil office. In 1703, Bute's grandfather, James Stuart, was created First Earl of Bute in recognition of his support of the Act of Union with England, a cause he later deserted, thus establishing a Stuart-family tradition for abandoning political careers at times of heightened controversy. The First Earl was succeeded in 1710 by Bute's father, another James, whose most significant legacies were building the family seat at Mount Stuart and a strategic marriage to Lady Anne Campbell, daughter of Archibald Campbell, First Duke of Argyll, which placed the Stuarts at the centre of a powerful aristocratic family network. In 1723, the Third Earl succeeded at the tender age of nine and consequently spent his minority in the charge of his maternal uncles, John, Second Duke of Argyll, and Archibald, First Earl of Ilay and Third Duke of Argyll. Although Bute would later attempt to downplay his heritage by abandoning the family seat in the homeland and remarking to English colleagues that he was "not particularly concerned about [Scotland]," he was very much the product of this national and family background.[11]

His powerful uncles probably left the greatest impression on young Bute. The Duke of Argyll and Earl of Ilay were the most prominent figures in early eighteenth-century Scottish politics, and it was through their influence that Bute would secure his first civil post as Commissioner of Police for Scotland in 1737, thereby launching his career. But perhaps more importantly, these men served as significant role models for the adolescent earl. The cosmopolitan Campbell brothers were themselves exposed to art and architectural grandeur from a young age, having spent their own childhoods ensconced at the opulent Jacobean manor, Ham House in Surrey, the home of their maternal grandmother, the Duchess of Lauderdale. Dividing their time between Scotland, England and the Continent, both men went on to establish successful careers in the military and politics, but devoted much of their attention to intellectual and artistic pursuits. Perhaps inspired by the renowned picture cabinet at Ham House, the Second Duke of Argyll amassed a distinguished collection of paintings which included particularly fine examples of the Dutch and Flemish painting that his nephew would, in turn, grow to love.[12] The Earl of Ilay, meanwhile, was an avid amateur scientist with a particular passion for botany.[13] At Whitton Park, his Twickenham estate, he established an impressive botanical garden teeming with exotic plant specimens gathered from all corners of the globe. As an impressionable schoolboy, Bute visited his uncle at Whitton, and was likely furnished with inspiration for his own later botanical projects at Mount Stuart, Caen Wood House and Kew Gardens.

It was evidently important to Bute's uncles that the young earl received a suitably genteel and well-rounded education. Following in his uncle Archibald's footsteps, Bute was sent to Eton College, and afterwards, at the age of seventeen, to study civil law in Holland, first in Groningen and later at the University of Leiden, where he received his degree in 1732. At this time, Dutch universities were renowned across Europe for their innovative scholarship and particularly attracted the progeny of the Scottish gentry and professional classes.[14] Though studying law, Bute would have received a typically comprehensive humanist education which included courses in science, history and philosophy. It was likely here that the young earl first developed a serious interest in the study of botany and made connections with eminent Leiden-based natural scientists like Jan Frederik Gronovius, a patron of Linnaeus with whom Bute would later correspond.[15] What is more, at Leiden, Bute would have been immersed in the virtuoso culture which flourished in Dutch urban centres amongst the educated elite. Here, learned men conversed on diverse subjects ranging from anatomy to antiquities, and physics to philology. They accumulated and shared both ideas and tangible specimens of their learning, like plants, minerals, books, artworks and archaeological artifacts. Like his uncle before him, Bute would have left this setting with broad intellectual interests and a taste for collecting.

Typical of the many Scotsmen educated in Holland at this time, Bute returned home with the aesthetic and intellectual values of his host country. Indeed, his formative years spent in Leiden seem to have irrevocably shaped his tastes, interests and outlooks. This manifested itself in his art collection in both direct and indirect ways. Certainly, the quintessentially Dutch landscapes of Golden Age masters like Ruisdael and Meindert Hobbema (cat. 15) – with their broad, brooding skies and low flat terrains dotted with windmills, church spires and bleaching fields –

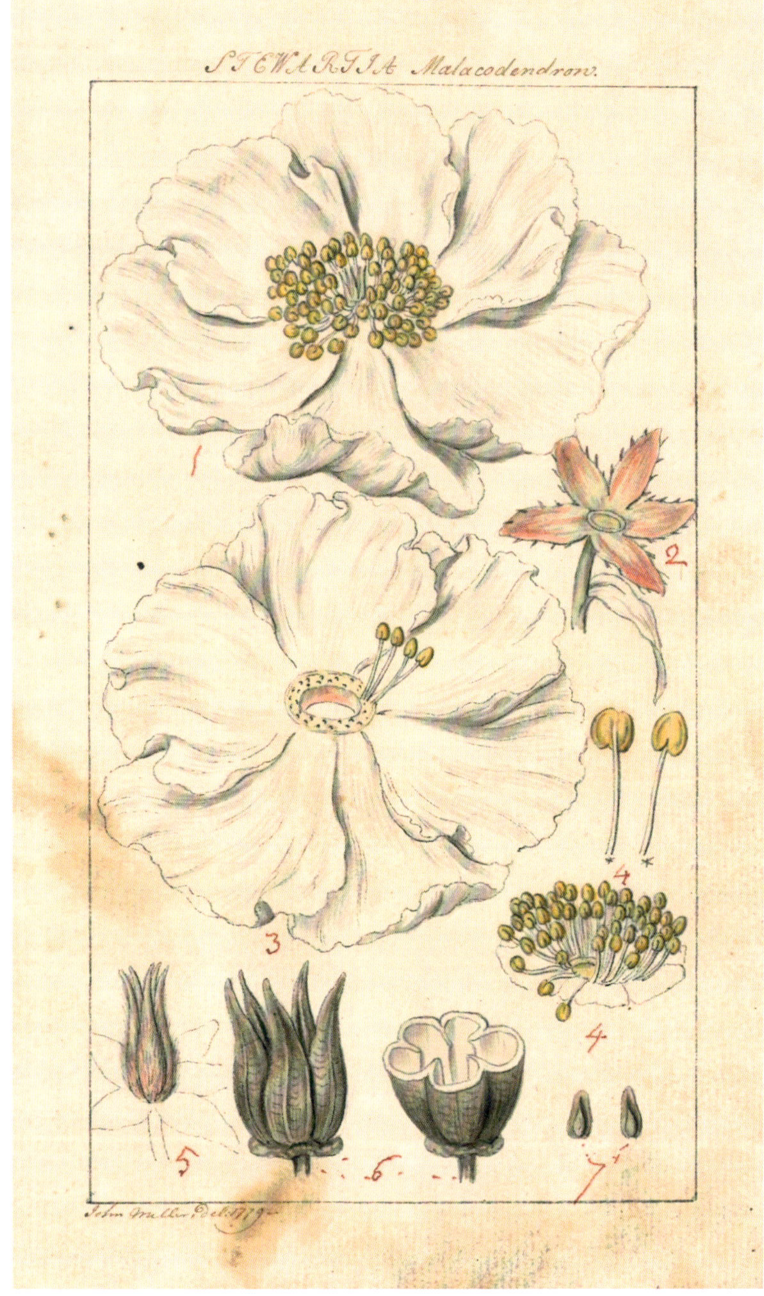

5 Johann Müller (1715–ca. 1792), *Stewartia*, 1779, 22.8 × 13.8 cm, pen and watercolour design for the *Botanical Tables* (1785), The Bute Collection at Mount Stuart, BU/124/50, 27.

must have been familiar and nostalgic to the collector. But Bute also collected less obviously Dutch landscapes in the Italianate style by artists such as Jan Both, Aelbert Cuyp (cat. 7) and Nicolaes Berchem (cat. 4), as well as genre paintings by Jan Steen (cat. 29–30) and Cornelis Bega (cat. 2–3), portraits by Gerard ter Borch (cat. 5–6), and marine subjects by Willem van de Velde. In particular, he displayed a clear preference for the artists from his temporary home of Leiden, including Gabriël Metsu (cat. 16), Gerard Dou, and at least two pictures attributed to the most famous former denizen of the city, Rembrandt.[16]

Moreover, the earl gravitated not only to Dutch painting, but also to the empirical and pragmatic forms of scholarly study that flourished in the Low Countries at the time. Rather than being mutually exclusive, his interests in art and science seem to have intersected. In retirement at Luton, and later at his seaside retreat, Highcliffe in Hampshire, Bute divided his time between scientific study, and art collecting and patronage. While both were popular pastimes for the Georgian aristocracy, the earl seems to have approached these endeavours as more than just casual hobbies. His serious dedication to botany, no doubt fostered by his time spent amongst the community of leading natural scientists at Leiden, was duly recognised by his professional counterparts, including Linnaeus, who named the genus of flowering plant, *Stewartia* (fig. 5), in his honour.[17] The result of many years of tireless study was the earl's magnum opus, *Botanical Tables Containing the Families of British Plants* (1785), an ambitious nine-volume treatise on botanical taxonomy.[18] Dedicated to Queen Charlotte, twelve copies of this luxurious publication were produced and illustrated with over 600 copiously detailed yet elegant, hand-coloured botanical engravings (fig. 6), which the earl commissioned from the German draughtsman, Johann Sebastian Müller. These illustrations were no doubt valued for their didactic quality as well as their aesthetic beauty, as evidenced by the fact that similar illustrations were often removed from any textual context and pasted into albums, such as they were in Bute's collection, which included hundreds of botanical illustrations by artists like Müller and Maria Sibylla Merian.[19]

That the earl was drawn to seventeenth-century Dutch painting, a school of art renowned for its high degree of realism and close observation of the natural world, is not at all surprising. What is somewhat more unexpected, given Bute's keen interest in plants, is the notable dearth of floral still-life paintings in his otherwise comprehensive collection. Only a handful of small flower subjects were sprinkled throughout the display at Luton, and today just one of these remains in the Bute Collection – *A Festoon of Flowers* (cat. 18) by the Frankfurt-born, Utrecht-based artist Abraham Mignon.[20] One would assume that the careful studies of plant specimens featured in the works of specialist flower painters like Mignon would have particularly appealed to the earl. Despite their realism, however, such works were not scientifically accurate visual documents but rather contrived floral fantasies which commonly combined plants that bloomed in different seasons and parts of the globe. It is for this reason that Francis Russell has speculated that Bute generally eschewed flower paintings.[21] Whatever the case may be, their absence at Luton is suggestive of the earl's selective personal taste.

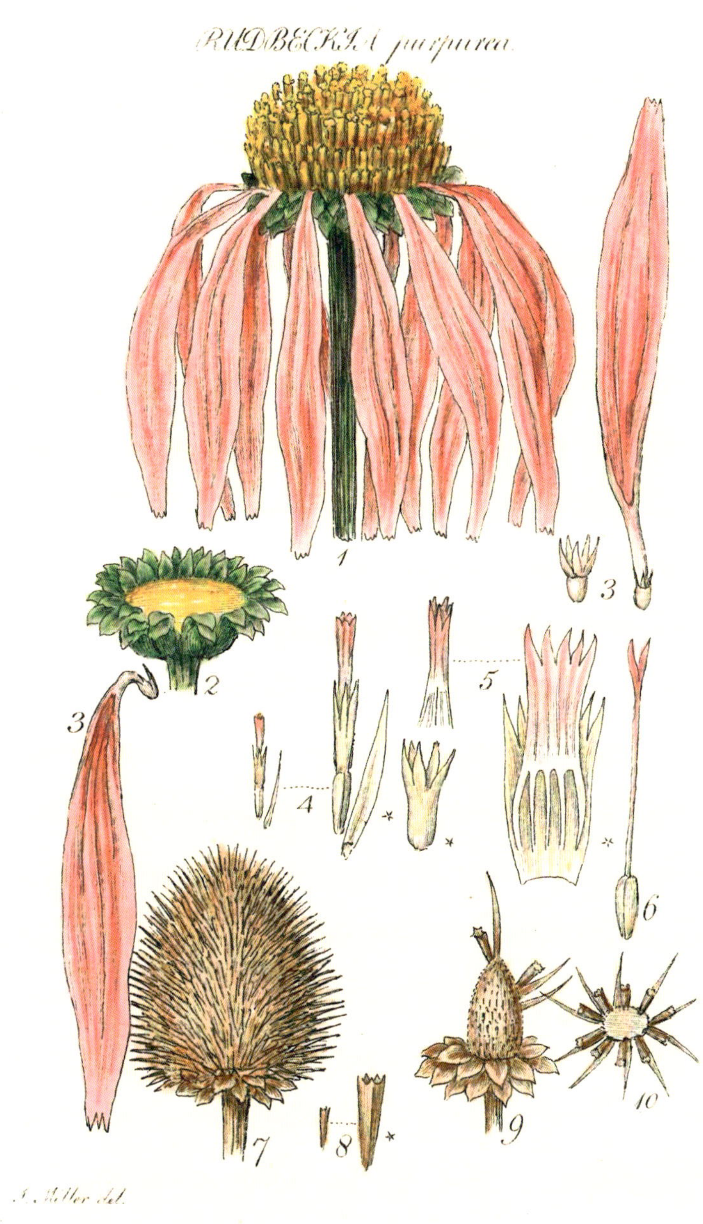

6 Johann Müller (1715–ca. 1792), *Rudbeckia purpurea*, 19.4 × 12.3 cm, hand coloured engraving from the *Botanical Tables* (1785), The Bute Collection at Mount Stuart, BU/125/6.

II

Like most Georgian stately homes, Luton had on the main floor a number of grand, public state rooms designed to receive, entertain and impress visitors. Though, as we will see, Bute entertained considerably fewer guests than his more sociable contemporaries, he nevertheless saw fit to install several elegantly appointed reception rooms, including Luton's main drawing room. This sumptuous space was one of several rooms in the house for which Bute's architect-designer Adam produced dozens of watercolour designs for bespoke furniture (fig. 7), fixtures and whole interior schemes articulated in his delicate, Neoclassical idiom.[22] Adam's holistic approach to room design resulted in a harmoniously unified aesthetic, and the drawing room, in particular, possessed an overriding Italian flavour. It was purpose-designed to showcase some of the treasures Bute had acquired on a recent trip to

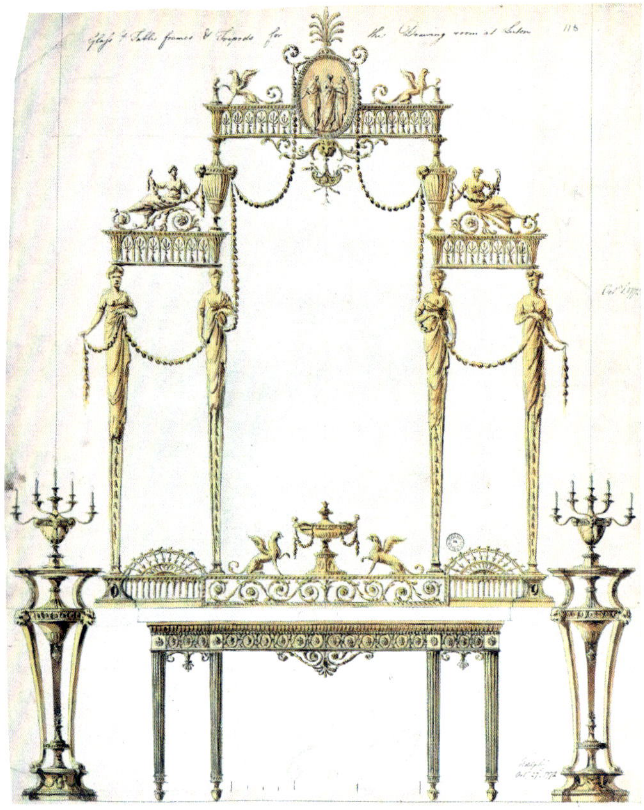

7 Robert Adam (1728–1792), *Glass and Table Frames & Tripods for the Drawing Room at Luton*, 1772, Sir John Soane's Museum, SM Adam Volume 20/116.

the Continent, including side-tables that supported mosaic tops from Venice, candelabra made from "bronzes executed in Italy in the Style of Mich Angelo [sic]," and, of course, paintings by Venetian Cinquecento masters, including Veronese and Tintoretto, which were displayed in matching rococo gilt frames.[23] The ceiling above (fig. 8), adorned with roundels depicting classical scenes by the Venetian painter, Antonio Zucchi (1726–1796), completed the fantasy of a princely Palladian villa.

For a distinguished art collector like the Third Earl, it would have been remiss not to include Italian art in the display at Luton. According to contemporary British art theory, which in turn was based on earlier Continental writing, Italian (or "Italianate") painting occupied a position at the very top of the artistic hierarchy.[24] In particular, Italian Renaissance history paintings depicting mythological or biblical subjects were the most highly valued by those collectors who self-identified as men of taste and erudition (as Bute undoubtedly did). Dutch painting, however, was placed on the other end of this theoretical spectrum. It was a school of art that was increasingly losing ground in the eyes of British art theorists, artists and elite collectors, who argued vociferously for the supremacy of Italian art over that of their Northern counterparts.[25] Where the Italian school was lauded for its lofty narratives, moralising messages and idealised aesthetics, the Dutch school was often chastised for its focus on lowly subject matter and minute material detail rather than grand universal truths. A typically negative comparison comes from Walpole, that prolific cultural commentator, writing in the 1740s, around the time that Bute was making his first art purchases. Walpole exclaimed:

"... as for the *Dutch* Painters, those drudging Mimicks [sic] of Nature's most uncomely coarsenesses, don't their Earthen Pots and Brass Kettles carry away Prices only due to the sweet neatness of [Francesco] *Alban*[i], and to the attractive delicacy of *Carlo Maratt*[a]?"[26]

Lamenting the continued currency of supposedly "low" Dutch genre paintings amongst British art buyers, this aristocratic arbiter of taste believed that truly refined connoisseurs preferred Italian history painting. Bute, evidently, was of a different opinion. But although his preference was clearly for the Northern school, the earl bought Italian art, too. Indeed, there were just under a hundred Italian pictures at Luton by the end of the century. Again, the collector's purchases in this area are revealing of a selective taste shaped by experience and circumstance.

Unlike so many of his peers, the Third Earl did not embark on the Grand Tour following his studies in Leiden. A popular rite of passage for wealthy Britons in the eighteenth century, the Grand Tour, a kind of cultural pilgrimage to Europe, primarily served to introduce the well-bred youth of the British Isles to the art, architecture and customs of their Continental cousins.[27] While it was not uncommon for tourists to pass through the Low Countries and France, the ultimate destination was Italy, the perceived cradle of polite civilisation in the West. The young

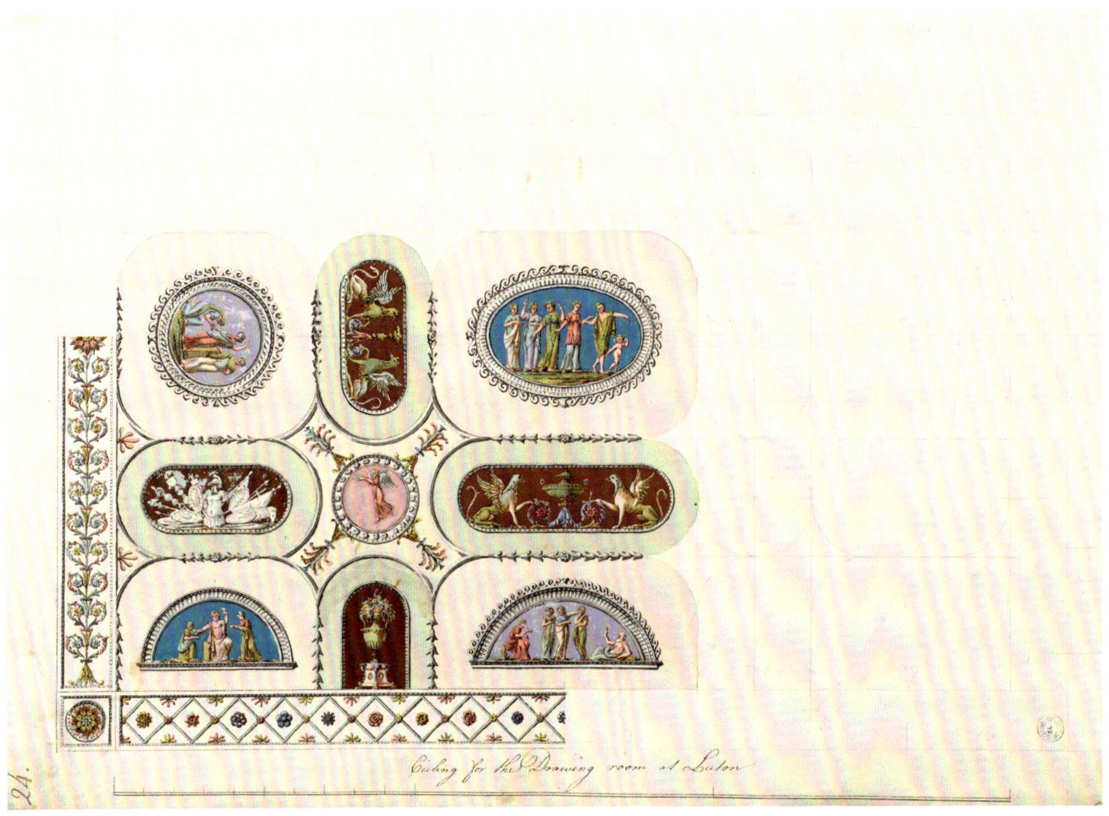

8 Robert Adam (1728–1792), *Ceiling for the Drawing Room at Luton*, 1769, pencil and watercolour, Sir John Soane's Museum, SM Adam Volume 12/24.

earl, however, did not make it beyond Dutch borders, and it would not be until he was in his mid-fifties that he would take in the iconic sites of Rome, Florence and Venice in person. Why Bute bypassed this standard initiation rite is unclear. One possibility posited by Russell is that he feared the taint of being aligned with his paternal uncle John, a Jacobite sympathiser, then in the entourage of the exiled Pretender in Rome.[28] Or, it could have been that Bute was merely eager to head home to claim his birthright after coming of age in May 1734. In any case, the Third Earl's earliest exposure to European culture was staunchly Northern.

While his first-hand experience of Italy was considerably delayed, perhaps influencing his artistic tastes, Bute was by no means ignorant of the art produced there. In his library at Mount Stuart, where he resided with his young family until their immigration to England in 1746, the earl had many volumes relating to Italian art and architecture.[29] These included Palladio's *Four Books on Architecture*, Leonardo's *Treatise on Painting*, and Dryden's 1695 translation of du Fresnoy's *The Art of Painting*, the first English-language art treatise to champion the Italian school over that of the Dutch. The earl's remote education in Italian art was furthered through the aid of reproductive prints in his collection after Raphael, Cortona, Albani and others.[30] By the time he was serving as a trusted advisor to George III, Bute was extremely well informed and instantly recognised the singular importance of a particular Italian art collection that had come up for sale. In 1762, Bute and his brother, James Stuart Mackenzie (fig. 9), the Minister at Turin, arranged the purchase of the famed picture collection and library of Consul Joseph Smith, a former British diplomat in Venice.[31] This landmark acquisition endowed the Royal Collection with some five hundred works, mostly Italian, including a large and distinguished group of *vedute*, or cityscapes, by the fashionable Canaletto. That Bute ceded such works to the Royal Collection and chose primarily to concentrate

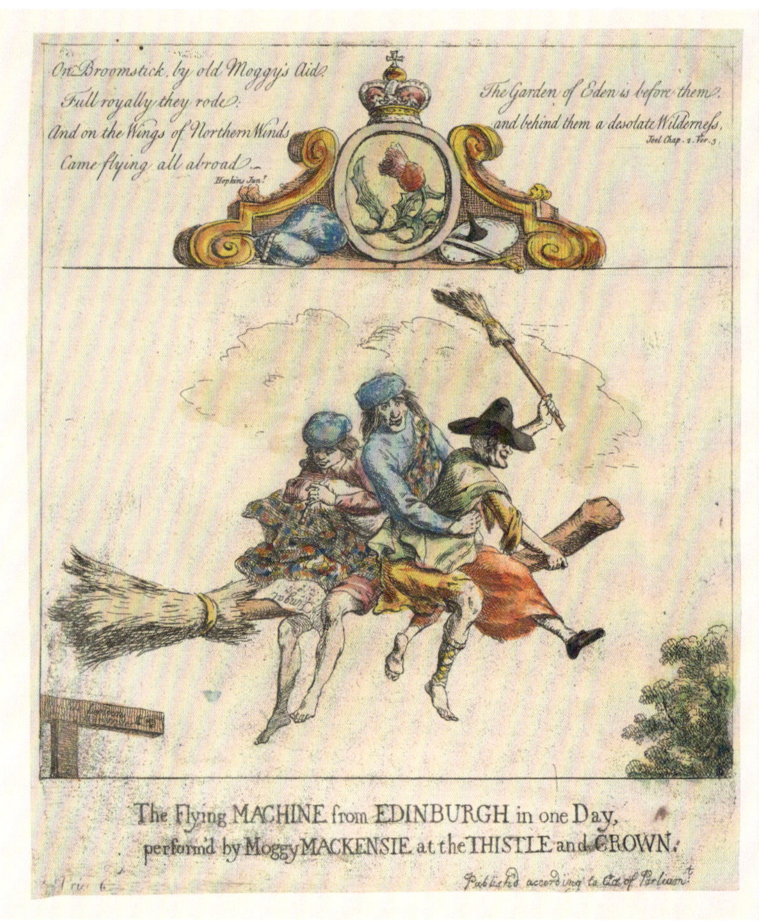

9 *The Flying Machine from Edinburgh in one day performed by Moggy Mackenzie at the Thistle and Crown*, 1762, hand coloured etching by Paul Sandby (1731–1809), 26.9 × 23.0 cm, Scottish National Portrait Gallery PGE 31. Sandby ridicules Bute's appointment of his brother James Stuart Mackenzie as Keeper of the Privy Seal in Scotland, a position of power and influence.

on the Northern school has been interpreted as a deliberate act of deference to the king, whom he likely did not wish to overshadow.

In the summer 1768, the Third Earl finally embarked on the Grand Tour at a mature age. This came seven years after his heir, Lord Mountstuart, had set out on his own tour at the more conventional age of seventeen, a trip that was commemorated in a stock souvenir portrait (fig. 10) by Pompeo Batoni (1708–1787), the favoured portraitist of British Grand Tourists. Unlike his son's excursion, the primary purpose for the elder Bute's trip was medical rather than recreational. He had been suffering from a battery of physical ailments, including stomach pains, digestive issues and insomnia, all likely brought on by stress. For even at this time, Bute was the regular target of abuse by the press and the public, which were operating under the mistaken assumption that he continued to exercise influence over the King. In reality, the earl and his former pupil had broken ties in 1766 over Bute's bitter feelings towards George's alliance with his former political rival, William Pitt. Moreover, the earl was also experiencing family troubles with his second son, James behaving badly at university and eloping with the daughter of a lowly baronet. Feeling fragile after recent events, Bute decided to take the healing waters at Barèges in the French Pyrenees, which was to be the first port of call on a Continental trip that would span nearly three years and include sojourns in Italy's great cities: Venice, Rome, Florence and Naples. Leaving behind his wife and an unfinished house, the earl, along with his favourite son, Charles, departed from Dover in August, travelling via France. By late November, Bute, at long last, arrived in Italy, where he first took up residence in Venice. He hoped the warmer climate and civilised culture would improve his low spirits.

For most of Bute's peers, the Grand Tour was just as much a social occasion as it was a cultural education. The earl, however, spent little time fraternising with the *cognoscenti* that congregated in Italy's cultural centres. Though hundreds of miles away from the angry mobs in London, Bute was still stinging from the hostile treatment of his countrymen and felt it necessary to keep a low profile. Among the trusted members of his inner circle while in Rome was Abbé Peter Grant, a fellow Scot and regular host to Grand Tourists. In August 1769, Grant reported to William Hamilton, the British Ambassador in Naples:

"Here [Bute] orders himself to be called Mr Stuart, he never wears his ribbon or garter, sees no mortal but Mr [James] Byers [another trusted guide] and your humble ser^{v}t, as for the

Marquis Tannucci [Prime Minister of Naples], or any of your great folks, he'll certainly have nothing to do with, nor even exchange one word with them ..."[32]

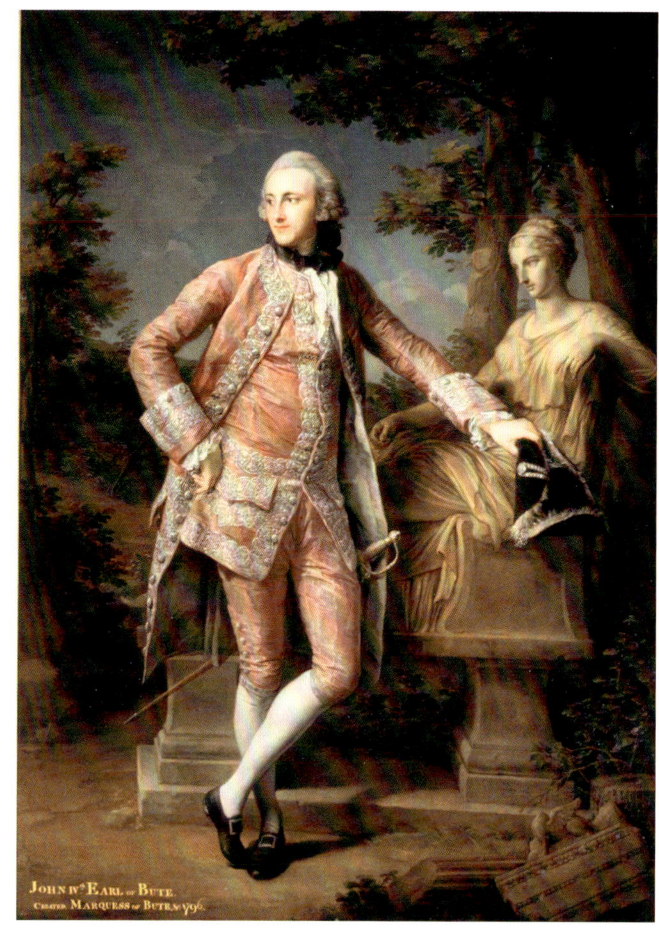

10 Pompeo Batoni (1708–1787), *Lord Mounstuart*, 1767, oil on canvas, 236.4 × 144.7 cm, The Bute Collection at Mount Stuart. John Stuart, later First Marquess of Bute (1744–1814), was the Third Earl's eldest son. He inherited the house at Luton and added to the collection of pictures formed by his father.

Once one of the most powerful men in Britain, the Third Earl now shirked the ostentatious ornaments that outwardly signified his lofty position and attempted to assume the safe guise of anonymity in a foreign land.

Yet, despite his relative reclusiveness, Bute did form a few key relationships with men who not only served as his hosts but helped him to expand his art collection – a project which had taken on increasing urgency as the renovations at Luton progressed in his absence. These men were, for the most part, British diplomats and emissaries who supplemented their civil salaries by moonlighting as art agents. For example, in Naples, there was Hamilton, another Scottish compatriot and connoisseur, from whom Bute acquired Etruscan snuff boxes, folios of drawings of Neapolitan views by Pietro Fabris, as well as fossils and volcanic rock specimens for his geological collection.[33] In Florence, Bute was likewise assisted by the envoy, Horace Mann, who sold him a rare self-portrait then attributed to Poussin.[34] But the bulk of his Italian purchases were made in Venice with the assistance of his friend and fellow collector, Sir James Wright.[35] The British Minister at Venice was responsible for obtaining many of Bute's Italian pictures, including a *Mystic Marriage of St Catherine* by Paolo Veronese (cat. 33), a *Venus and Cupid* by Pietro Liberi, a *Descent from the Cross* by Jacopo Tintoretto, and a *Finding of Moses* by Giovanni Battista Tiepolo (then ascribed to Carletto Caliari), all of which were subsequently installed in the drawing room at Luton.[36]

A survey of the pictures at Luton would show that the earl had more than a penchant for Venetian painting. Canvases attributed to Veronese, Tintoretto, Liberi, as well as Bellini, Titian, Bordone, and Zuccarelli were hung not only in the Drawing Room, but spilled over into the adjacent saloon, and nearby library. The monumental scale and lofty subject matter of many of these pictures, such as Bordone's six-by-ten-foot masterpiece, *Christ and the Centurion* (fig. 12), made them practical purchases for display in Luton's formal state rooms.[37] But again, such works may have had a special appeal for the collector. Though he did own examples of the Roman, Florentine and Bolognese Schools, including works attributed to Cortona, Carracci and even Leonardo (a work now ascribed to Cesare da Sesto), the Venetian school was the best represented.[38]

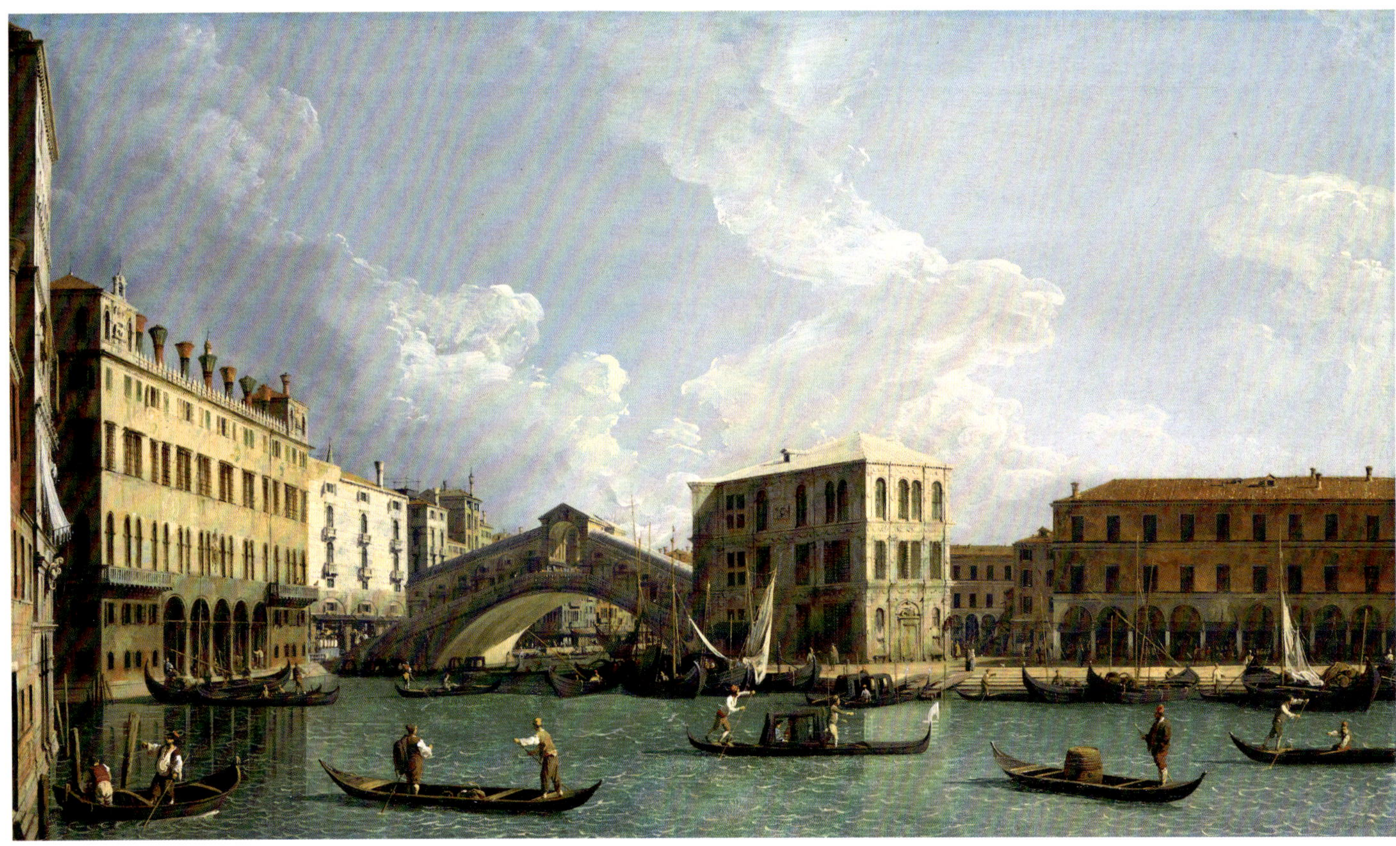

11 Canaletto (1697–1768), *A View of the Rialto, Venice*, 1734–1735, oil on canvas, 64.1 × 109.7 cm, Sir John Soane's Museum, P61. This painting was kept at Highcliffe with Bute's collection of marine paintings.

In particular, he seems to have favoured the sixteenth-century circle of Veronese. Perhaps Bute responded to the characteristically rich colouring and careful handling of sumptuous fabrics in paintings like the *Mystic Marriage*, which, as critics observed, was akin to the sensuous Flemish school. Moreover, the earl seems to have responded to the city of Venice itself, where he spent his longest residency while in Italy. He commissioned hundreds of drawings of Venetian architecture, and enthusiastically embraced the wider cultural offerings of the city; he frequently attended theatrical and musical performances, and collected (and even published his own) books of Italian poetry in Venice.[39]

Yet, the floating city apparently failed to buoy the Third Earl's spirits completely. On an excursion to take the healing waters at Valdagno in summer 1770, he wrote to his friend Wright, who was then back in England, complaining, "I would not pass such another winter [in Venice] for the universe where besides too Constant pain, I was a Hermit in a great City, no Society to make life happy, no friend of similar turn, & congenial ideas ..."[40] Owing to his fragile health, Bute nevertheless remained in Italy until the following spring, when he finally felt fit enough to endure the arduous trip home. His month-long expedition back, following a large circuit through France and Holland, was documented in the last of a series of travel notebooks that the earl kept during his time abroad. These journals mostly contained clinically-detached descriptions of the sites on route, apart from the odd personal aside, such as his comment on Holland, which he described as "a country so familiar to me from my long stay there that I can add nothing to former

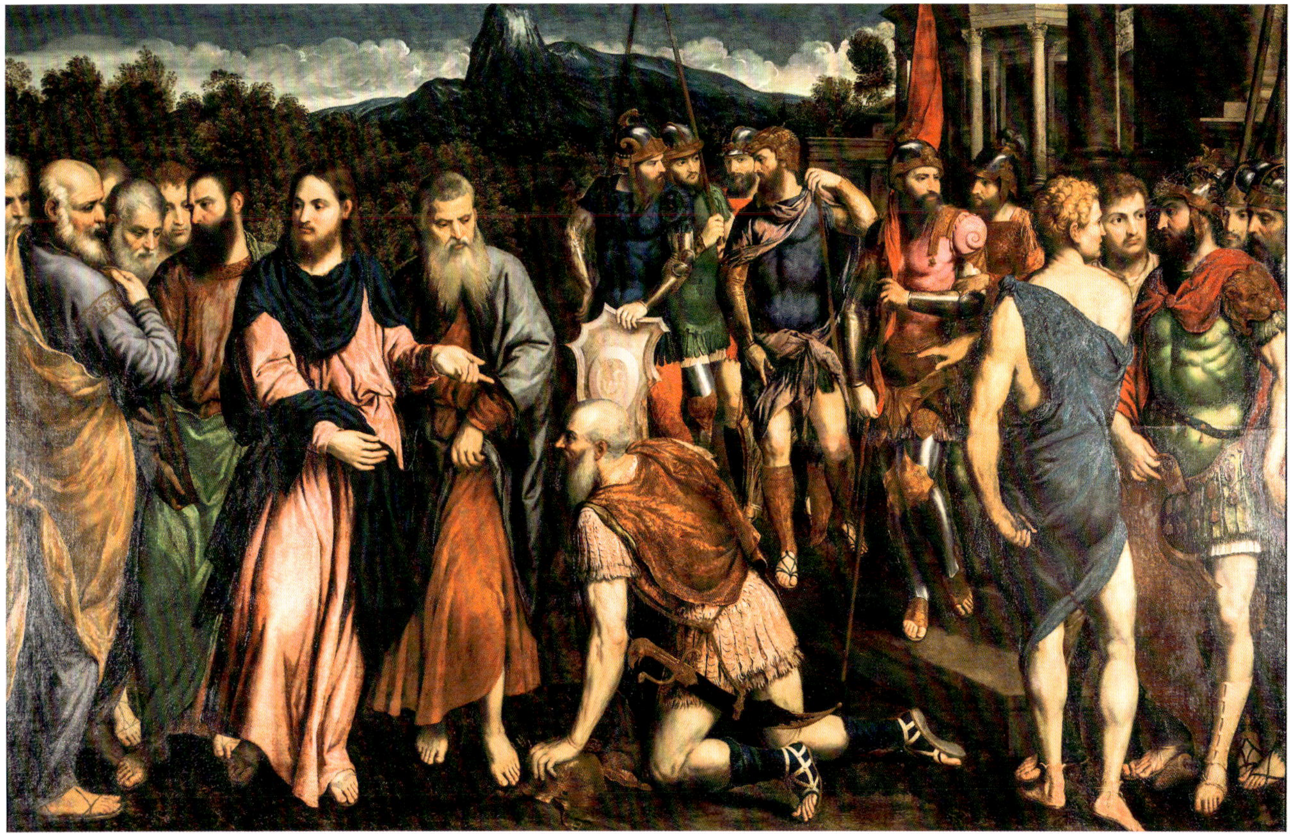

12 Paris Bordone (1500–1571), *Christ and the Centurion*, ca. 1555, oil on canvas, 194.5 × 305 cm, The Bute Collection at Mount Stuart. This impressive work was bought by the Third Earl in Venice in 1770–1771. It was hung in the saloon at Luton with large Italian works, including Guercino's *Assumption of the Virgin* (Detroit).

observations."[41] In May 1771, the earl finally returned to England to find his country house transformed by renovations, and his Italian art purchases, earlier sent back by Wright, cleaned and awaiting his arrival. Once work at Luton was more or less complete two years later, and the grand state rooms were fitted with his large Venetian canvases, the earl's interest in Italian art seemed to subside.

III

Moving to the upper floor at Luton, the East Bow Window Dressing Room contained twenty paintings, a mixture of landscapes, portraits and genre subjects, mostly of the Northern School, which were hung closely together in tiers of two and three, and above mantle pieces and doorways, in a dense display that would have covered much of the available wall space.[42] Like fitting together the pieces of a puzzle, this kind of picture hang required careful planning in order to create a display that was both balanced and aesthetically pleasing. In this room, and others at Luton, it seems apparent that picture placement was dictated not only by practical considerations like size but also thoughtful curatorial decisions. Here, and elsewhere, the placing of particular works created both complementary pairings and intriguing contrasts, the most dramatic of which was the juxtaposition of Jan Steen's *Cock Fight* (cat. 29), a comic genre subject depicting peasants competing for a woman's attention, flanked on either side by Claude Lorrain's idyllic classical

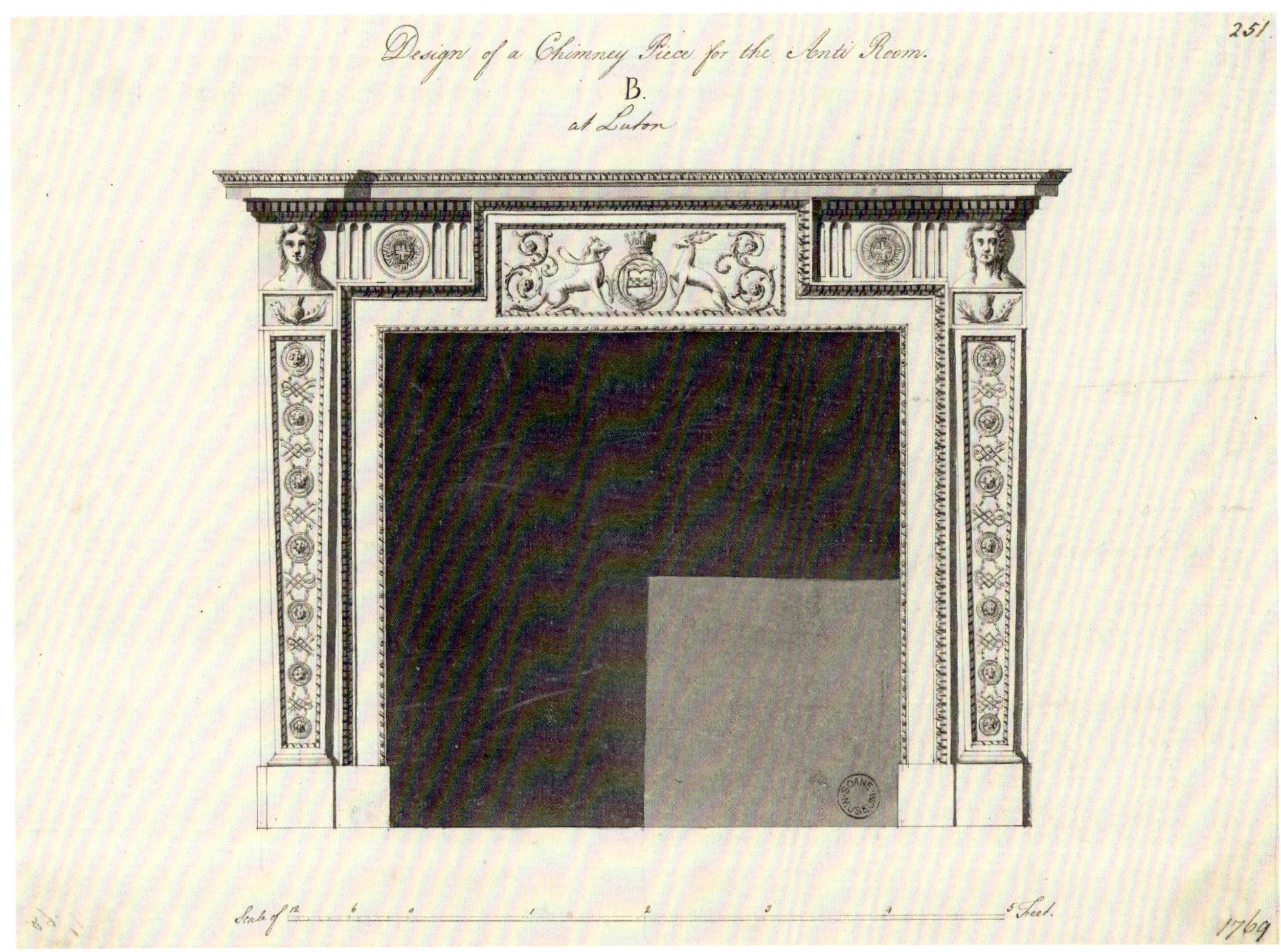

13 Robert Adam (1728–1792), *Chimney Piece for the Anti Room at Luton*, 1769, pen and ink wash, Sir John Soane's Museum, SM Adam Volume 22/251.

landscapes, *Morning: A Wooded Landscape* (cat. 11) and *Evening: A Seaport at Sunset* (cat. 10). Perhaps conceived as a visual joke, the contrast would have highlighted the great divide between the bucolic countryside of Claude's *Morning* and the rough rural life pictured by Steen. Though vastly different and representative of the two poles of the theoretical spectrum of painting – the "low" Dutch droll versus the "high" Italianate landscape – both artists were regarded as the respective masters of their field, and these pictures are undisputed masterpieces. Their presence in a dressing room in the domestic quarter of the house rather than on more conspicuous display in a public room on the main floor is noteworthy. It is illustrative not only of the generally high calibre of the paintings at Luton but also of the occasionally unorthodox display decisions that were made there.

Though there were not necessarily codified rules for the hanging of paintings in eighteenth-century country houses, there were general conventions which often reflected the function of the spaces in which pictures were displayed.[43] So, for example, visitors to a stately home may have sat down to a feast in a dining room surrounded by still-life subjects of game and produce, or topographical depictions of the estate illustrating where the food on their plates originated. Additionally, the size of a room may have dictated the types of work used to adorn the walls. As

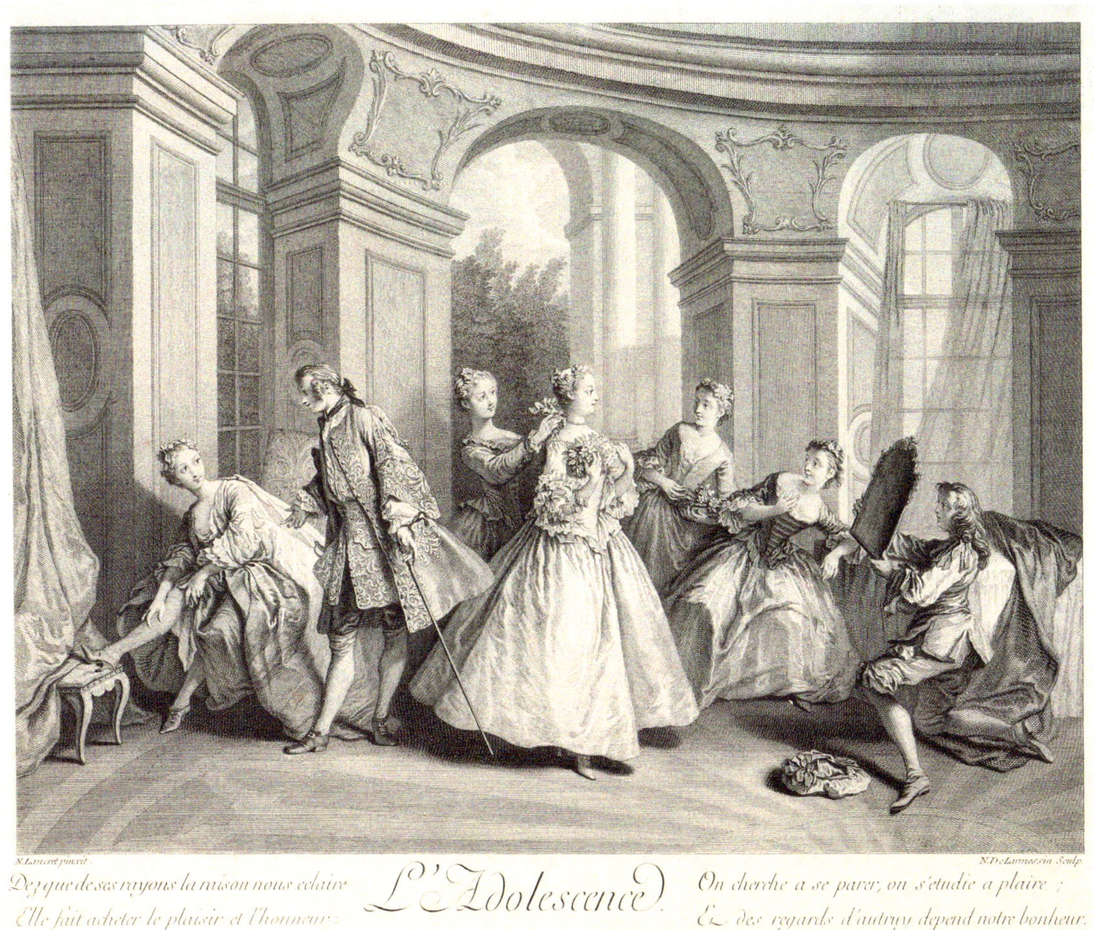

14 Nicolas de Larmessin III (1684–1755) after Nicolas Lancret (1690–1743), *L'adolescence*, 1735, engraving, 37.7 × 46.1 cm, British Museum, 1873,0712.333. Lancret's *Four Ages of Man* paintings, which are now in the National Gallery (NG 101–104), hung at Luton in the South Green Dressing Room among other French works. Bute's print collection included sets of engravings after Lancret.

we have seen, large scale mythological or biblical subjects were deemed appropriate for grand, formal reception rooms. Alternatively, smaller, more highly detailed pictures, like Dutch genre paintings, small-scale religious subjects and framed prints, would have been relegated to more intimate spaces, like closets, bedrooms and picture cabinets, which were rooms specially designed for small-scale paintings that could be held in the hands, or at least looked at from close-to, in order to appreciate the painterly skill which was often the justification for their acquisition. Most country houses would also have had a gallery with portraits of ancestors, family members, friends and allies, serving as a visual illustration of the homeowner's illustrious heritage and personal network. In many respects, Luton appears to have followed such customary practices as well as responding to contemporary trends, but in others, it notably broke with convention.

Luton's earliest surviving picture inventory, produced at the turn of the century at the behest of Bute's heir, is assumed to document his father's original hang.[44] From the inventory, we can surmise that the earl approached art display in the same methodical manner as his scientific studies. In many rooms he grouped schools of art together, forming a kind of taxonomy. Thus, he had a Venetian drawing room; there was a dressing room devoted to French paintings, featuring works by Lancret (fig. 14), Le Nain, and Pierre and Pierre-Antoine Patel; there were also several

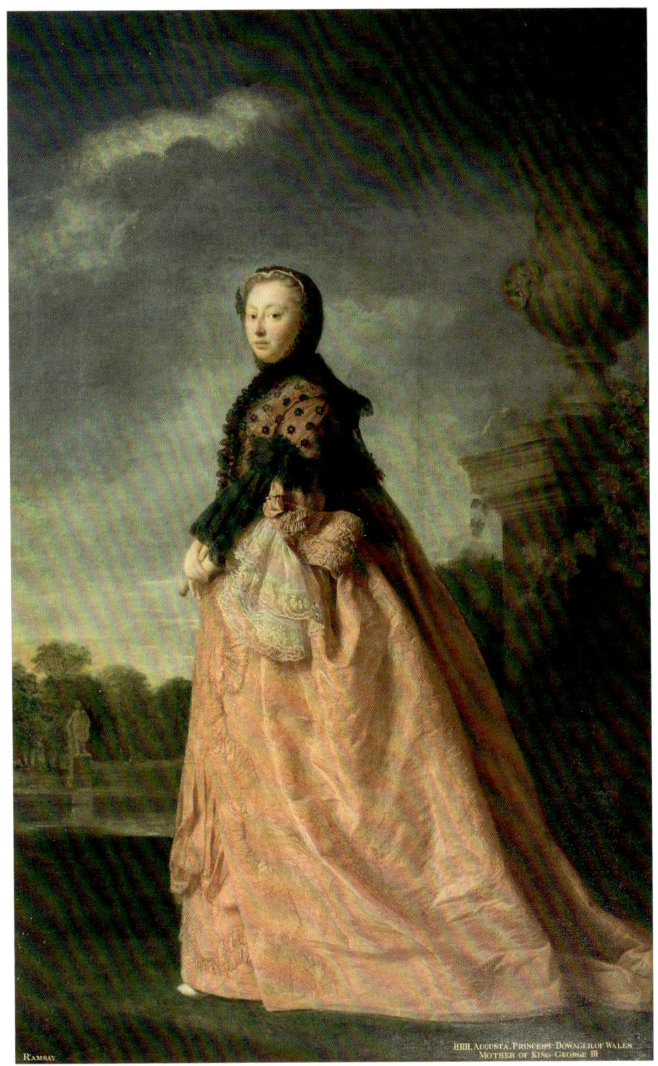

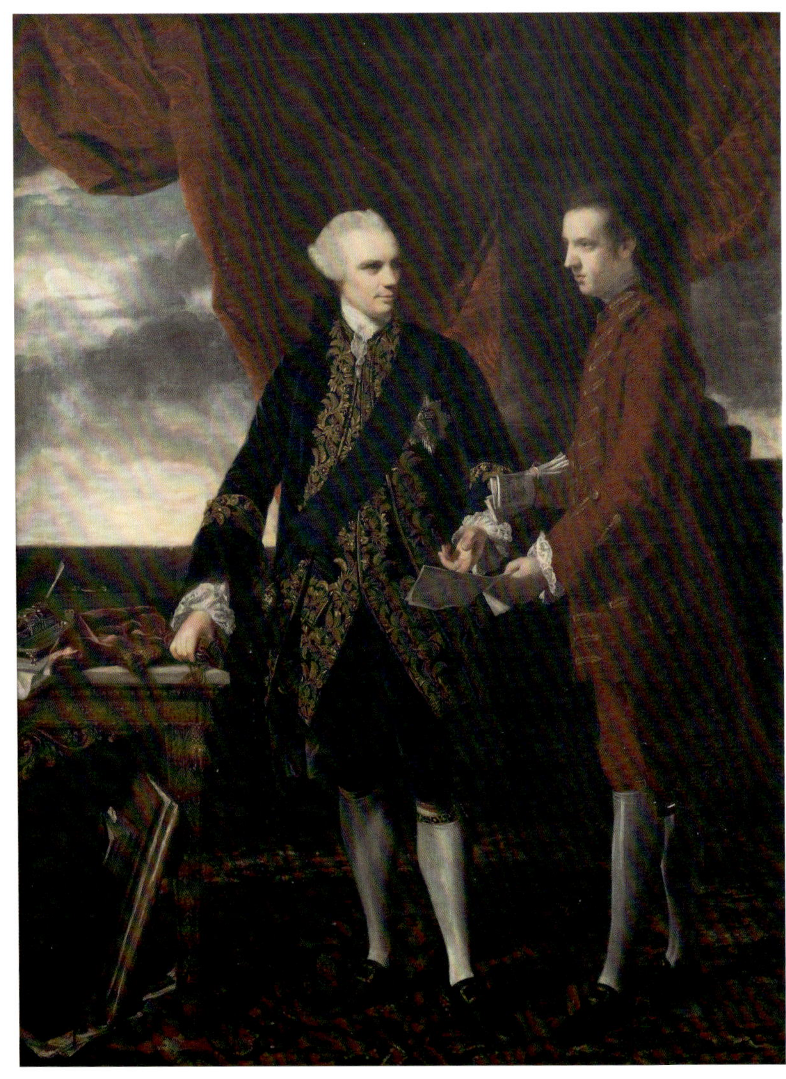

15 Allan Ramsay (1713–1784), *Augusta, Princess of Wales* (1719–1772), 1764, oil on canvas, 236.2 × 147.3 cm, The Bute Collection at Mount Stuart.

16 Sir Joshua Reynolds (1723–1792), *John Stuart, Third Earl of Bute with his Secretary Charles Jenkinson*, 1763, oil on canvas, 244 × 211 cm, The Bute Collection at Mount Stuart. Commissioned while Bute was still in office, this portrait was paid for by the king in December 1763. George III gave the painting to Bute's heir, Lord Mountstuart in 1783.

rooms, including his picture cabinet, that were filled almost entirely with Netherlandish paintings.[45] Bute's attempt to group schools together was a relatively novel approach to picture display at the time, though it became standard practice by the middle of the nineteenth century.[46]

In other rooms, various display decisions were seemingly made to encourage thoughtful reflection, make a visual point or otherwise complement the overriding aesthetic of the room. In his entrance hall, Bute hung a *trompe-l'œil* bas-relief by Jacob de Wit (1695–1754), a painted grisaille which would have blended well with the surrounding white stucco work, and which was in keeping with a decorating trend observable in other Adam's-designed houses of the period, such as Kedleston Hall and Osterley Park.[47] The De Wit was paired with a copy of the mosaic of doves from the Villa Adriana, further contributing to a classicising aesthetic and evoking the grand country retreat of an emperor. For his library, instead of the standard portraits of authors and philosophers, Bute opted for mostly Old Masters, just as his erstwhile pupil would do at Buckingham House.[48] In the Luton library, there were many landscapes, including Arcadian vistas by Francesco Zuccarelli (1702–1788), and Cuyp's much-admired *River Landscape with Horseman and Peasants* (fig. 35).[49] Such pleasingly pastoral scenes must have been conducive to the earl's quiet study. Rather than still life subjects, Luton's dining room was filled with portraits of Bute's relations and associates, including a suite of pictures by Allan Ramsay depicting George III when Prince Wales (fig. 27), another of the king after his coronation (cat. 22) and one of his mother (and dear friend of the earl) Augusta, Dowager Princess of Wales (fig. 15).[50] Additionally, there was Reynolds's 1763 double portrait of Bute and his then-secretary Charles Jenkinson (fig. 16), a canvas undoubtedly installed by his son, the First Marquess, who received the picture from the king in 1783.[51] While the entire scheme in this room was likely laid out by the younger Lord Bute, it is tempting to think that it was his father who, in the absence of visitors to Luton, sought to surround his dinner table with old friends.

What truly set the Luton display apart from other country houses of the period was the high quality of the pictures on the upper storey.[52] As we have seen, masterpieces by Ruisdael, Claude and Steen were displayed in dressing rooms, where they hung alongside distinguished works by Van Dyck, Rembrandt, Poussin and Rosa. Moreover, Bute's picture cabinet – containing thirty-four Dutch and Flemish masterworks described in the inventory as "select jewels of the first water" – could also be found on the bedroom floor, an unusual location for a room that was usually intended to impress visitors to the house.[53] Of course, the distinction between "public" and "private" space in a grand stately home could be nebulous, and select guests certainly would have been invited into these ostensibly private rooms. However, it seems that the house and picture display at Luton catered more to the owner's personal use and enjoyment than the expectations of visitors.

In comparison with most country houses of the period, the earl's estate was comparatively inaccessible.[54] It was, at that time, customary for proprietors of impressive country seats to welcome curious visitors in for a tour. So long as the guests were polite, well-presented and of a suitable social standing, it could be assumed that they would not be turned away, even if the lord of the manor were not at home.[55] This was a social convention from which the wary, eremitic earl understandably shied away. Indeed, there were reports that visitors to Luton were routinely refused entrance, including the likes of Walpole, who complained to Lady Ossory, "I was as unlucky at Luton; I sent in a memorial, begging only to see the chapel – the lord was not at home, and admittance was denied."[56]

The earl was not only discriminating in his taste in art. Indeed, he could be just as selective about who he let into his house. The privileged few included his cousin, Lady Mary Coke, and family friend, Mary Delany, the bluestocking artist, both of whom provided detailed accounts of their visits in which they marvelled over the astounding quantity of paintings. "Every room is filled with pictures," remarked Mrs Delany, "many capital ones: and a handsome screen hangs by each fireside, with ye plan of ye room, and with the names of the hands by whom the pictures were painted, in the order as they stand."[57] Lady Mary said much the same, writing, "... almost every room has fine pictures. The quantity Ld Bute has collected astonish'd me."[58] Other guests included connoisseurs and intellectuals known to Bute, such as the Italian art enthusiast, the Earl of Exeter, whose picture-buying expedition to Italy overlapped with the earl's own, and Samuel Johnson, the distinguished man of letters for whom the earl had secured a government pension.[59] Like the other guests to Luton, Dr Johnson left awestruck by the art collection,

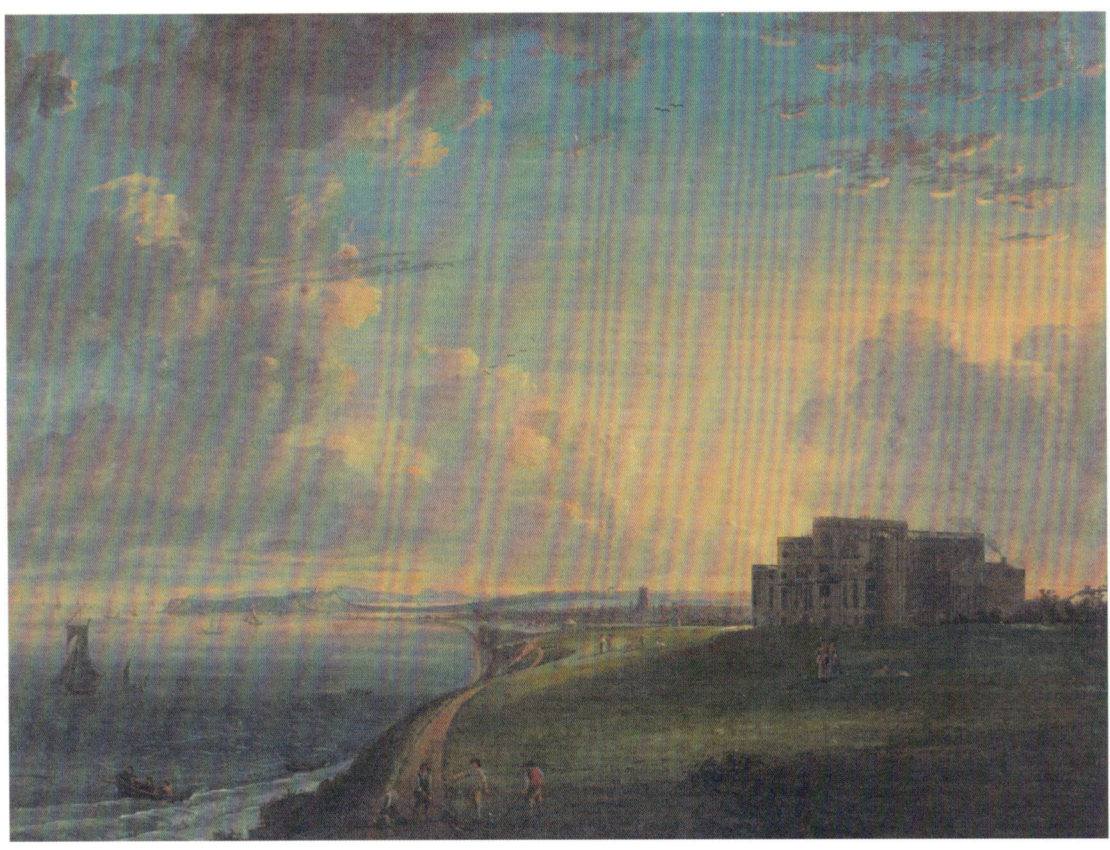

17 Adam Callendar (fl. 1780–1811), *High Cliffe*, 1783, watercolour after Charles Steuart (fl. 1760–1790), 47 × 64.5 cm, Victoria and Albert Museum, P.39–1953. At Highcliffe, Bute kept marine paintings as well as his collection of prints and drawings.

reporting, "The quantity of pictures is beyond expectation, beyond hope."[60] Given that Bute had now withdrawn from public life, it is hardly surprising that most of these visitors were family members, close friends and fellow connoisseurs, rather than casual acquaintances drawn from the political and social elite. It perhaps also explains the absence of any overt political or associational symbolism in the art and architectural programmes at Luton. Where some great houses of the age used the estate to express the public identity and allegiances of the owner – such as in the well-known case of the "Whig" sculpture gardens at Stowe – Luton sent no such message, aside from, perhaps, a perfunctory fealty to the king. More than anything, it expressed the tastes (and great wealth) of the detached collector.

Apart from occasional visitors, and the company of his immediate family, Bute led a relatively solitary existence at Luton. In 1775, writing to John Strange, one of his connoisseurial contacts in Venice, Bute claimed to have been living behind a locked door for eight years, seeing no one.[61] This was obviously something of an exaggeration as the earl did continue to socialise with a small circle of like-minded friends and associates, such as his trusted art agent Baillie, as well as the botanist John Hill and writer John Home.[62] However, the fragile, world-weary earl was circumspect of strangers and felt it necessary to turn his back on society, just as it had done to him. As he wistfully expressed to Strange:

"I live entirely out of the world my Friend partly to avoid giving the least handle to the Venom dayly darted at me & also from Inclination & bad health; had I been a Younger Man, the calm pursuits of philosophy and nat[l] history my darling Studys might have restored a Constitution once excellent [sic]..."[63]

This evocative image of a bookish recluse, self-imprisoned in a gilded cage of his own making, is similarly captured by one further guest to Luton. Following his visit in 1775, the expatriate French writer, Louis Dutens (fig. 36), wrote, "[It is at Luton] since the year 1766, when he declared in the House of Peers that he no longer saw the King, and that he took no future part in public affairs, Lord Bute has lived more like a philosopher than a man of the world."[64]

IV

Once renovation work at Luton drew to a close in summer 1773, and the house was packed to the rafters with paintings, the Third Earl's activities as an art collector slowed down considerably. In his later years, he spent less time at Luton, preferring instead the comforts of a humbler abode. In 1775, Bute secured the services of architect Robert Nasmith (d. 1793) to oversee construction of Highcliffe (fig. 17), a building described by the earl as "a cottage for the sea air and bathing between Christ Church and Lymington on the verge of the New Forest, alone by the cliffs, above 100 feet high."[65] While Bute did purchase paintings for his new home (fig. 11), including many marine subjects suitable for the seaside setting, he had less need for pictures in this comparatively modest dwelling (though in subsequent building phases, "High Cliff" would grow to be rather more than a mere cottage).[66] Here, the earl invested most of his time, energy and money on scientific experiments and botanical study. In the end, it was this passionate pursuit of science that led to his ultimate demise. In autumn 1790, while searching for plant specimens on a cliff edge, Bute tumbled twenty-eight feet, and sprained his ankle. Though it was a minor injury, the already enfeebled seventy-seven-year-old would never make a full recovery. A year and a half later, on 10 March 1792, the Third Earl of Bute died at his London home on South Audley Street.

Unfortunately, Bute's retirement project at Luton failed to make much of a mark on posterity. Even within his lifetime, it was viewed as a something of a mistake. While visitors to the estate almost always acknowledged the impressiveness of the art collection, the house itself, though undeniably opulent, received mixed reviews, with many guests remarking on its unfinished appearance. In 1787, the statesman and connoisseur, Lord Palmerston, summed up the regrettable state of the house as follows:

"... it is now only half a house and what is built is so imperfect in appearance without the remainder, which will probably never be added, that the general idea of grandeur and magnificence, which must have been Lord Bute's great object throughout, is lost, after an expense which, on a judicious plan, would have been much more than sufficient to have one of the completest seats in England."[67]

Indeed, Adam's proposed plan was never actually seen to completion, most likely because Bute had lost interest in the project, shifting his attention to Highcliffe. Luton would remain unfinished until the earl's great-grandson, the Second Marquess of Bute, finally completed it in

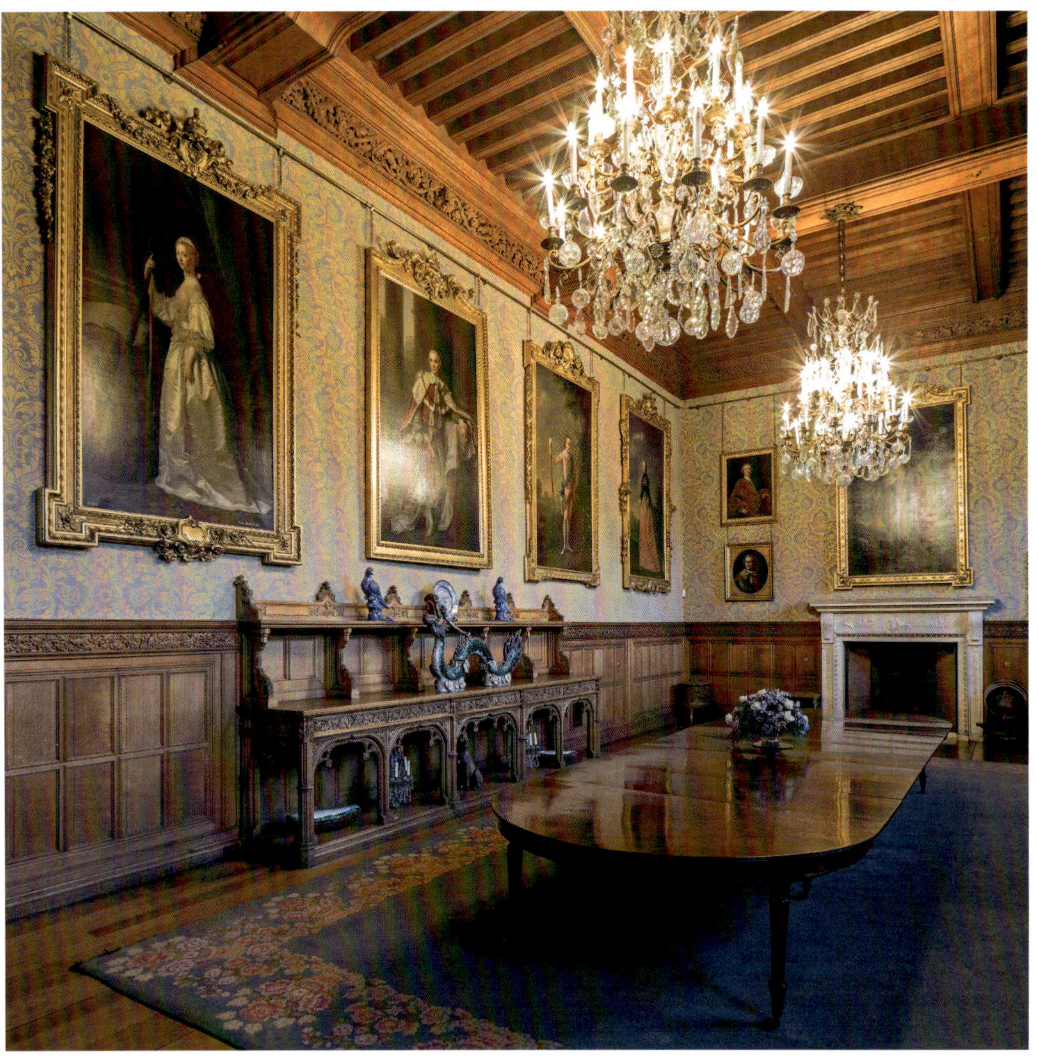

18 The Dining Room at Mount Stuart with Bute family portraits by Ramsay.

1829.[68] A devastating fire gutted the building in 1843, and five years later it was sold from the Bute family.[69] Today, little of the original building survives.

Fortunately, however, much of Bute's picture collection has remained intact, and though its inception lay in the decorative programme of a failed architectural project, its inherent value clearly transcended the original context. Public recognition of the earl's paintings came as early as the 1760s, when the publisher John Boydell included engravings after the earl's pictures in his successful print series, *A Collection of Prints, Engraved after the Most Capital Paintings in England* (1763–1792).[70] Its illustrious reputation was to last beyond Bute's death and into the following century. The earl's Dutch and Flemish pictures, in particular, were held up as exemplars in the Regency-era writings of art historian Gustav Waagen, artist Joseph Farington and art dealer John Smith.[71] Further recognition of the collection's national significance came in 1845, when, following the fire at Luton, the Scottish Royal Academy proposed to erect new galleries in Edinburgh to house the pictures on long-term loan. Similar offers came from the Royal Institute and the Board of Manufactures (the predecessor of the Scottish National Galleries), which likewise sought to safeguard the earl's masterpieces for the nation. These plans were ultimately rejected, though members of the public would get the opportunity to view the collection in its near entirety on exhibition at the Bethnal Green Branch Museum in 1883, the Glasgow Corporation Galleries in 1884 and the Queen's Park Museum and Art Gallery in Manchester in 1885.[72] For the two centuries since his death, the Luton picture collection – the foundation of what is now known as the Bute Collection – has remained in the possession of the earl's descendants. Today, the collection is preserved at the family seat, Mount Stuart on the Isle of Bute, where it endures as the Third Earl's lasting legacy.

Notes

1 For focused discussion of Bute's political career, see Brewer, 1973; Schweizer, 1988.

2 For the architecture and design at Luton, see Adam, 1775, part 3; Russell, 2004, pp. 155–172.

3 Bute employed several art agents; however, Baillie made the largest contribution to the collection. In addition to arranging the purchase of paintings, prints and drawings, Baillie also made copies of Old Masters for the earl, as well as reproductive engravings after paintings in Bute's collection. The inscription on Baillie's portrait by Lemuel Francis Abbott states, "William Baillie Esq. Under whose direction and management the Luton collection of Pictures and Drawings were Formed." For Baillie, see *Oxford Dictionary of National Biography*, online edition, 2004, http://www.oxforddnb.com.

4 *General Evening Post* (18 November 1783).

5 Quoted from a letter printed in *The St. James's Evening Chronicle* (9 June 1737) in which Hogarth writes under the pseudonym "Britophil."

6 The earliest surviving picture inventory for Luton (Luton, 1799) is a document entitled *Catalogue of Pictures at Luton Park Bedfordshire*, dating to ca. 1799. It is written by an unknown hand identified as a "Mr. Slace," with additional annotations by the First Marquess of Bute. Some of the pages are watermarked "JWilliams/1797." This document seems to have been based on a pre-existing catalogue, likely produced within the Third Earl's lifetime, as indicated by a comment made by the Marquess stating, "in this room [the Antiroom] I have committed a great error in not altering the old Catalogue." An annotation on the title page indicates that it is a "rough" draft, apparently for the 1800 catalogue, *List of the Pictures at Luton as they were in January 1800*, in which many of the paintings are described in new locations. Russell surmises that the ca. 1799 catalogue is, therefore, the most accurate representation of the Third Earl's collection, as it is unlikely that his heir would have made major alterations to the display in 1800 if he had already done so after his father's death in 1792. For the inventory, see Luton, 1799; Russell, 2004, p. 193.

7 For example, William Baillie after Jacob van Ruisdael, *Landscape with Two Trees and a Shallow Pool* (1773), British Museum Reg. No. F,2.185; Richard Earlom after Gerbrand van den Eeckhout, *Triumph of Mordecai* (Boydell, 1787) BM Reg. No. 1868,1212.23. Five of Bute's pictures were also included in John Boydell's print series, *The Most Capital Paintings in England* (1763–86), see below, note 70.

8 Luton, 1799, p. 20, "North Blue Dressing Room."

9 Waagen, 1838, p. 359.

10 For the history of the Stuarts, see Mount Stuart Trust, 2001.

11 According to the Duke of Newcastle, Bute described himself "as having little to do in Scotland; or at least, as being in no degree, particularly concerned about it." Quoted by Alexander Murdoch in "Lord Bute, James Stuart Mackenzie, and the Government of Scotland," Schweizer (ed.), 1988, p. 117.

12 The painting collection in the Green Closet at Ham House contained over fifty Dutch and Flemish paintings by the late seventeenth century. For the Ham House art collection, see Rowell, 1996. The painting collection of the Second Duke of Argyll was evidently renowned. It was named in connection to Carlo Gambarini's project to engrave the most "Cappital pictures" in England in 1731. Argyll's collection was housed at Adderbury House in Oxfordshire and was described by Walpole in 1767. For Argyll's collection, see Vertue, Notebook IV, 1930–1955, p. 19; Walpole, 1927–1928, p. 66; exhib. cat. Edinburgh, 1992, p. 158.

13 For Ilay's scientific interests, see Emerson, 2002.

14 For Scottish students in the Netherlands, see exhib. cat. Edinburgh, 1992, pp. 27–31; Mijers, 2012.

15 Leiden's importance in the field of botany at this time is explored in Stearn, 1962.

16 See discussion by Peter Black, below, pp. 59–60.

17 For Bute's botanical study, see David P. Miller, "'My favourite studdys': Lord Bute as Naturalist," in Schweizer (ed.), 1988, pp. 213–240.

18 Bute published twelve sets of the nine-volume book at a cost of £1,000. Ten of these were bound in fawn calf leather with the earl's coat of arms, while the remaining two were bound in red goatskin with gold edged pages, which were intended for the Royal Family. The book aimed to explain Bute's view of Linnaeus's taxonomical system to the "fairer sex." As such, he distributed most of the sets to women, including Queen Charlotte, Catherine II, Empress of Russia and the Duchess of Portland. Male recipients included botanist Joseph Banks and diplomat and writer Louis Dutens. For more on the *Botanical Tables* and the present locations of ten of these sets, see Lazarus and Pardoe, 2011.

19 For Bute's botanical illustration collection, see Russell, 2004, p. 200.
20 Luton, 1799, p. 19.
21 Ibid., p. 198.
22 Many of Adam's designs for Luton are preserved both in the Bute Collection (MS BU/165/S-5) as well as at the Soane Museum (SM Adam vols. 6, 8, 12, 17, 20–22, 25, 37, 39, 51, 53).
23 Adam's design for the bronze candelabra at Luton was engraved and published in Adam, 1775, part 3, plate 8. For paintings, see Luton, 1799, p. 5, "With-Drawing Room." For a discussion of Bute's bespoke picture frames, see Russell, 2004, pp. 191–192.
24 For the hierarchy of art in eighteenth-century Britain, see Lipking, 1970.
25 For the reception of Dutch art in eighteenth-century Britain, see Mount, 1991.
26 Walpole, 1747, p. xi.
27 For the Grand Tour, see, for example, Stourton and Sebag-Montefiore, 2012, chapters 7 and 9; Wilton and Bignamini, 1996.
28 Russell, 2004, p. 6.
29 For Bute's art books at Mount Stuart, see ibid., p. 13.
30 Ibid.
31 For the purchase of Consul Smith's collection, see exhib. cat. London, 1993.
32 A letter from Grant to Hamilton (13 January 1769) preserved in the National Library of Scotland (A cc 456 O), as quoted in Russell, 2004, p. 83.
33 For Hamilton's letters to Bute regarding such purchases and commissions, see MS BU/118/3/46–48.
34 This painting is now attributed to the "Circle of Poussin." While in Mann's collection, it was engraved by Thomas Patch; it remains in the Bute Collection (Inventory No. B00498). See Luton, 1799, p. 17, "North Green Dressing Room"; Blunt, 1966, no. R2.
35 Wright was likely introduced to Bute by his mother-in-law, Lady Mary Wortley Montagu, who lived in Venice for several periods. He first offered his services to Bute in 1766, and the following year wrote to him about a large group of Venetian pictures he hoped would entice George III (he had overestimated the earl's influence on the king at this time). Surviving letters from the summer of 1769 indicate that Bute purchased a number of Venetian paintings through Wright, including two Veronese pictures, a Tiepolo (then attributed to Carlo Caliari), a Fasolo, and a Liberi. Wright also sold paintings to Bute's son-in-law, Sir James Lowther. For Wright's letters, see MS BU/118/7/150-2.
36 The Tiepolo is now at the National Gallery of Victoria, Melbourne (accession no. 95-5); the Tintoretto was sold in the Bute sale at Christie's, 7–8 June 1822 (Lugt, *Répertoire* 10271), second day lot 42; the Liberi was also sold (Christie's, 1967).
37 The Bordone remains in the Bute Collection (Inventory No. B00438), see Luton, 1799, p. 6, "Saloon."
38 Bute's "Leonardo" of the Virgin and Child (now assigned to Cesare da Sesto) remains in the Bute Collection (Inventory No. B00115), see Luton, ibid.
39 Bute acquired 650 drawings by various artists which were arranged into fifteen volumes, five of which were devoted to the architecture of Venice. He funded the publication of a set of volumes of poems by Ludovico Ariosto in Venice in ca. 1772. For Bute's Italian books and his drawings collection, see Russell, 2004, pp. 96–97.
40 From a letter to Wright (26 May 1770) now preserved in the British Library (BL, Egerton MS. 1648/II), as quoted by Russell, 2004, p. 91.
41 Quoted from an entry dating to an earlier part of his tour (12 July 1769). For Bute's travel notebooks, see MS BU 142 S-4.
42 Luton, 1799, p. 27, "East Bow Window Dressing Room."
43 For picture display in eighteenth-century country houses, see Christie, 2000, pp. 215–224; Russell, 1989.
44 See note 6.
45 For French paintings, see Luton, 1799, p. 19, "South Green Dressing Room." For Dutch paintings, see ibid., pp. 29–32, "Cabinet"; pp. 15–16, "West Bow Window Dressing Room"; p. 17, "North Green Dressing Room"; p. 20, "North Blue Dressing Room"; p. 21, "South Blue Dressing Room"; p. 23, "North Red Dressing Room."
46 Russell, 1989, pp. 146, 149.
47 De Wit's *An Allegory of Painting* remains in the Bute Collection (Inventory No. B04215), see Luton, 1799, p. 1, "Hall."
48 Luton, 1799, pp. 11–13, "Library" (3 Rooms). For Buckingham House Library, see Russell, 1989, p. 146.

49 A pair of Zuccarelli landscapes remain in the Bute Collection (Inventory No. B00962); the Cuyp is now in the National Gallery, London (Inventory No. NG6522).

50 Luton, 1799, p. 3, "Old Dining Room."

51 Description of the Reynolds portrait in the Luton inventory reads, "This picture was originally painted for Alexander Earl of Eglintoune [sic], and afterwards taken by His Majesty George the Third, who bestowed it on the present Lord Bute in 1783."

52 This was first noted by Russell and reiterated by Anthony Crichton-Stuart, see Crichton-Stuart in exhib. cat. Edinburgh, 2012, p. 15; Russell, 2004, p. 196.

53 Luton, 1799, pp. 29–32, "Cabinet."

54 Russell, 2004, p. 165.

55 For country house tourism in Early Modern Britain, see Tinniswood, 1989.

56 Letter to the Countess of Upper Ossory (18 July 1772), see Walpole, 1937–1983, vol. 32, p. 84.

57 Letter to Bernard Granville (16 September 1774), see Delany, 1862, p. 35.

58 Journal entry (2 September 1774), see Coke, 1896, p. 390.

59 Brownlow Cecil, Ninth Earl of Exeter travelled to Italy in 1768, and his time in Naples and Rome overlapped with Bute's visit. Exeter evidently knew James Wright and also bought pictures by Veronese from him. He visited Luton in ca. 1776 and made a list of pictures he saw there in a copy of Pellegrino Antonio Orlandi's *Abecedario Pittorico* (1753 edition) now in the library at Burghley House. For Exeter's Italian pictures, see Humfrey, 2013; Russell, 2004, p. 193. Johnson travelled to Luton with James Boswell and Charles Dilly on 4 June 1781, see Boswell, 1885, pp. 373–375.

60 Ibid., p. 375.

61 Letter to John Strange, British Resident in Venice (15 May 1775), see MS BU/122/1/16.

62 Russell, 2004, p. 111.

63 Letter to Strange (22 December 1775), see MS BU/122/1/18.

64 Dutens, 1806, pp. 114–115.

65 Letter to Strange (22 December 1775), see above, note 63. Highcliffe has traditionally been attributed to Robert Adam, but there is nothing to indicate that he was directly involved; however, his younger brother William's firm was retained as evidenced by payments made from Bute's Coutts bank account in 1776, along with payments to Nasmith, who seems to have overseen the construction. The house was expanded in 1778, 1783 and 1787. For Highcliffe, see Russell, 1984; Russell, 2004, pp. 123, 175–179.

66 Seventy-four out of the eighty-seven pictures sold at the posthumous Highcliffe sale were marine subjects (Christie's, 1796; Lugt, *Répertoire* 5423). Russell points out that some of these were already in Bute's collection prior to 1775. For the Highcliffe pictures, see Russell, 1984; Russell, 2004, pp. 123, 175–179.

67 Connell, 1957, p. 170.

68 Later renovations were carried out by architect Robert Smirke from 1826 to 1829.

69 Luton was sold to the Liverpool solicitor, John Shawe Leigh in 1848. It was purchased in 1903 by the diamond baron, Sir Julius Werner, whose descendants retained ownership until 1991. It was purchased by Elite Hotels in 1999 and opened to the public as a luxury hotel, spa and golf course in 2007.

70 Boydell's print series was begun in 1763 and was available in bound volumes from 1769 onwards. By 1792, it comprised 572 prints in nine volumes. The engravings after Bute's pictures are William Elliott after Cornelis van Poelenburch, *The Flight into Egypt* (ca. 1764), British Museum reg. no. 1861,1109.230; William Walker after Willem van Herp, *A Flemish Entertainment* (1764), BM reg. no. 1872,0608.37; Isaac Taylor and Richard Earlom after Van Herp, *A Flemish Collation* (1765), BM reg. no. 1876,0708.2443; William Elliott after Aelbert Cuyp, *A View of the Maese near Maestricht* (1764), BM reg. no. 1877,0609.1559; Pierre Charles Canot after Ludolf Bakhuizen, *A Moderate Gale* (1766), BM reg. no. 1861,1109.7.

71 For Farington, see introduction, note 10; for Waagen, see above. Smith compiled the nine volume *Catalogue Raisonné of the Works of the Most Eminent Dutch, Flemish, and French Painters* (1829–1842) in which he provided detailed descriptions, locations and provenance of works by highly regarded Northern artists, including several works at Luton, see for example Smith, 1829–1842, vol. 1, no. 40; vol. 2, no. 915; vol. 3, no. 354; vol. 4, nos. 26, 67–8, 159–60, vol. 5, nos. 106, 249; vol. 6, no. 103; vol. 8, no. 31.

72 For the catalogues of these exhibitions, see exhib. cat. London, 1883; exhib. cat. Glasgow, 1884; exhib. cat. Manchester, 1885.

OLIVER COX

CREATING A KING:

THE THIRD EARL OF BUTE

AND GEORGE III

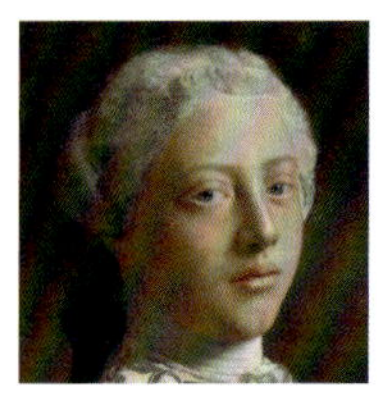

Reacting to the death of George II on 25 October 1760, Thomas Hollis, political philosopher, publisher of seventeenth-century political literature and active member of the Society for the Encouragement of Arts, Manufactures and Commerce, confided to his diary his hopes for the throne's new incumbent, George William Frederick: "May his grandson, a youth of fine dispositions, avoid his imperfections and excel his virtues, and pursue and adhere to, unswervingly, every manly and regal accomplishment! – May his pattern be that of Alfred, as historiated by the incomparable John Milton!"[1]

Hollis hoped that George III's youthful vigour would be supported by "wise and faithful parliaments and ministers, and by the affections of his people" so that "the constitution may be preserved, the age reformed, science and art encouraged, posterity attended to, [and] mankind in general benefited."[2]

George's most faithful, if not his wisest minister, was John Stuart, Third Earl of Bute. First entering George's life in 1747, Bute became the major pedagogic influence on his charge from 1755 on, assuming control of the prince's education. The relationship between the two men would drastically transform not only the political but the cultural landscape of the eighteenth-century British Atlantic world.

This chapter explores the complex and ever-changing relationship between the Third Earl and George, his erstwhile pupil and then king, charting the ways in which a particular understanding of the nature of the British constitution, inherited from his father – Frederick, Prince of Wales – and developed with Bute, created at least a decade of political instability and change.

Yet politics should not be seen as distinct from the two men's artistic patronage and collecting. Bute, inheriting the legacy of Frederick, Prince of Wales, shaped George's early adventures in the art world, and this relationship contributed, both directly and indirectly, to the establishment of the Royal Academy in 1768.

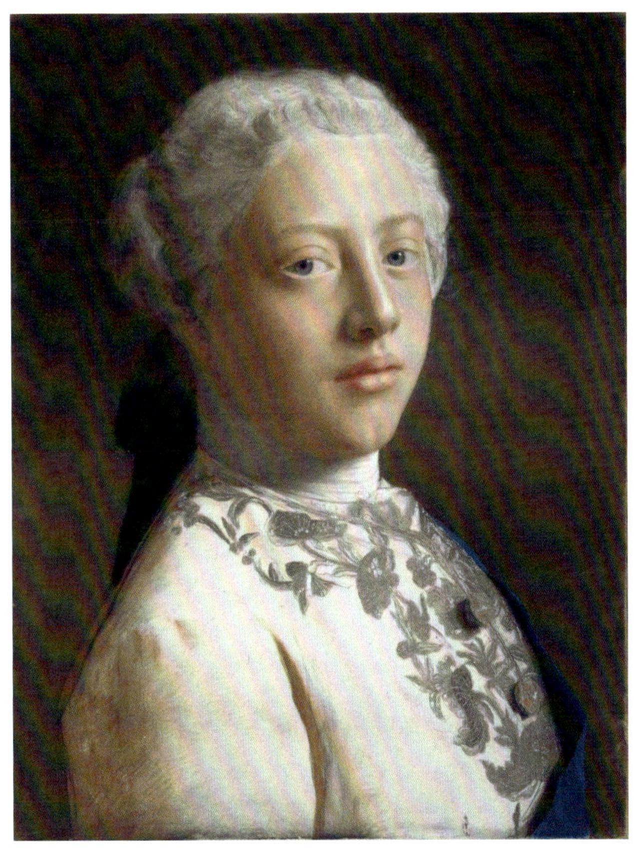

19 Jean-Étienne Liotard (1702–1789), *George, Prince of Wales* (1738–1820), 1754, pastel on vellum, 40.6 × 29.8 cm, Royal Collection Trust, RCIN 400897.

Early Years: Education and Marriage

Born in Edinburgh, John Stuart succeeded to his father's titles and lands in January 1723, aged nine, under the guardianship of his uncles, the Duke of Argyll and the Earl of Ilay. Between 1724 and 1730, Bute was at Eton College. He was a near contemporary of the catty commentator on eighteenth-century life, Horace Walpole, and William Pitt the Elder, Earl of Chatham. His was a rigorous classical education, requiring him during Whitsun 1728, for example, to learn 700 lines of Latin and 300 of Greek by heart.[3] He studied civil law at the University of Leiden, which Francis Russell suggests may have opened his eyes (and later his purse) to Dutch genre painting,[4] and married Mary, only daughter of the early-eighteenth-century phenomenon Lady Mary Wortley Montagu and her husband Edward, in 1735. Bute dabbled, rather unsuccessfully in politics, for the next six years before retiring to Mount Stuart on the Isle of Bute in 1741. By 1744, Bute was struggling at Mount Stuart, confiding to his school friend from Eton, Thomas Worsley:

"Judge you how much occasion I have for books horses &c. More than any lady you know, I try all I can to banish Melancholly [sic], but I own my friend it has often Incapacitated me."[5]

Yet it was Bute's passion for horses and for horse racing that was to provide him with his big break. In 1746, the Butes relocated to Twickenham before receiving the estate of Caen Wood in Hampstead (later renamed Kenwood by its subsequent owner, Lord Mansfield[6]) from his uncle, formerly Earl of Ilay, now Third Duke of Argyll. A meeting at Egham Races was to change the direction of the Butes' lives.

Mrs Boscawen described to the political memoirist, Nathaniel William Wraxall, this meeting in some detail. Bute, "as he did not at that Time keep a Carriage, or did not use it to convey him to the Race Ground," shared a lift with his Apothecary.

"Frederic, Prince of Wales, who then resided at Cliefden, honoured the Races on that day with his presence; where a tent was pitched for his accommodation, and the Reception of the Princess, his Consort. The weather proving rainy, it was proposed, in order to amuse his Royal Highness before his return home, to make a party at Cards: but a difficulty occurred about finding persons of sufficient rank to sit down at the same table with him. While they remained

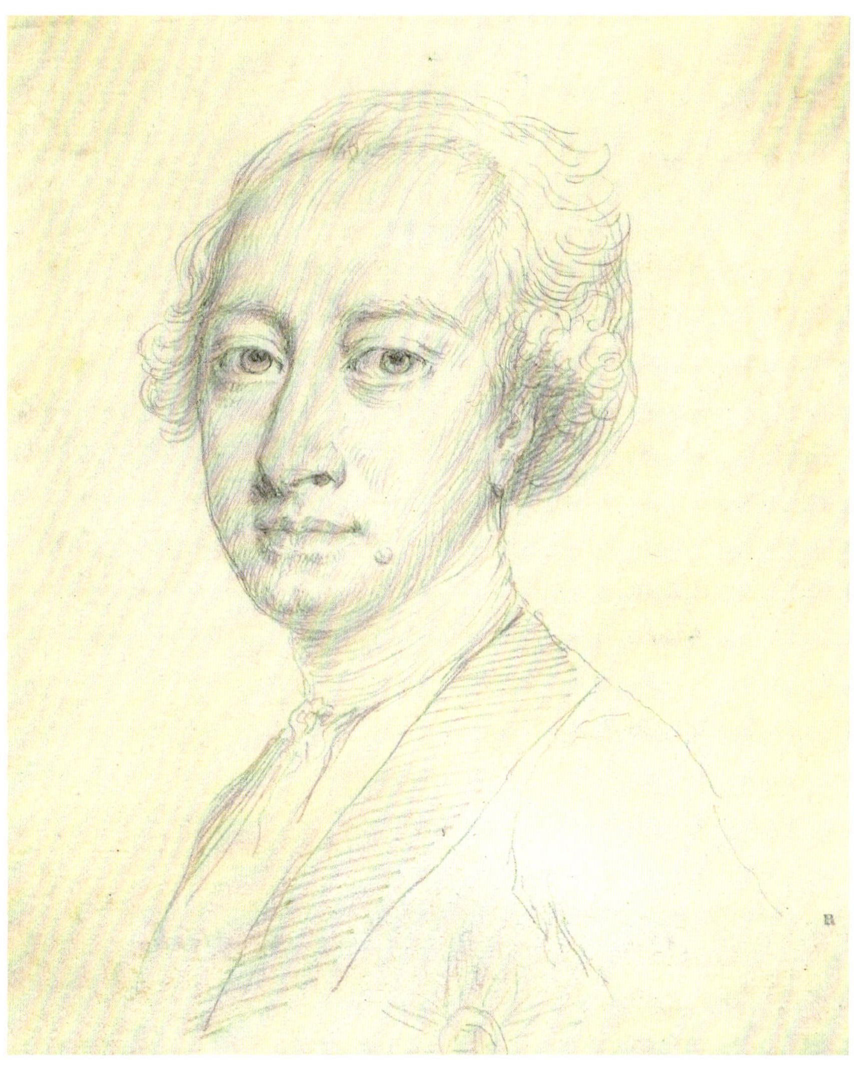

20 Jonathan Richardson (1667–1745), *Frederick, Prince of Wales, at the age of twenty-nine*, 1736, graphite on vellum, 16 × 13.7 cm, British Museum, 1902,0822.19.

under this embarrassment, somebody observed that Lord Bute had been seen on the Race Ground; who, as being an Earl, would be peculiarly proper to make of the Prince's party."

Bute, as Boscawen relates, dutifully played cards with the Prince, whilst his original companion, his apothecary, left Egham in his carriage.

"The Prince was no sooner made acquainted with the Circumstance, than he insisted on Lord Bute's accompanying him to Cliefden, and there passing the night. He complied, rendered himself extremely acceptable to their Royal Highnesses, and thus laid the Foundation, under a succeeding Reign, of his political elevation, which flowed originally in some measure from this strange contingency."[7]

For later commentators, reflecting on the enormous political upheavals of the 1760s caused in part by Bute's relationship with Frederick's son, this unorthodox meeting could be interpreted as laying the foundations for improper influence. Yet, for Bute, this chance meeting with Frederick, Prince of Wales, and the subsequent friendship and honours that followed, thrust him into the centre of British political life.

Lessons from a Patriot Prince: The Influence of Frederick, Prince of Wales

Frederick, Prince of Wales (fig. 20) , much like the Third Earl of Bute, divided his contemporaries and continues to divide historians. It is only recently that a full re-evaluation of the prince's political and cultural activities in life and influence in death has revealed the crucial position he played in mid-eighteenth-century Britain.[8] Historians have finally moved away from a reliance on eminently quotable, yet distinctly partial sources, such as Lord Hervey's *Memoirs of the Reign of King George II* and Henry Etough's *Free and Impartial Reflexions on the Character, Life and Death of Frederick Prince of Wales*.[9] In place of the "Poor Fred" of previous generations,[10] the Prince can now be seen as an important political and cultural figurehead, a patron of the arts and the most important royal collector since Charles I. As just one example, fourteen of the twenty Old

Master paintings catalogued in *The First Georgians* exhibition at the Queen's Gallery in 2014 were acquired by Frederick.[11]

Frederick's "mercurial character and early demise have left him difficult to assess,"[12] yet historians of eighteenth-century Britain are increasingly minded to see the Prince of Wales's political and artistic patronage as an attempt to create a new image of monarchy, derived from patriotic, British building blocks and a rejection of the men and measures of Frederick's father, George II, and his Prime Minister, Sir Robert Walpole.

When Frederick first arrived on English shores from Hanover in 1727, the political terrain was shifting towards what historians now term the "Robinocracy."[13] Britain's first "prime minister," Sir Robert Walpole had occupied his position as First Lord of the Treasury since 1722. Walpole was able to monopolise the counsels of the king, closely superintend a growing administration, ruthlessly control patronage and lead an election-winning party in parliament. Sir Robert (fig. 21) attracted criticism precisely because he was a new form of politician, halfway between the early-modern royal favourite and the modern prime minister.

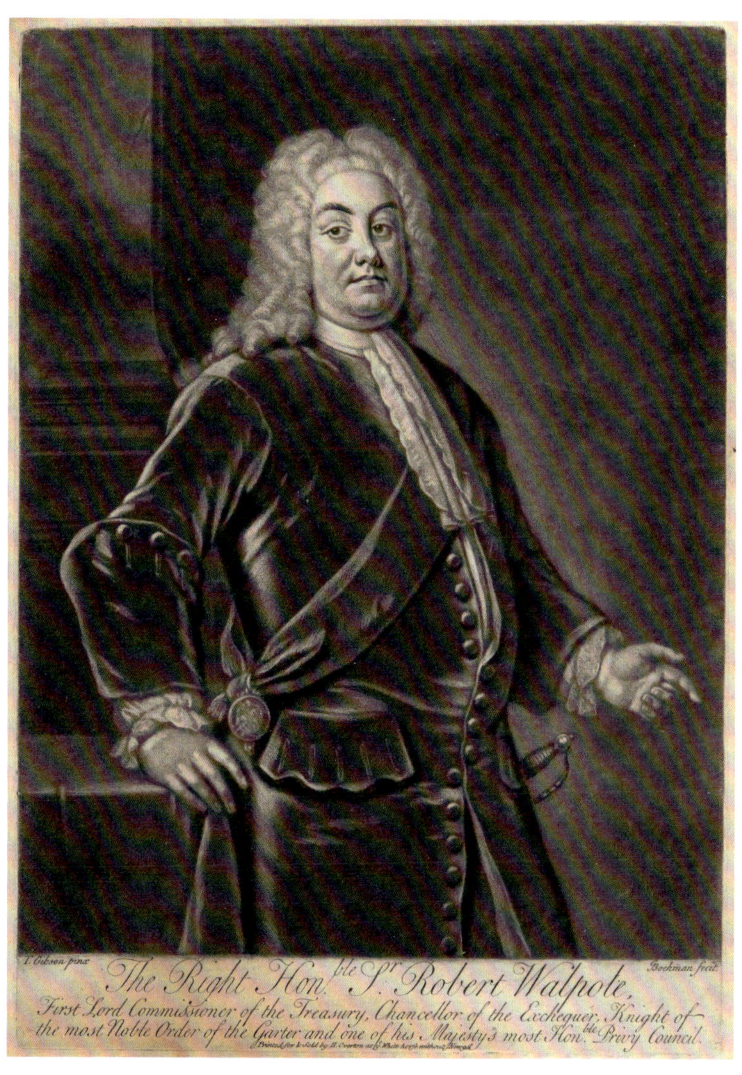

21 Gerhard Bockman (1686–1773) after Thomas Gibson (ca. 1680–1751), *Sir Robert Walpole*, ca. 1740, mezzotint, 36.8 × 26.4 cm, Hunterian Art Gallery, GLAHA:3974.

For Walpole's opponents, who clustered around Frederick, Prince of Wales soon after his arrival in England, this Robinocracy embodied something even worse than the private greed and abuse of power symbolised by his vast art collection and palatial country house, Houghton Hall.[14] They believed that Walpole's use of the patronage available to his ministry – government offices and pensions – allowed him to buy the support of both Houses of Parliament and of the electorate. In this way, Walpole was not only corrupting individuals, but he was destroying the balance of the British constitution by securing for the Crown an illegitimate and corrupt influence over the legislature.[15]

During the 1730s and early 1740s, this "Patriot" opposition to Sir Robert Walpole used a combination of politics, patronage and paternalism to create a coherent attack on the canker they believed was corrupting the British state. Men like Richard Temple, First Viscount Cobham – who with the help of William Kent and others created the richly iconographical landscape of Stowe – were portrayed as buttressing the constitution and a bulwark against the creeping, insidious corruption symbolised by Walpole. Temple's generation also included Bute's uncles, the Earl of Ilay and Second Duke of Argyll. The duke broke with the Walpole ministry in 1737, whilst Ilay remained loyal.[16] The next generation – scornfully labelled as "Boy Patriots" – looked

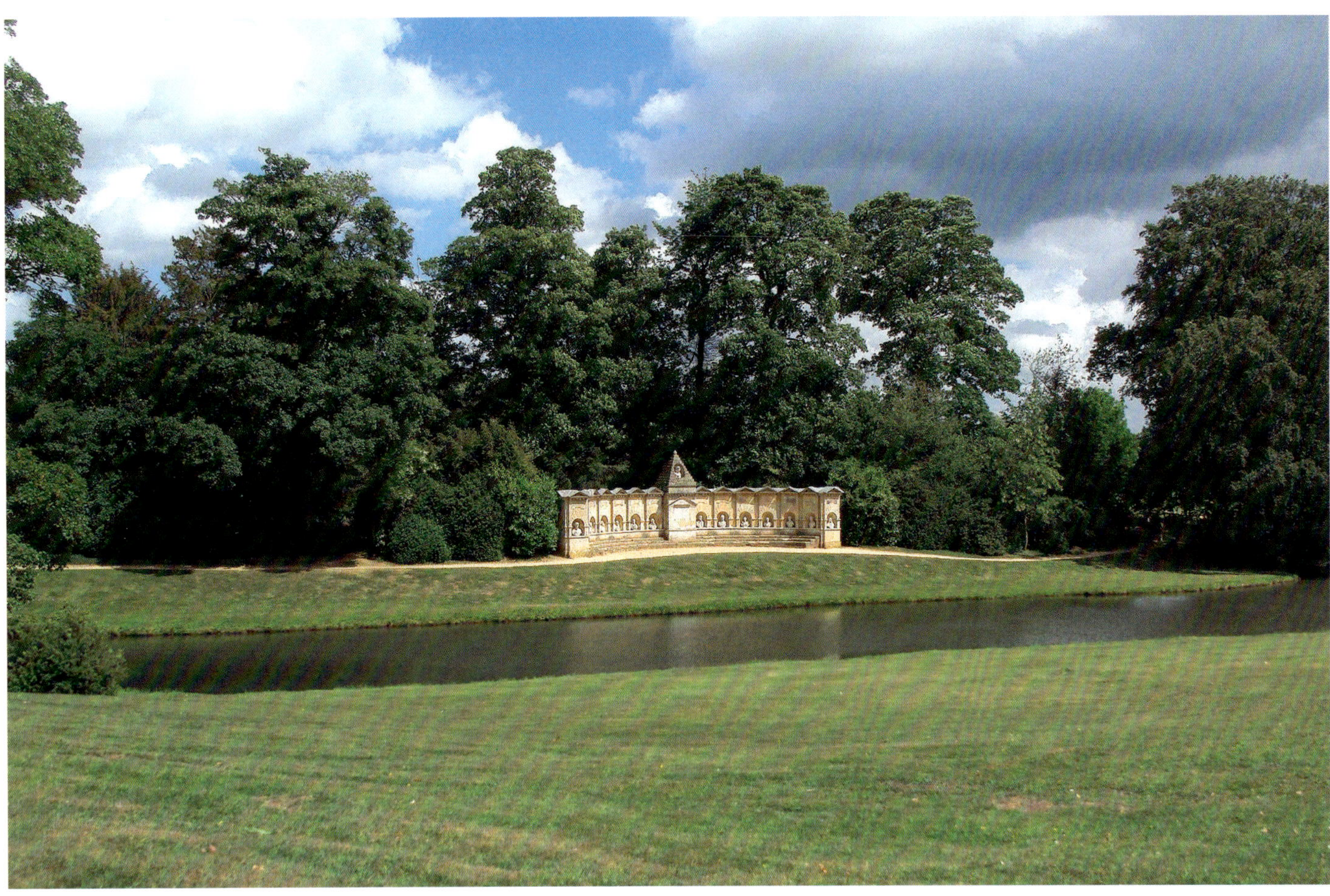

22 The Temple of British Worthies, Stowe, Buckinghamshire (photo: the author).

to Cobham for guidance and Frederick, Prince of Wales to legitimise their opposition to George II's men and measures.

Lord Chesterfield would write, in 1737, that with the prince in a position of political leadership against his father and Sir Robert:

"We have a prospect of the Claud[e] Lorraine kind before us, while Sir Robert's has all the horrors of Salvator Rosa. If the Prince would play the Rising Sun he would gild it finely; if not he will never be able to shine through."[17]

Frederick and the "Patriot" opposition developed a shared political and artistic language. One historical figure that symbolised this shared language was King Alfred, who first appeared in the gardens of Stowe (fig. 22) between 1735 and 1737. Alfred featured prominently as the wellspring of that uniquely English liberty that was under threat from Walpole:

"The Mildest, Justest, Most Beneficent of Kings;
Who Drove Out The Danes, Secured The Seas, Protected Learning;
Establish'd Juries, Crush'd Corruption, Guarded Liberty,
And Was The Founder Of The English Constitution."

What the figure of Alfred offered Frederick and his political allies was a standard of kingship against which his father could consistently be found wanting. If Alfred, as the gardens at Stowe proclaimed, "crush'd corruption" and "guarded liberty," George II and Walpole promoted venality and encouraged tyranny. Whereas Alfred founded the Royal Navy, promoted trade and ensured the nation's maritime security, Frederick and his allies believed contemporary governmental foreign policy to be too pacific and inappropriately European. Alfred, therefore, was both a stick with which to beat the administration and a figure that offered the possibility of a reformation of the role of the monarchy through a restoration of idealised Anglo-Saxon kingship.

In the summer of 1740, the association between Alfred and Frederick would be rendered in a way that has endured as a core plank of British national identity to this day.[18] On 2 August, the *London Daily Post and General Advertiser* reported the performance of a new masque with music composed by Thomas Arne, "of two Acts, taken from the various fortunes of *Alfred* the Great, by Mr Thomson," at Frederick's rented home, Cliveden.[19] The audience, comprised of members from Frederick's court, Princess Augusta and the two-year-old Prince George, listened to the final, rousing ensemble piece. Writing to Lord Guilford two weeks later, Bussy, Fourth Baron Mansel, observed:

"The Entertainment you had Here [Mansel's estate at Briton Ferry] was very short of that at Clifden, but Had I Known your Passion for a Chorus, I would have summon'd the Neath Choir ... to sing yours & Lady Norths [sic] Praises. Methinks I saw you stretching your Melodious Throat in the Greatest Extasy, pronouncing Those Delightful Words; Britons Never Will Be Slaves."[20]

Frederick's after-dinner party piece had political clout. The first performance of "Rule, Britannia!" at the climax of the masque of *Alfred* was seen by the anti-Walpole press as a mission statement for the kind of king that Frederick would be:

"A *Prince of Wales's* pleasing himself with such a Representation, is a Sort of Pledge, that he will join sincerely in *Alfred's* Prayer in the *fifth Scene* of the *first Act*; that he will endeavour to build the publick [sic] Weal on *Liberty and Laws*; and that he will disdain to think of establishing his Throne upon the *Tongues* or *Swords* of those, who count for Gain, what they villainously earn by sacrificing the *Constitution* and *Liberties* of their Country."[21]

Crucial to the cultural and political endeavours from Frederick's arrival in 1727 to his premature death in 1751 was a shared sense of the importance of the British constitution. In 1749, politics and theatre once more collided as Frederick's children took to the stage for a performance of Joseph Addison's *Cato*, a classical hero to match Alfred. The eleven-year-old Prince George recited a specially composed prologue:

"A boy in England born – in England bred;
Where freedom well becomes the earliest state,
For here the love of liberty's innate.
Yet more; before my eyes those heroes stand,
Whom the great William brought to bless this land,
To guard with pious care that gen'rous plan
Of power well bounded, which it first began."[22]

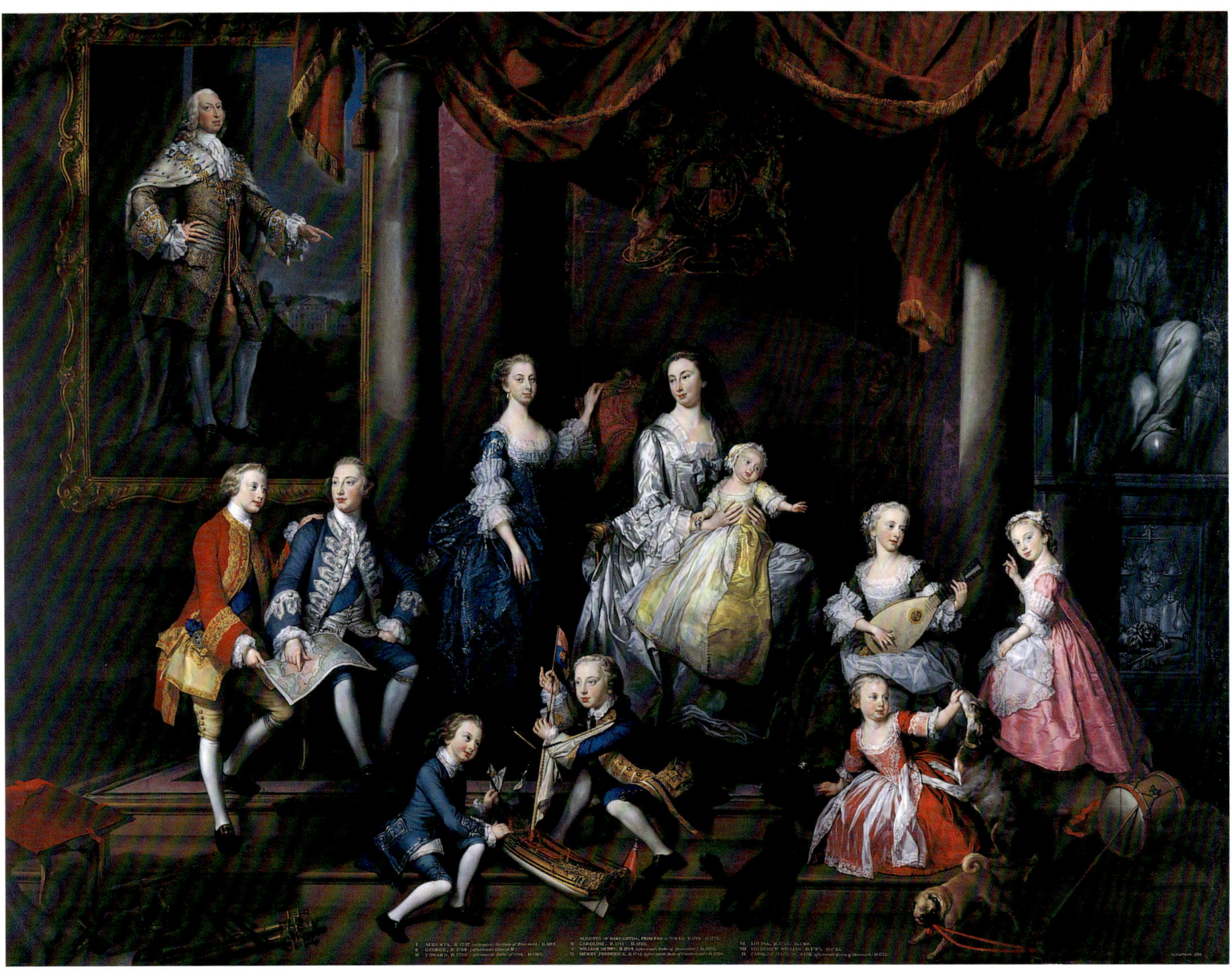

23 George Knapton (1698–1778), *The Family of Frederick, Prince of Wales*, 1751, oil on canvas, 350.8 × 461.2 cm, Royal Collection Trust, RCIN 405741.

In the same year, Frederick composed "Instructions for my Son George." This manuscript, one of the few to survive Princess Augusta's bonfire, "drawn by my-self, for His good, that of my Familys, and for that of His People," informed George that in order to succeed he would need to follow "the Ideas of my Grand-Father, and best Friend, George I."[23] Frederick warns that "flatterers, courtiers or ministers are easy to be got, but a true friend is difficult to be found."

Frederick clearly took the education of his children seriously, which was a view shared by his courtiers at Leicester House. The following year, when Lord Guilford was appointed governor to the princes, Frederick provided a detailed set of teaching instructions for his sons and daughter, with four-and-a-half hours of lessons in the morning and three between dinner and supper.[24] George Lyttelton wrote to Guilford to express his "Joy upon hearing now that your Lordship has accepted A Trust of so much Importance to the whole Nation," and that he could not "wish my Country more happy hereafter than there is a great reason to hope it will be under a King whose Heart has been form'd by your Lordship."[25] Within a year, however, Prince Frederick was dead. Nonetheless, his wife, Princess Augusta, dedicated herself to keeping aspects of Frederick's political outlook alive.

One way in which she achieved this was through commissioning a remarkable group portrait from George Knapton in 1751. *The Family of Frederick Prince of Wales* (fig. 23) was an attempt to capture the constitutional ideals articulated by her husband and her supporters in paint. The life-sized work shows the late Frederick as a portrait on the wall, flanked on the other side of the canvas by a statue of Britannia. Around the base of the statue, a bas-relief explains the British constitution. Scales hold a crown and a liberty cap in balance; a lion guards another liberty cap whilst reclining on the twin documents which secure the constitution: Magna Carta and the Act of Settlement. The prince and the constitution, held in balance, signify the component parts of the constitution and the role the Crown could play in securing liberty for all. Prince George, with his garter sash and star, examines "A Plan of the Town and Fortification of Portsmouth," connecting him once more with the mercantile and "blue-water" policies dear to the "Patriot" Opposition's heart since, at least, the mid-1730s.[26]

Creating a King: Bute and George, 1755 to 1760

Frederick's premature death may well have hastened Bute's move to the heart of the Leicester House circle. Appointed a Gentleman of the Bedchamber in 1750, Bute developed a close friendship with Princess Augusta, because, as Bute's future under-secretary Charles Jenkinson observed, the princess "liked Lord Bute as the only person about her husband who was attached to her on her own account."[27] For the ever-expanding popular press, this friendship had all the trappings of a sexual relationship, and historians have tied themselves in knots ever since in working out the accuracy of these rumours.[28] True or not, they led to an outpouring of satirical cartoons (fig. 24),[29] many of which remain in the Mount Stuart collection.

From 1751, Prince George, and his brother Edward, Duke of York, spent part of their time at Savile House, next door to his father's London home, Leicester House.[30] Sir George Savile of Rufford, working with James Gibbs, extensively renovated the house on purchase from Queen Caroline in 1729. Plaster heads of British worthies were inserted into the ceilings: Shakespeare, Milton, Newton and Samuel Clark in the drawing room; King Alfred, the Black Prince, William III and the Duke of Marlborough in the dining room.[31] Despite not being commissioned by Frederick, or a member of his immediate circle, his two eldest sons enjoyed their formative years surrounded by an iconography that had been developed twenty years previously in opposition to their grandfather.

Bute became George's principal tutor and advisor in 1755, melding the "Patriot" inheritance from George's father Frederick with further focus on the British constitution and an increased interest in, and discussion of, collecting tastes and habits. As John Bullion has suggested, Bute succeeded in educating the prince where others had failed, because he gave him a "vision of what a virtuous king could achieve."[32]

John Brooke, in his biography of George III, hinted at the strange atmosphere in which George conducted his schooling. "As a child [he] lived in an adult world, the most terrible

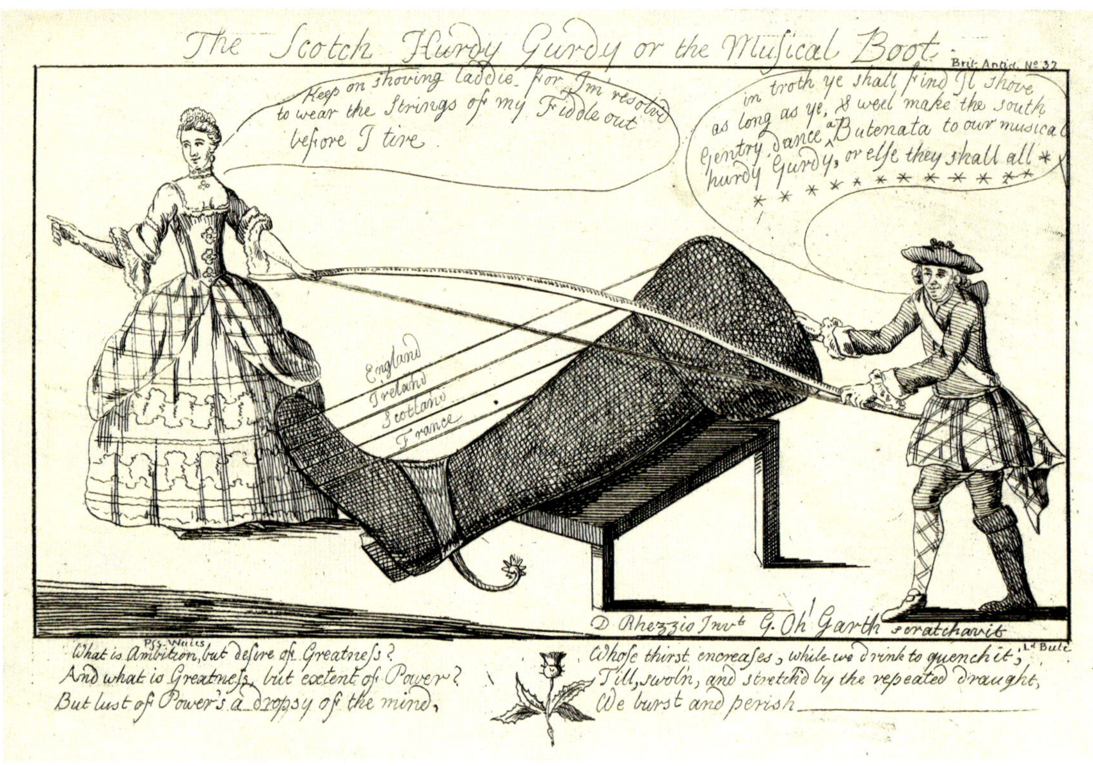

24 *The Scotch Hurdy Gurdy or the Musical Boot*, ca. 1762, etching, 18.1 × 26.8 cm, British Museum, Cc,3.43. During Bute's time as Prime Minister, he was attacked in a stream of anonymous satirical prints. Many alleged a relationship with Princess Augusta, the king's mother.

situation that can befall a child."[33] Despite the destruction of Bute's letters to George, seven large boxes of the Prince's essays and academic exercises survive in the Royal Archives[34] and, along with collections at Mount Stuart, allow the historian to piece together Bute's strategies for engaging his new charge. In seeking to teach the prince to become a king, Bute "sought in books the answer to the mystery of statecraft."[35]

At the start of July 1756, George having "had the pleasure of Your Friendship during the space of a year," wrote to Bute, full of anger at the way in which he was being treated by his grandfather and his ministers, and in so doing connected the specific and topical challenge of who was to be part of his new household with a more general critique of the situation into which British politics had descended.

"It is very true that the Ministers have done everything they can to provoke me, that they have call'd me a harmless boy, & have not even deign'd to give me an answer when I so earnestly wish to see my Friend [Bute] about me. They have also treated My Mother in a cruel manner (which I will neither forget nor forgive to the day of my death) because She is so good as to come forward & to preserve Her Son, from the many snares that surround him. My Friend is also attack'd in the most cruel & horrid manner, not for any thing he has done against them, but because he is my Friend, & wants to see me come to the Throne, with Honor & not with Disgrace & because he is a friend to the bless'd Liberties of His Country & not to arbitrary notions."[36]

Personal desire had collided forcefully with national politics. George's eighteenth birthday was of political significance, for if the aging George II should die there would be no regency, and

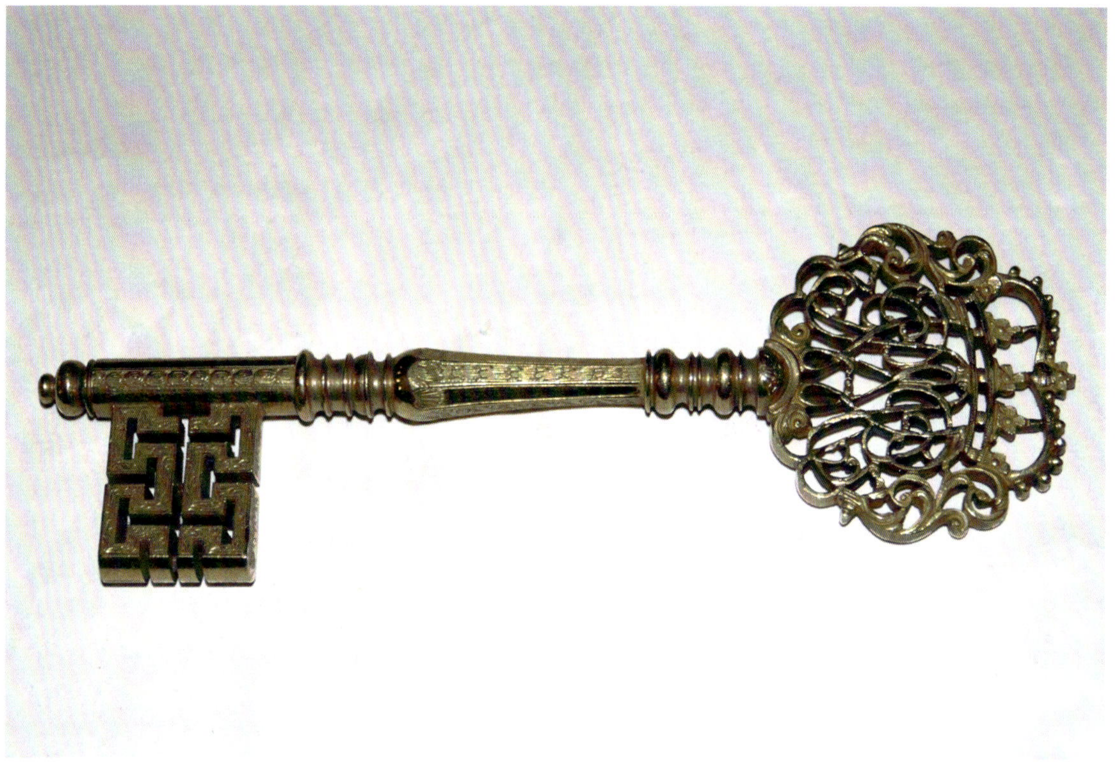

25 Gilded key provided for Bute when he was appointed Groom of the Stole in 1756.
The Bute Collection at Mount Stuart.

there was the opportunity for the prince to choose his own Royal Household. As with the battles his father had faced twenty years previously, all sides shared the understanding that an independent Royal Household centred around George, Prince of Wales, could become the nucleus for a new and enlarged opposition. One significant aspect of this debate centred on George's "earnest wish, that the E. of B. might be plac'd, in some principal Station, about my person."[37] The king eventually conceded this point and, "being desirous to shew all marks of tenderness, & affection, for ye P. of W. is dispos'd to comply with his most ardent Request, by appointing ye E. of Bute, to be Groom of ye Stole to His R.H."[38] The gold keys belonging to the Office of the Groom of the Stole remain in the Mount Stuart collection (fig. 25), where in a 1792 "Account of George's Medals of St Andrew and Gold Keys belonging to my late Father John 3^d Earl of Bute," the Fourth Earl, later First Marquess, noted:

"The one with the hollow pipe was given on the first establishment of the Prince's household; and no key being prepared George the Second made use of the one used by his Court."[39]

Bute's was an unpopular appointment, and the fact that no new key had been prepared highlights the unwillingness of George II to acquiesce to his grandson's demands. With Bute at the heart of the Leicester House establishment, George started to explore and consider the role of the monarch and the British constitution.

The clearest expression of George's own "thoughts on the British Constitution" lie in draft treatises in the Mount Stuart archives.[40] These show the extent to which George had absorbed the "Patriot" rhetoric of his father's generation, which had also been captured in George Knapton's family portrait. George began by observing, "We must necessarily mention the three kinds of

Government, to one of which that in every Dominion must resemble, the English one indeed is a mixture of all three." It was for the ideal of the balanced British constitution, articulated in Knapton's portrait, that George proposed to "lay down some Rules that we esteem necessary to preserve this Constitution."

"Every form of Government has some principle to which its Laws & rules of action ought to be agreeable; in Democracys & Aristocracys this is Virtue, in Monarchy Honour; in Despotism, pride, avarice & sloth. The British Constitution being a Mixture of the free forms of Government, Honour & Virtue ought to be equally thought of."[41]

What is most striking about George's rules is the extent to which they connect an idealised conception of the British constitution based on historical study with the tenor of political debate in the late 1750s. Take, for example, the idea of a militia. The importation of Hessian and Hanoverian troops to protect Britain from invasion was a cause for much patriotic soul-searching.[42] Mercenaries, combined with a standing army, were seen as both a menace to the liberties of Englishmen and a source of political patronage. Charles Jenkinson, who would become Bute's under-secretary in 1761 (fig. 16), used King Alfred as a way of highlighting how a domestic militia secured the Anglo-Saxons' defence of English liberty against the Danes in the ninth century.[43] George, as part of his preparation to rule, looked to work out his own response to these issues. He argued that:

"'tis freemen who serve for the defence of their Country who we look upon as the true preservers of the Laws, as they would be loosers [sic] if that most estimable of all treasures Liberty was destroy'd."[44]

When considering the role of trial by jury, George applauded the extent to which the crime was calibrated to the defendant's peer group – with peers tried by peers and "the rest of the People have a Jury compos'd of their equals for the same purpose." He disapproved, however, of "the Commissioners of Excise," perhaps demonstrating the extent to which he had been indoctrinated by the "Patriot" worldview of his father. The Excise Bill of 1733 had been a seminal moment in the development of an organised opposition to George II, and Prince George, almost thirty years later, felt the activities of excisemen, perhaps those proposed by Bute in the hugely unpopular cider tax,[45] would be "difficult to be chang'd yet it ought because entirely Contrary to our Constitution."[46]

George's essays and notes combined the current with the historical and created an outlook that despaired of contemporary politics and looked forward to a new era when liberty would be restored and the constitution upheld. Bute shared this outlook, as he explained his ambition for Prince George to Gilbert Elliot in 1756:

"My Young friend, My hopes, the only Hopes, the *Spes ultima* [last hope] of this poor country, grows every day more firm, More steady; May his future subjects be as fond of Liberty as he is; May they have as Strong an aversion to Vice, Corruption & Arbitrary Power, & they will be a happy people; He a happy [prince]."[47]

George's sense of his own ability was somewhat lacking. Writing to Bute in December 1758, George's paranoia reached new heights:

"I will frankly own that throughout the negligence, if not wickedness of those around me in my earlier Days, & Since perhaps through my own indolence of temper, I have not that degree of knowledge & experience in business, one of My age might reasonably have acquired, therefore if I should Mount the Throne without the assistance of a Friend, I should undoubtedly be in the most dreadful of situations."[48]

Ultimately, George may have found it easier to express his situation and his ambition through the use of historical proxies. At some point, between 1755 and 1758, George returned to his father's hero, Alfred the Great, to sketch his future direction:

"He had the happiness of being bred up in the school of adversity ... excellent were his laws, and vigorously kept to; for he examined into everything himself, impenetrable in his secrets.

"When Alfred mounted the Throne, there was scarce a man in office that was not totally unfit for it, and generally extremely corrupt in the execution of it ... he got rid of the incorrigible, reclaimed others, and formed new subjects for to raise his own glory and with it the glory and happiness of his country ... When all this is carefully examined, we may safely affirm that no good and great Prince born in a free country and like Alfred fond of the cause of liberty, will ever despair of restoring his country to virtue, freedom and glory, even though he mounts the Throne in the worst corrupted times, in storms of inward faction and the most threatening circumstances without.

"Let him be but true to himself, true to religion, virtue, honour, freedom; such a Prince has a right to expect, and will most certainly have the support of that Almighty Power that decides the fate of kingdoms, and baffles all the black designs and wrecks the cunning of proud, ambitious and deceitful men."[49]

George, influenced and encouraged by Bute, sought to act like a latter-day Alfred. On the question of marriage, George would write to Bute that, "He has thoughly [sic] convinc'd me of the impropriety of marrying a Country Woman," reassuring his mentor that, "the interest of my Country ever shall be my first care, my own inclinations shall ever submit to it."[50] For the influential historian Sir Lewis Namier, these assertions were merely "flapdoodle,"[51] but given that they formed the mainstay of the prince's education, there is every reason to believe that he accepted all of them as completely true. George imagined himself as Alfred, purging the political nation of his grandfather's corrupt cronies; those proud, ambitious and deceitful men.[52] As he confided to Bute, "I am born for the happiness or misery of a great Nation."[53]

Bute's influence was not just confined to a constitutional education. As Francis Russell's comprehensive work has demonstrated, George's actions as a patron and a collector were "encouraged, indeed formed, by Bute."[54] Here again, the ghost of George's father was never far away. From 1749, Frederick had employed George Vertue as his art adviser and was committed to repatriating the Old Master and tapestry collections of Charles I; and Francis Hayman expressed Frederick's aim for an academy for British painters in his 1751 *The Muses Paying Homage to Frederick, Prince of Wales and Princess Augusta*.[55] Hopes for Frederick's future reign were such that the future founding president of the Royal Academy, Sir Joshua Reynolds, while travelling

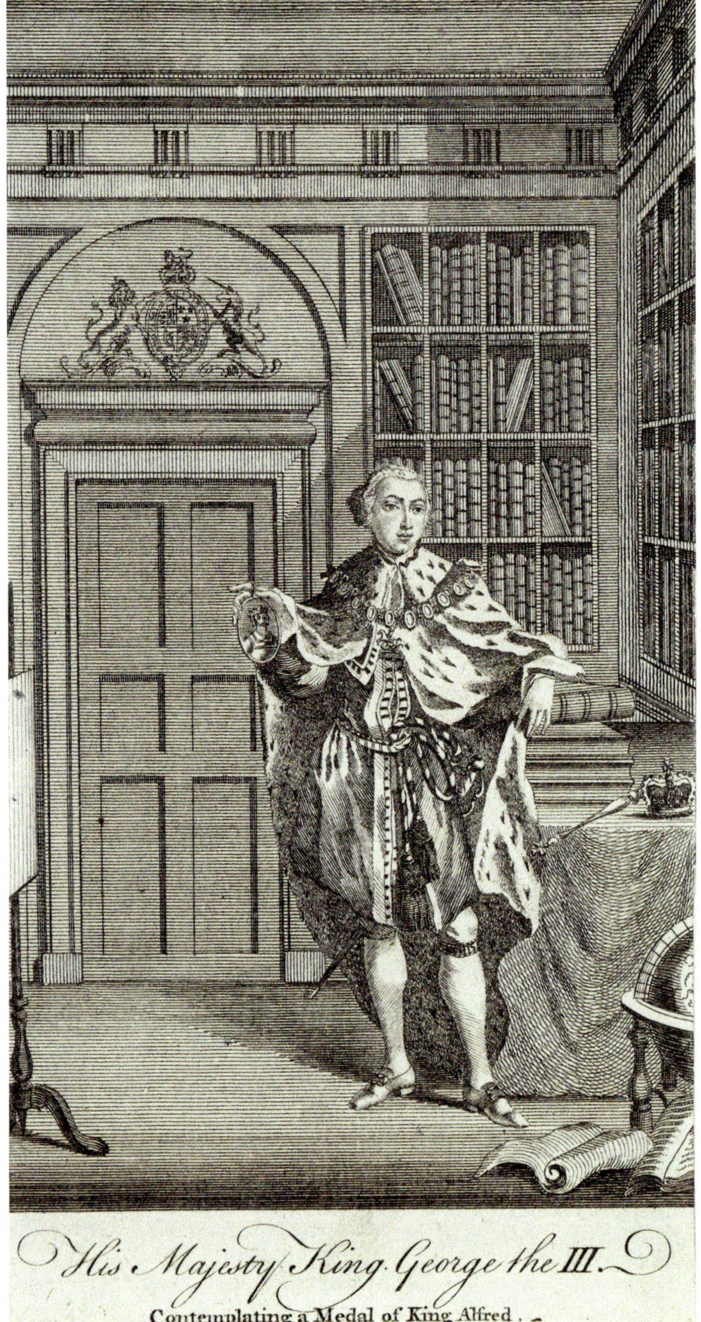

26 *His Majesty King George the III. Contemplating a Medal of King Alfred*, ca. 1750–1800, engraving, Royal Collection Trust, RCIN 630058.

in Italy wrote, "We are all extremely afflicted for the loss of the Prince of Whales [sic] who certainly would have been a great Patron to Painters as he already was to Mr. Dalton."[56]

"Mr. Dalton" – Richard Dalton – was, by the early 1740s, one of the most active English art dealers, spending long periods of time in Italy cultivating both potential aristocratic clients (as buyers and sellers) and a generation of influential artists and architects, including Joseph Wilton, Matthew Brettingham and Robert Wood.[57] Dalton was appointed librarian to George, Prince of Wales in 1755, and Russell has documented how Dalton's visit to Italy in 1758–1759 had the aim of enriching the prince's (and Bute's) collection in medals, drawings and prints.[58] Dalton wrote to Bute from Florence on 17 November 1758:

"I have the pleasure to say that a fine collection of Drawings are sent to Leghorn carefully packt [sic] for HRH to the number of near 700, one Rafaele amongst them, about 40 fine Ones of Guercino and several of the Carracci & other eminent Masters, in a box several small Portraits painted by the Lombard school; besides which the day before I came away bought a good collection for your Lordship that cost not more y^{n} a hundred pound, amongst which are many very fine ones."[59]

Such activities clearly delighted the prince, who wrote:

"My D. Friend; I have this instant received from Dalton the collection of Guercinos You gave him for Me; they are very beautiful, but their value is much increased from the pleasure whenever I examine them that must occur, of knowing from whom I have got them."[60]

The Mount Stuart collection holds a number of items that speak to the close connoisseurial relationship between Bute and George. On 2 April 1792, John Stuart newly elevated to his father's titles as Fourth Earl, created an "Account of the Badges belonging to my late Father the Earl of Bute." An "Onyx Badge with plain Gold Back was given by the King, who took it out of a drawer where there were many of the same sort: but His Majesty said he selected it, knowing it had belonged to the Stuart's Kings of England."[61]

"The Diamond George" in the Mount Stuart collection, "was given by the King in return for a valuable Onyx St Andrew presented to him by my Father, formerly the property of the

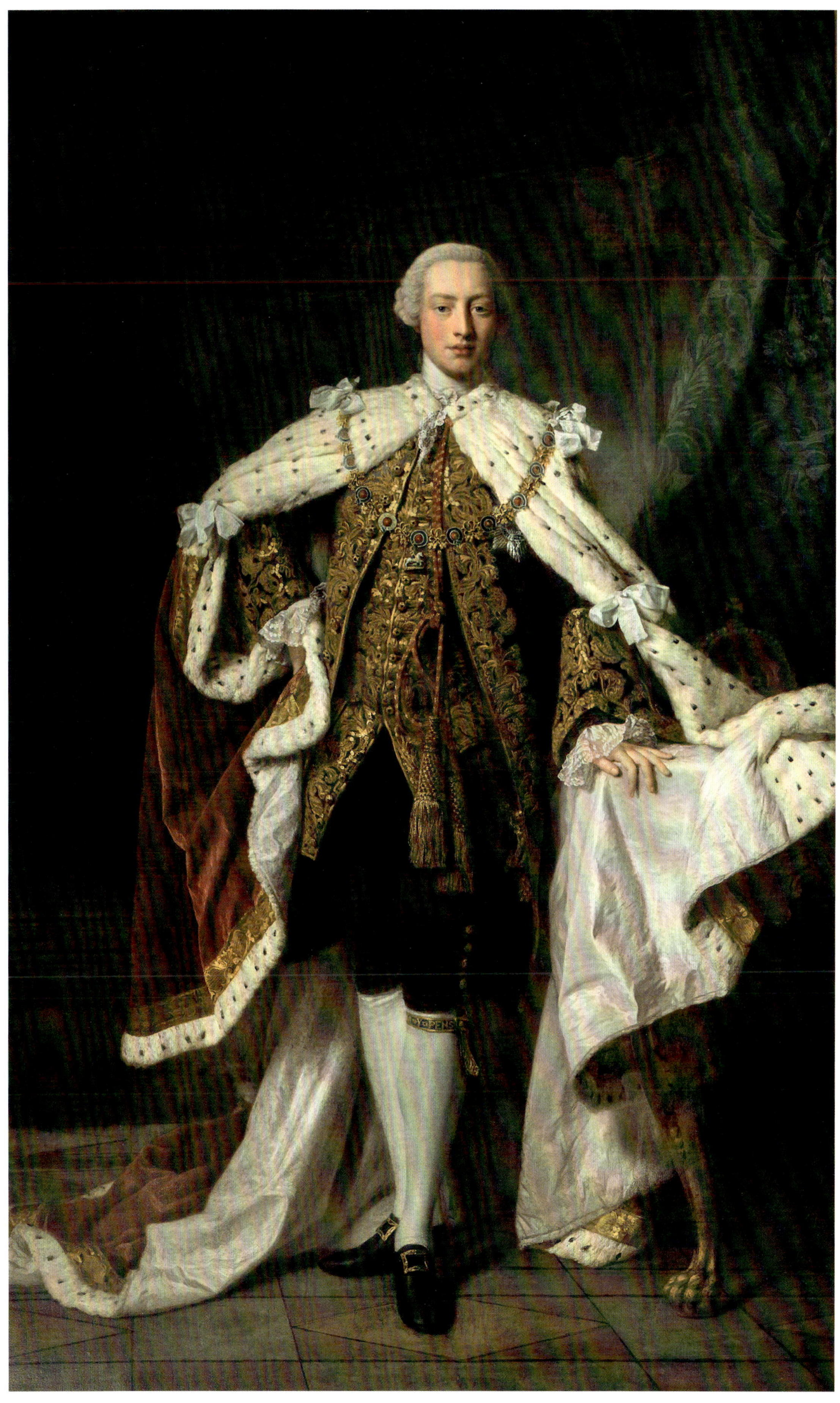

27 Allan Ramsay (1713–1784), *George III as Prince of Wales*, 1757–1758, oil on canvas, 236.2 × 144.8 cm, The Bute Collection at Mount Stuart.

King's of Scotland." The memory of his "Dearest Friend" was important to George, who set the onyx in diamonds, "and always wears it to this day on the Festival of St Andrew." Bute also received a "George, Onyx with blue enamelled back" from "Her Royal Highness the Princess Dowager of Wales."[62]

King and First Minister: Bute and George, 1760–1763

On George's accession to the throne, he was indeed burnished by comparison to his boyhood hero, Alfred the Great. Alongside Thomas Hollis's remarks which opened this chapter, 'Britannicus,' writing to the *Public Ledger or The Daily Register of Commerce and Intelligence*, was inspired "to consider the character of many antient [sic] British Kings; and, with peculiar veneration and delight, that of the Great Alfred."[63] Likewise, the publishers of *The Christian Magazine* were keen to advertise that the first edition of their new magazine carried a copper plate representing "his present Majesty contemplating a Medal of King Alfred." George is presented as the embodiment of the scholar king, a connoisseur and collector (fig. 26) surrounded by books. The pose and dress of the sitter is taken from Allan Ramsay's portrait of *George III as Prince of Wales*,[64] (fig. 27) with the cameo medal of Alfred, the embodiment of the balanced British constitution, added in. Clearly, the publishers expected George, like Alfred, to maintain the delicate equilibrium at the heart of the British state.

The bitter irony for George III was that, in attempting to act as the Patriot King his father never had the chance to be, new political groups energised by the fear of a renewal of the royal prerogative in a manner not seen since the ill-fated reigns of Charles I and James II, turned George's understanding of the British constitution against him. His ambitions were those of a scholar king with no conception of the political realities of the 1760s.

George III, eager to enact his vision for patriot politics, quickly brought Bute into the heart of government. Within two days of George's accession he was sworn of the Privy Council, and in early 1761 received the seals as Secretary of State for the Northern Department and a seat in the cabinet. Bute's rapid elevation created confusion and strife both within parliament and out-of-doors, and the early years of George's reign were to prove that the king's conception of liberty did not necessarily coincide with that of career politicians.[65]

Politics and art, would prove difficult to disentangle. As Holger Hoock's important work on the founding of the Royal Academy during the 1760s documents, "discussion of the arts, artists'" activities and institutional politics reflected, or contributed to, wider political discourses which crystallised around Crown and government involvement. Writings on art, and art itself, "refracted contested notions of monarchical authority, representation, oligarchic monopoly, corruption and reform."[66] George III's close involvement with the Royal Academy certainly enhanced the organisation's standing, but it also opened up questions of improper influence and the role that the monarch could, should or ought to play in the promotion of art.[67]

Once more, the spectre of the royal favourite, Lord Bute, and the fear of creeping Crown prerogative, encouraged a broadening of parliamentary political discourse to be applied to the art world. For those outside the Academy, and sceptical as to the aims of the new king, this new cultural institution was nothing more than a cabal of royal favourites.

By 1788, in one of the last letters from George to Bute in the Mount Stuart collection, the king was more sanguine, and certainly more worldly, about the realities of eighteenth-century political and social life:

"I owne every day makes me more a Phylosopher [sic], and attempt to keep my desires within a narrow compass, that my disappointments may be fewer. When one is within a few months of fifty one has acquired little advantage from the experience of a toilsome life if one has not learnt to be moderate in expectation and thankful to Divine Providence for the good one possesses, and full of diffidence of one's attempts and therefore not surprised when they prove abortive."[68]

Conclusion

Writing in 1764, one year after Lord Bute's resignation of the premiership, Philip Dormer Stanhope, fourth Earl of Chesterfield recorded his impressions of the man:

"Here the new scene opened: Lord Bute arrived from the greatest favour to the highest power and took no care to dissemble or soften either, in the eyes of the public, who always look upon them with envy and malignity; but on the contrary avowed them both openly. He interfered in every thing, disposed of every thing, and undertook every thing, much too soon for his inexperience in business, and for at best his systematic notions of it, which are seldom or never reducible to practice."[69]

John Stuart, Third Earl of Bute was a phenomenon, and yet historians have tended to treat the various component parts of his personality in isolation.[70] Politics occupies one set, his botanical works the other,[71] and his collecting habits the third.[72] It is Bute's political significance that until recently has dominated historical scholarship. As Karl W. Schweizer notes, "his presence and actions [evoked] responses and counter-responses that collectively altered the basic patterns of Georgian political life."[73] The myth of Bute's secret influence, rather than the man himself, shaped the direction of aristocratic factional politics during the 1760s and 1770s, and gave rise to a potent new form of popular radicalism embodied in the figure of John Wilkes.

Yet, more work needs to be done to connect Bute's political life to his intellectual and artistic life. The two are, of course, connected. In 1761, he received the seals of state and immense wealth upon the death of his father-in-law, Edward Wortley Montagu. His wife, Mary, the sole inheritor, was left a life interest in the Wortley estates in West Yorkshire worth £17,000 per annum, whilst her personal fortune was estimated at over £1 million. Time on the political front line may have initially prevented Bute from indulging his artistic and botanic passions, but with the Grenvillite condition that George ceased consulting his favourite on public affairs, Bute agreed to leave London in September 1763. His departure from the political scene opened up a world of artistic and scholarly opportunity.

Perhaps John Brooke was right when he observed in his 1972 biography of George III that "[Bute] should never have gone to Court. His proper place was in an Oxford common room. He is the most finished example in British history of the don in politics."[74]

Notes

1 Blackburne, 1780, pp. 98–99. Extracts of Hollis's memoirs were printed in *The London Magazine or Gentleman's Monthly Intelligencer*, 44 (1780), p. 397.
2 Ibid.
3 Russell, 2004, p. 3.
4 Ibid., p. 6.
5 Hovingham MS. 13/3/5: Bute to Worsley (12 January 1744), quoted in Russell, 2004, p. 15.
6 For an admirably detailed overview of Kenwood's history see English Heritage's website, "Kenwood: History and Stories," English Heritage, accessed 28 November 2016, http://www.english-heritage.org.uk/visit/places/kenwood/history-stories-kenwood.
7 Wraxall, 1815, vol. 1, pp. 431–432.
8 For the most recent re-evaluation of Frederick's role, see Eagles, 2016, pp. 140–156; see also Eagles, 2014, pp. 223–242.
9 Smith and Taylor, 2009, pp. 283–312.
10 Marples, 1970; Walters, 1972; De-la-Noy, 1996. The most recent biography is, if anything, too uncritical of the prince: Vivian, 2006.
11 Shawe-Taylor, 2014, p. 18.
12 Eagles, 2016, p. 140.
13 Langford, 1989, pp. 9–58.
14 Dukelskaya and Moore, 2002.
15 For the culture wars occasioned by Walpole's rule, see Urstad, 1999; and Gerrard, 1994.
16 Murdoch, 2004.
17 Wyndham, 1924, vol. 2, pp. 60–61.
18 Cox, 2013, pp. 931–954.
19 *London Daily Post and General Advertiser* (2 August 1740).
20 Bodleian Library, Oxford: MS. North d. 5. fo. 22^{r}. Mansel to Guilford (14 August 1740).
21 *The London Magazine*, 9 (August 1740), p. 393.
22 *The London Magazine, or, Gentleman's Monthly Intelligencer*, 18 (1749), p. 37. Other actors included Lord Guilford's son, Frederick, Lord North who would be George III's Prime Minister during the loss of the American colonies.
23 RA/GEO/Main/54227-32: reproduced in Shawe-Taylor, 2014, p. 51; see also Young, 1937, pp. 172–175.
24 Bodleian Library MS. North b.3 fo. 307-8 (14 October 1750).
25 Bodleian Library MS. North adds. C. 19^{r-v}: Lyttelton to Guilford (6 October 1750).
26 For further commentary on Knapton's work, see Shawe-Taylor, 2014, p. 22; Christine Gerrard, "Queens-in-waiting: Caroline of Ansbach and Augusta of Saxe-Gotha as Princess of Wales," in Campbell-Orr, 2002, p. 157.
27 Russell, 2004, p. 20.
28 See, for example, Bullion, 1992, pp. 245–26; Berridge, 2015.
29 Atherton, 1974, pp. 208–227; George, 1959, pp. 119–132.
30 Sheppard, 1966, pp. 441–454.
31 Queen Caroline commissioned a similar set of busts for her hermitage at Richmond, which featured Samuel Clark, among others: Shawe-Taylor, 2014, p. 281.
32 Bullion, 1989, p. 46.
33 Brooke, 1972, p. 41; Brooke's account of George's education remains the most thorough, pp. 26–72.
34 RA Add 32: approx. 2,500 sheets (folio & quarto) and notebooks.
35 Brooke, 1974, p. 47.
36 Mount Stuart Archives BU/108/6: George to Bute (31 [sic] June 1756); see also Sedgwick, 1939, pp. 2–4.
37 Mount Stuart Archives BU/104/7 [1756].
38 Mount Stuart Archives BU/108/8: George II to George, Prince of Wales (4 October 1756).
39 Mount Stuart Archives BU/20/17/138: "Account of George's Medals of St Andrew and Gold Keys belonging to my late Father John 3^{d} Earl of Bute" (2 April 1792).
40 Mount Stuart Archives BU/109/424 [undated].
41 Mount Stuart Archives BU/109/424 fo. 4; see also Thomas, 1987.

42 Conway, 2001, p. 889.
43 Jenkinson, 1757.
44 Mount Stuart Archives BU/109/424 fo. 5.
45 Walsh et al., 1996, pp. 69–90.
46 Mount Stuart Archives BU/109/424 fo. 6.
47 Bute to Gilbert Elliot (16 August 1756), quoted in McKelvey, 1973, p. 48.
48 Mount Stuart Archives BU/108/27; see also Sedgwick, 1939, pp. 20–21.
49 Namier, 1961, p. 93.
50 Mount Stuart Archives BU/108/45.
51 Namier, 1961, p. 68.
52 Tim C. W. Blanning has recently made the case for historians approaching the idea of "representation as therapy rather than the pursuit of power"; see "The representation of Frederick II and George III: A Comparison," *Friedrich300 Colloquien*, accessed 25 November 2016, http://www.perspectivia.net/content/publikationen/friedrich300-colloquien/friedrich_repraesentation/blanning_representation.
53 Mount Stuart Archives BU/108/45.
54 Russell, 2004, p. 37.
55 Kimerly Rorschach's work laid the foundations for the resuscitation of Frederick's artistic patronage and collecting; see Rorschach, 1989–1990, pp. 1–76; and at greater length, Rorschach, 1985.
56 Hilles, 2015, p. 12.
57 Sunderland, 2014.
58 Russell, 2004, Appendix III, pp. 217–227.
59 Ibid., p. 219.
60 Quoted in ibid., p. 33.
61 Mount Stuart Archives BU/20/17/138: "Account of the Badges belonging to my late Father the Earl of Bute, taken Monday 2[d] April 1792."
62 Mount Stuart Archives BU/20/17/138 fo. 2.
63 *Public Ledger or The Daily Register of Commerce and Intelligence* (27 November 1760).
64 Fordham, 2010, pp. 161–162.
65 The ways in which George III and respective parliaments developed a working relationship has been the subject of extensive historical analysis, see Dickinson, 2011; Thomas, 2002; Brewer, 1981; Pares, 1951.
66 Hoock, 2003, p. 7.
67 Countering popular perception of the madness of King George, the 2004 "George III and Queen Charlotte: Patronage, Collecting and Court Taste" exhibition resulted in a collection of essays: Marsden, 2005.
68 Mount Stuart Archives BU/110/3: George III to Lord Bute (Saturday [1788]).
69 Mahon 1847, vol. 2, p. 472.
70 Scholarship on Lord Bute has been dominated by two historians, Karl W. Schweizer and John L. Bullion; see, for example, Schweizer, 1988; Schweizer, 2002; Bullion, 2013, which reprints five of Bullion's essays on Bute.
71 See, most recently, Phillips and Shane, 2014; and Berridge, 2015.
72 Russell, 2004.
73 Schweizer, 2014, p. 98.
74 Brooke, 1974, p. 47.

PETER BLACK

QUALITY *AND* QUANTITY:

BUTE AND

THE COLLECTING OF

DUTCH PAINTINGS

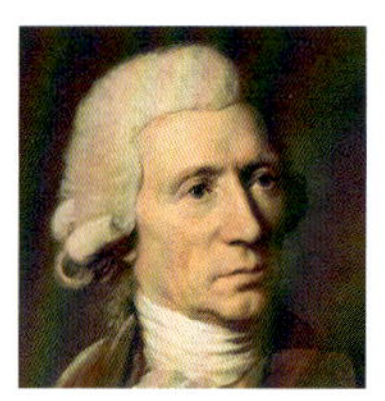

"Although not the first, it was arguably the greatest collection of seventeenth-century Dutch paintings in Britain ..."[1]

The collection of paintings formed by the Third Earl of Bute was kept in several great houses and included, by the time of his death in 1792, nearly 500 paintings at Luton Hoo alone. It was one of the greatest in Britain and outshone many noble European collections. It might seem that this collection came about simply as a function of Bute's wealth; but by looking at the kinds of painting he acquired, it is possible to reconstruct some of the ideas that motivated a man who was a prominent scholar of natural history as well as an expert on painting. Bute's collection is celebrated for its strength in Dutch and Flemish paintings, but in the mid-eighteenth century, while enthusiasm for these works was gaining strength among collectors, there was a dearth of theoretical writing with which to justify the strong market position even of a great master such as Rembrandt. The focus of critics, some of whom were part of a campaign to establish a Royal Academy of Arts, remained resolutely on Italian theory and practice. By about 1830, intellectuals would generally acknowledge the importance of the landscapes and scenes of daily life which characterise Netherlandish painting; but in 1750, the case still needed to be made – and there remained opportunities for adventurous collectors.

Bute's actual views are hard to recover as they are not documented; but glimpses of his thinking can be found in his writings, for example in relation to the Italian term *virtù*, which intellectuals used to parade their knowledge of art. Meaning rather more than our word "culture," *virtù* now lingers only as the name of a category of precious object in auction catalogues. Then it

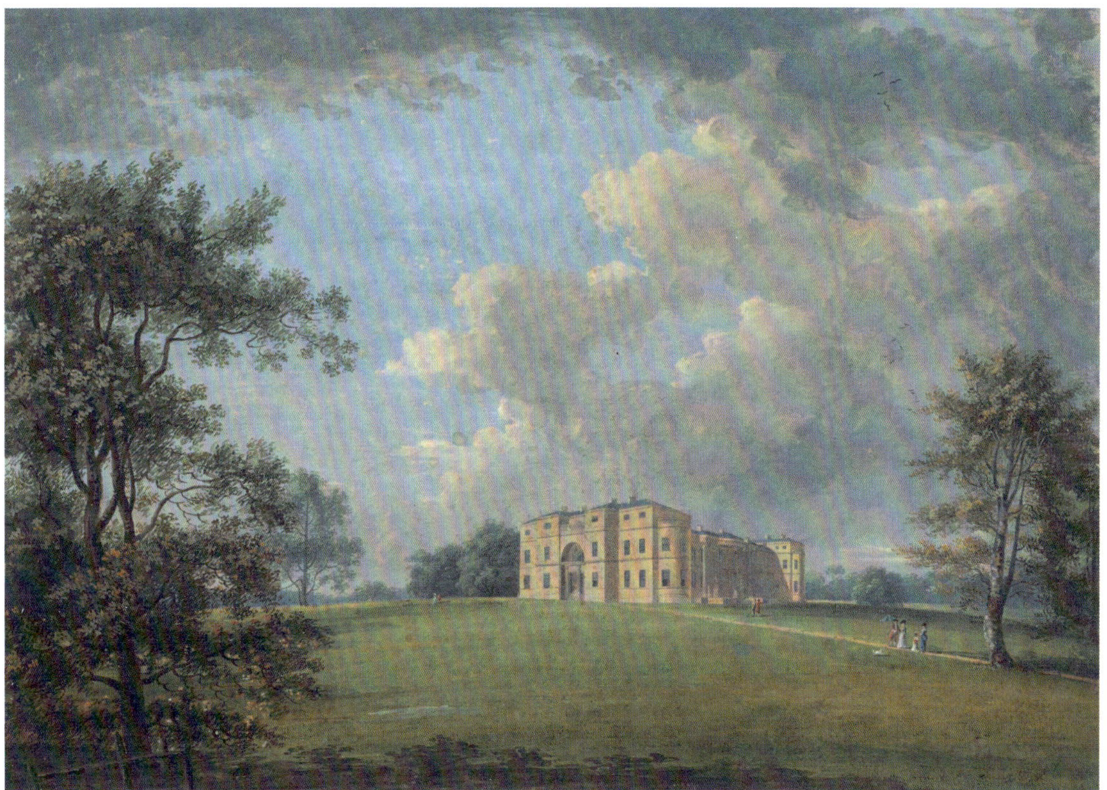

28 Adam Callendar (fl. 1780–1811), *Luton Hoo*, 1783, watercolour after Charles Steuart (fl. 1760–1790), 47 × 64.5 cm, Victoria and Albert Museum, P.42-1953.
Luton Hoo was on the crest of a hill, with gardens sloping down to the lake on the right.

meant, above all, theoretical and historical knowledge, but it also implied the practice of artistic skills, particularly drawing. Individuals who studied and collected art were known as *virtuosi*, and in both words lies a strong hint that culture requires a grounding in classical literature. A familiarity with the painters who were acknowledged as the greatest – the Italians rather than the Dutch – was an essential part of a civilising education, especially for those, like Bute, who held public office.

The word *virtù* was used in 1738, in an exchange of letters between the recently married Bute and his old school friend Thomas Worsley of Hovingham, who offered to assist in building the Bute collections that were evidently already under way.[2] Yet, in a manuscript essay on the art of travel writing, which Bute later addressed to his son, Charles Stuart (1753–1801), we see Bute distancing himself from *virtù*. Dismissing the standard travel books, he derides those who, "pretending to superior taste and understanding, condescend to initiate the readers into what the Italians call *Vertù*, from them we have also ample accounts of Pictures, Drawings, Statues, Medals &c."[3] He comes across as diffident, irritable even, with the predictable lists of works of art in Italy. We sense, in what he chooses to pass on to Charles, a depth of knowledge about art which he refrains from displaying; but there is also a down-to-earth quality which we could say he shared with the Dutch as a race and which empowered him to dismiss the authors of those "ample catalogues of every Palace in Italy," concluding that "the Travellers judgement can convey no knowledge to the reader, He must see the picture himself if he has a turn or any taste for these matters."

The taste of a typical eighteenth-century British intellectual has been characterised, seriously by theoreticians and facetiously by the popular novelists Sterne, Smollett, Goldsmith and Fielding, by one of those reassuring dichotomies. The distinction between art and nature, about which they joked, went back at least as far as Aristotle. Things are in reality never so simple, but the possibility of assigning objects or thoughts to a mere two categories turned the "art or nature" question into a long lasting, if not very useful, formulation, which gave ammunition to those who did not appreciate Dutch art. Although obviously not all painting could sensibly be assigned to one or other category, the idea nonetheless inhabited people's minds. And so great eighteenth-century collections, which were formed from a mixture of personal ambition, a desire to impress, but also – as was very much the case with Bute's – to form an understanding of the nature and production of art, focused on Italy because the Italians inherited a tradition that went back to the Ancients. Italian painters who treated mythological or religious subjects were depicting predominantly intellectual or spiritual rather than mundane subjects – ideas, not mere things.[4]

What is impressive about Bute's collection of pictures is his dedication not only to certain kinds of Italian painting, following the standard pattern, but also to Dutch and Flemish art, meaning, broadly speaking, landscapes and genre paintings, which are kinds of painting that in Bute's time received a mixed critical reception. Influential writers such as the Earl of Shaftesbury, Horace Walpole and Joshua Reynolds, made denigrating remarks about Dutch painters, whose work they saw as no more than the imitation of nature. But at the same time, Dutch paintings enjoyed wide popular appeal. Dutch pictures formed an important presence in many great art collections including, ironically, that of Reynolds, whose biggest passions were, if the significant numbers of works by these artists in his collection are any guide, Rubens (represented by twenty-one works), Rembrandt (seventeen), and Van Dyck (seventeen).[5] Through their experience of works in private collections, emerging British landscape painters such as Gainsborough, Turner and Constable, were gaining inspiration from the Dutch, a development which had a crucial influence on aesthetic developments in the nineteenth century, towards the end of which Impressionism would emerge. At that point, the establishment finally accepted that mere objects, or "nature," could have an important place in art.

In what follows, an indication will be given of the nature of Bute's collection and his taste will emerge in relation to that of his contemporaries. In the space of this essay it is not possible to construct a detailed intellectual argument in response to the idealising, Italo-centric rhetoric of Reynolds and others. We should note, however, that Dutch landscapes and figures subjects were not just popular, but, as Bute and others with a passion for natural history might have observed, the "sincere hand and faithful Eye," with which Dutch painters approached their work, allied them to Baconian science, ensuring that such pictures received an appreciative audience in the "Age of Observation."[6]

One famous picture collection which makes an interesting comparison with Bute's is that formed by Horace Walpole for his father, Sir Robert, who was Prime Minister 1721–1742, at his seat Houghton Hall in Norfolk, with a balance strongly in favour of Italian works. In the grandiloquent (though unillustrated) catalogue of 1747, the *Aedes Walpolianae*, we find an often-quoted example of anti-Dutch feeling. Walpole priggishly praises the breadth and strength of the Italian

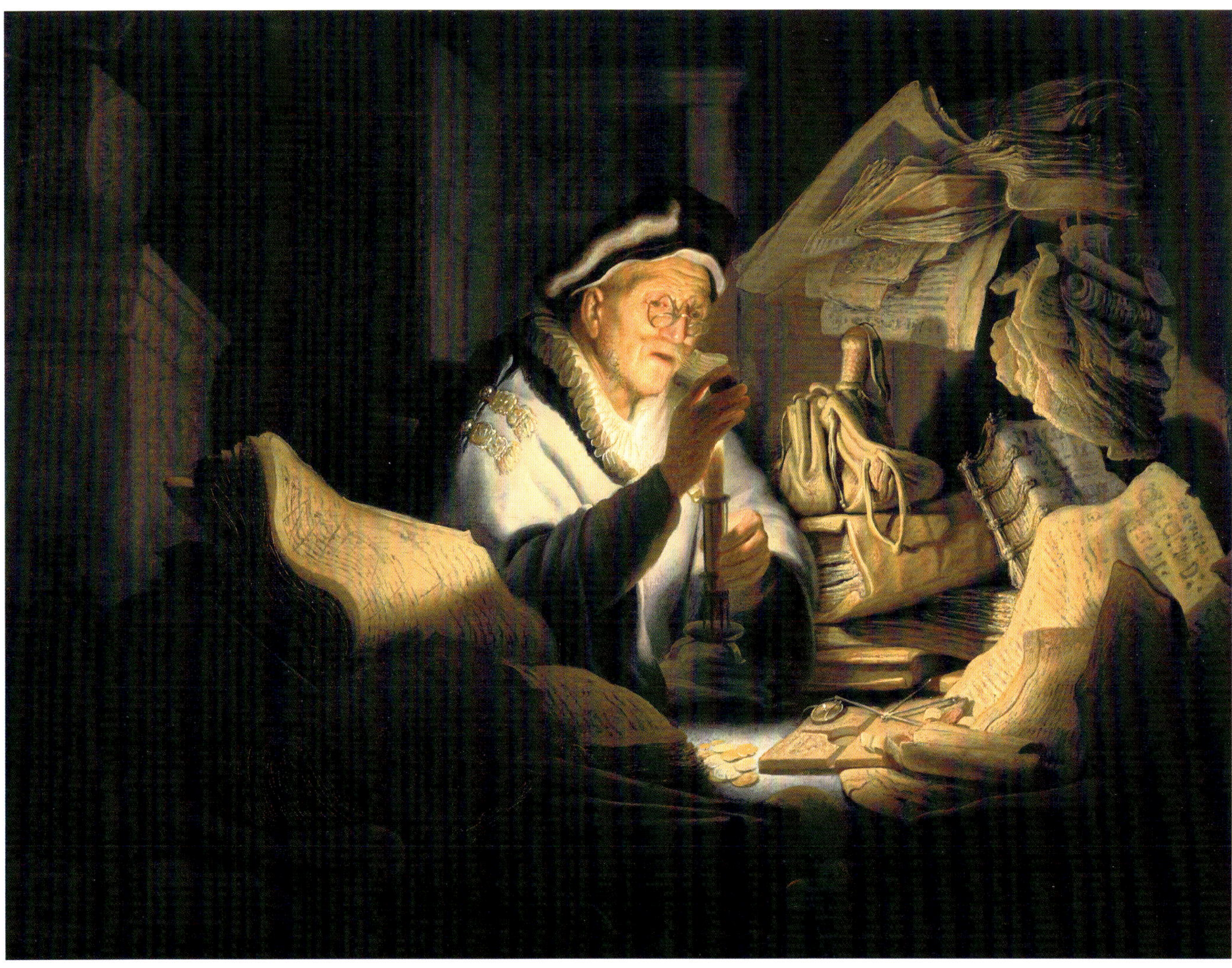

holdings. Among the Houghton pictures there were, of course, works by Dutch and Flemish painters, including the prolific and popular Teniers, but also the two great exceptions to the rule that Italian artists are best: Rubens and Van Dyck. Talking about the impossibility of equating artistic merit and price, Walpole undermines to some extent the intellectual principles on which the collection was built, by ridiculing Dutch works for their high monetary value: "As great as are the prices of fine Pictures, there is no judging from them of the several Merits of the Painters ... And as for the Dutch Painters, those drudging Mimics of Nature's most uncomely Coarseness, don't their earthen pots and brass kettles carry away prices only due to the sweet neatness of Albano, and to the attractive delicacy of Carlo Maratti [sic]?"[7]

We do not, unfortunately, have in Bute's own words any description of the programme that lay behind his collecting, often guided by Captain William Baillie (1723–1810), a retired soldier and expert in Dutch art. But because of the predominance of Dutch and Flemish works, we would expect him to take a very different line from Walpole, who was clearly more interested in the rising value of Dutch paintings than in their quality as works of art.[8] We might expect a

29 Rembrandt (1606–1669), *The Parable of the Rich Man*, 1627, oil on panel, 32.0 × 42.5 cm, Gemäldegalerie, Staatliche Museen zu Berlin, Preussischer Kulturbesitz. This unusual early Rembrandt painting has recently been identified as the "Usurer examining gold coin by candle light" listed in the Luton 1799 inventory.

wealthy collector to begin with Rembrandt, but compared to the passion which drove Reynolds, Bute seems to have bought few Rembrandts, with just two paintings ascribed to the artist in the Luton inventory of ca. 1799. The painting of "the Son of Rembrandt" that hung in the North Green Dressing Room has not stood the test of time. It is presumably the painting of a young man wearing a gorget, now ascribed to a follower of Rembrandt, which hangs at Dumfries House.[9] The subject of the other "Rembrandt," in the North Blue Dressing Room, which was listed as a "Usurer examining gold coin by candle light," is so unusual in Rembrandt's œuvre that it is probable that Bute owned the early panel of the *Parable of the Rich Man* (1627, Berlin, Gemäldegalerie), with its remarkable effect of candlelight and strong moral charge.[10] This painting (fig. 29) came onto the market in Holland in 1766 just when Bute was buying pictures there in large quantities, through Baillie and a major Amsterdam dealer, Pieter Fouquet (1729–1800). After Bute's death, the fate of this painting was to be downgraded – even now its monogram and date, in the dark bottom-left corner, are scarcely legible – and received an attribution to Rembrandt's pupil, Gerbrand van den Eeckhout (1621–1674). In this way the "Usurer" was disposed of by the Second Marquess, among pictures from Luton which were sold at Christie's in 1822.[11] It would be fair to say, however, that for Bute, and other collectors, there were a number of painters almost as highly esteemed as Rembrandt. Among the highlights of collections of the time were small, highly finished paintings by artists who now occupy rather less prominent positions in public museums. Extremely high prices were paid for works by artists such as Gerard Dou (1618–1675), a painter probably appreciated by Bute as an important master and not, as modern writers tend to regard him, a follower of Rembrandt's early manner.[12] Dou and his pupils were one of Bute's interests, as is demonstrated by paintings still in the collection by Dou as well as Domenicus van Tol, Abraham de Pape, Pieter van Slingelandt (cat. 28) and Pieter Verelst (cat. 32).

From the list of works at Luton, painters emerge whose reputation and value in Bute's time now seem inflated but whose presence should alert us to a programme of collecting which certainly included, as well as prestigious works, paintings by less-well-known artists such as Willem van Herp (cat. 12–13). We can see this market-driven phenomenon in the collections of various great men; many were attracted to small, highly finished works of a type made originally in large numbers for the open market. One example is the nearly ubiquitous David Teniers II, to whom Walpole may have been referring in his unkind remark about "earthen pots and brass kettles" quoted above. Teniers features, not surprisingly, in an important collection which Bute would have known, that of Sir Lawrence Dundas (1712–1781), a Scot who became extremely rich by supplying the British army in Flanders during the Seven Years' War. In 1794, 116 pictures from Dundas's house at 19 Arlington Street in London were sold, including the monumental Rembrandt double portrait of *Cornelis Claesz. Anslo and his wife Aeltje Gerritsdr. Schouten* (1641, Berlin, Gemäldegalerie) and the great collaborative painting of *Nature Adorned by the Graces* by Rubens and Jan Brueghel I (ca. 1615, Glasgow, Kelvingrove Art Gallery and Museum).[13] These masterpieces both sold for huge prices, at £546 and £882, but much of the sale proceeds came from pictures by fashionable artists such as Murillo, who was represented in the sale by six works, including the substantial *Holy Family* which Sir James Lowther, Bute's son-in-law, had missed out on buying in 1764.[14] Also in the sale were a dozen paintings by Teniers, including a *Fête de Village* which – it now seems astonishing – made £882, the same exceptional price as the Rubens/Brueghel *Nature* painting. As with many collections, that of Dundas, which was relatively small by the standards of Bute's, came together as the ornament of a great man's life but was quickly dispersed.

Another famous collection assembled by a public figure with whom Bute had important dealings was that of the Duc de Choiseul (1719–1785). As French Foreign Minister, Choiseul negotiated the Peace of Paris with Bute in 1763; this was the great event of Bute's premiership, bringing an end to the Seven Years' War. Immediately afterwards, Bute withdrew from public life. Unable to find peace and quiet, he set off for Europe in 1768, travelling first across France to take the waters at Barèges. He noted in his journal seeing Choiseul's Château de Chanteloup, "in going to the next post of Frillière we were in sight of a noble seat of the Duke de Choiseul, close to the River and surrounded by the great forest of Amboise."[15] Although, at that moment, he passed Choiseul's gates in silence, in October, having completed his cure at Barèges, Bute wrote to Sir James Wright, the British Resident in Venice, that his plan to travel *incognito* had not entirely worked, as "the extreme

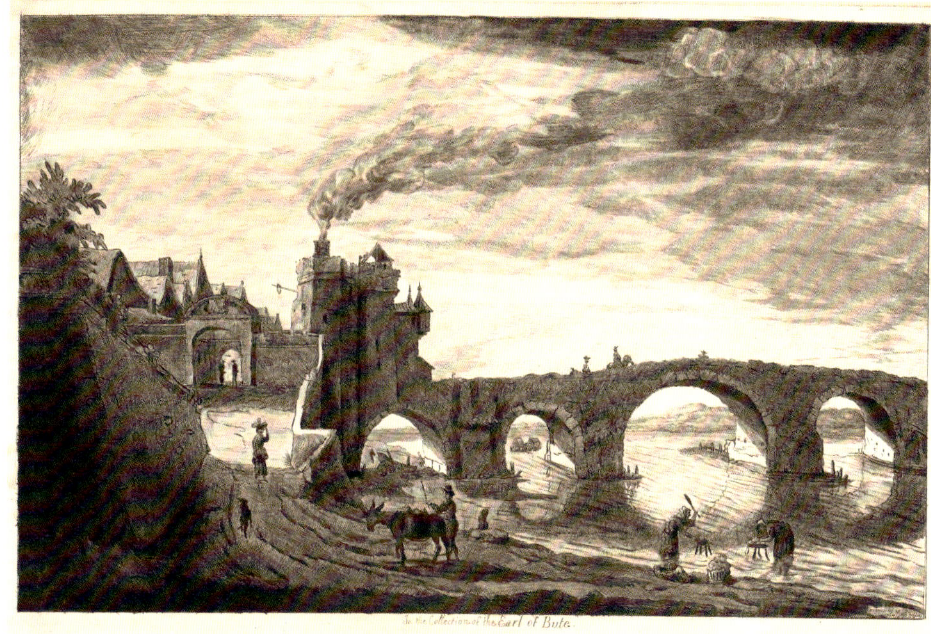

30 William Baillie (1723–1810) after Lambert Doomer (1624–1700), *Bridge at Amboise*, 1764, etching, 29.4 × 42.8 cm, Trustees of the British Museum, 1870,0813.651. Besides advising Bute on purchases, Baillie made several prints reproducing paintings and drawings in the collection. Doomer's drawing, of ca. 1646, is now in the Hermitage, St Petersburg, (inv 2827).

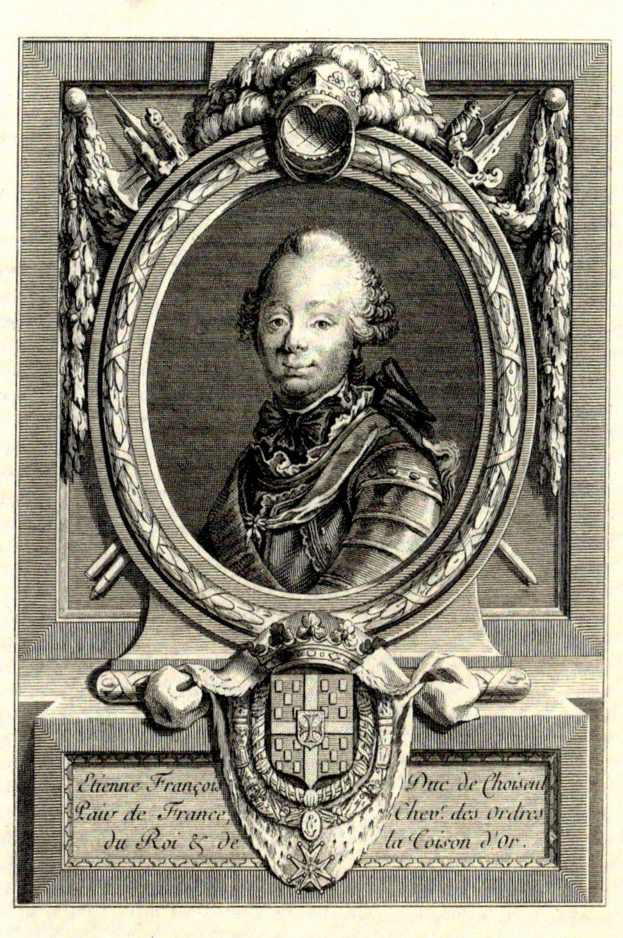

31 *Etienne François, Duc de Choiseul* from the *Cabinet Choiseul*, 1771, engraving, 20.2 × 14.4 cm, Trustees of the British Museum, 1858,0417.1211. Choiseul was the French Foreign Minister, with whom Bute negotiated the Peace of Paris in 1762–1763. The engravings of the Cabinet record his important art collection.

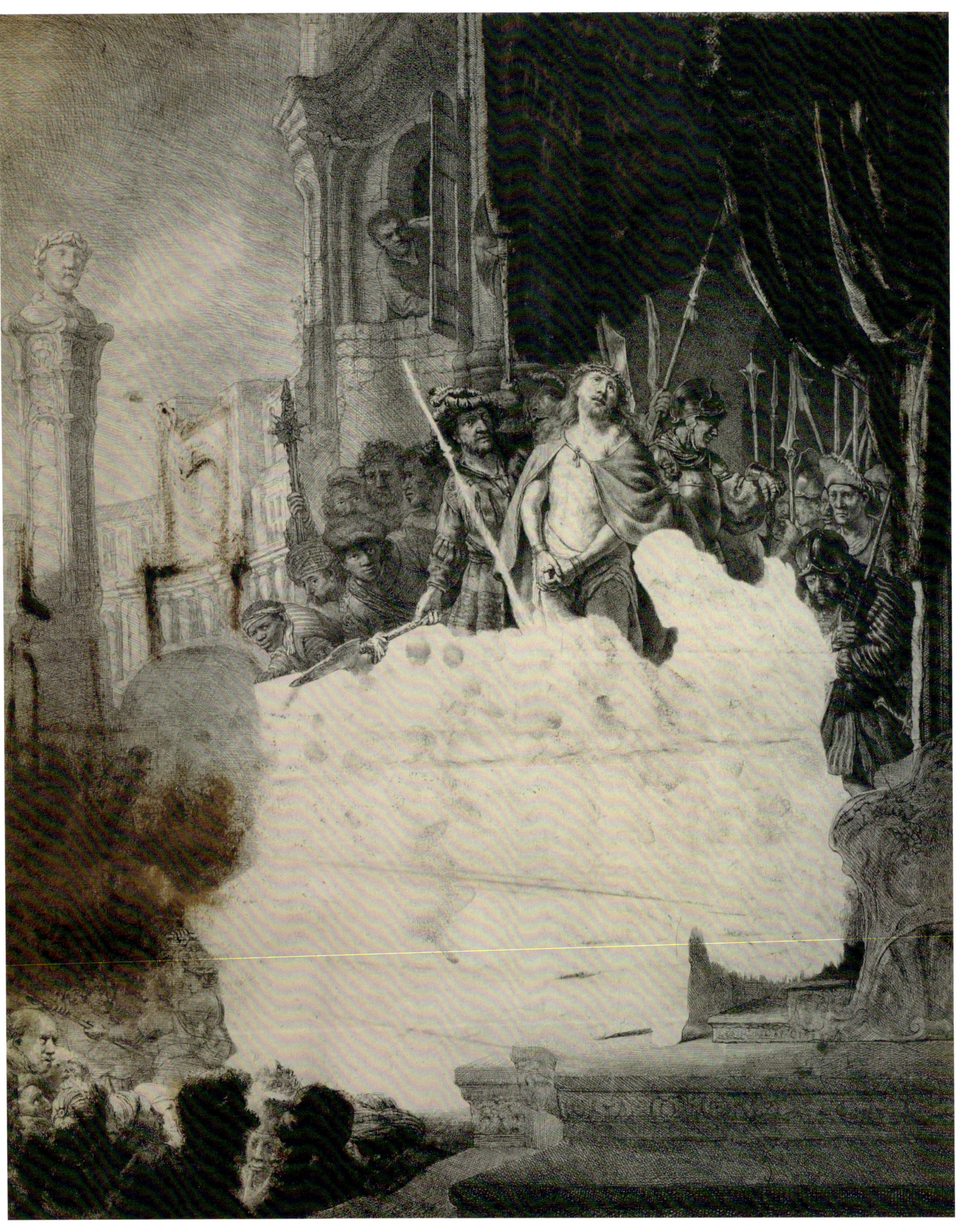

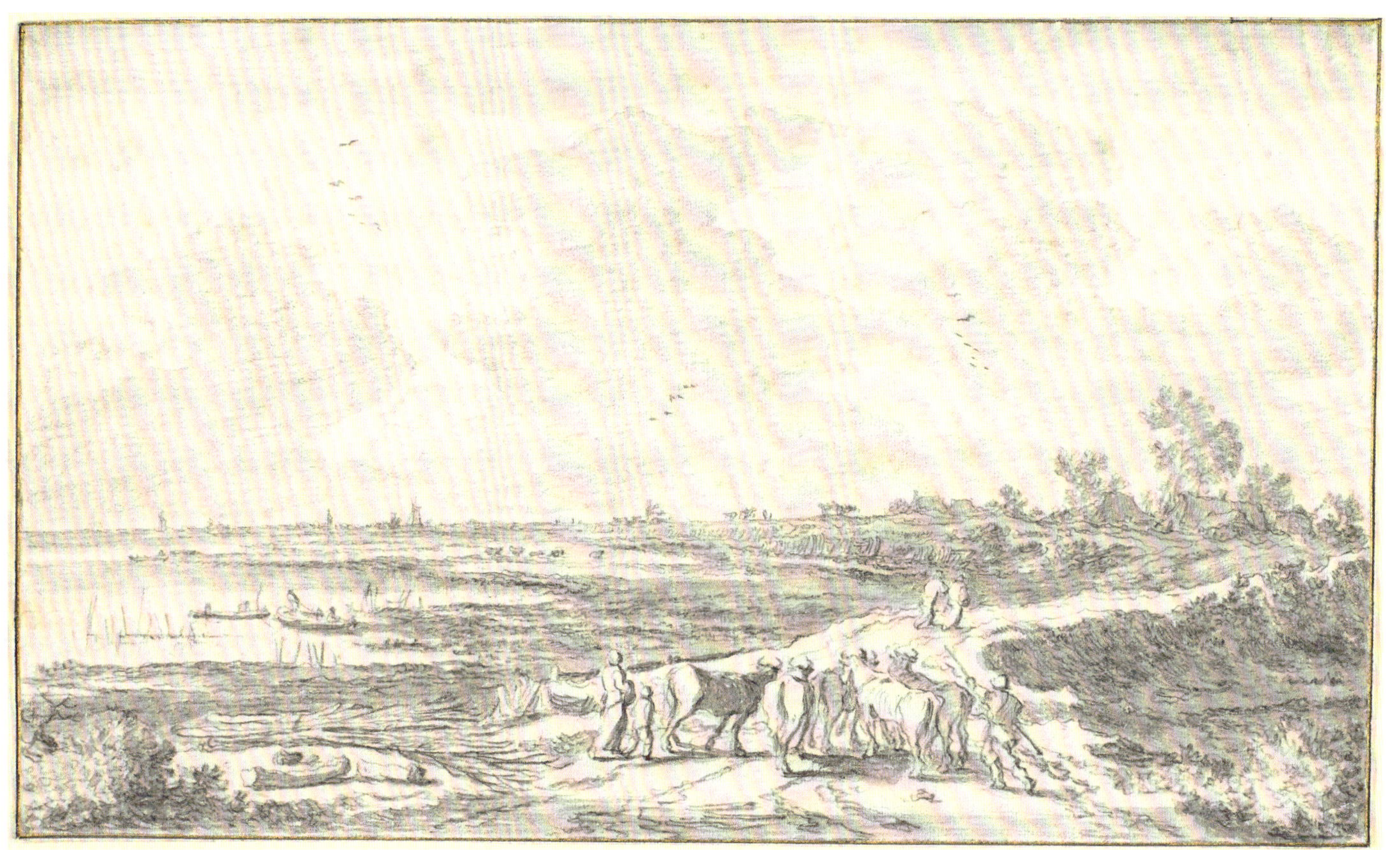

politeness of the French Monarch & Mr de Choiseul has a little interrupted my plan of privacy."[16] Bute and Choiseul must have had a lot to discuss. Back in 1762, the articles of peace had been drawn up by means of secret exchanges, which were forwarded between Bute and Choiseul by Bute's brother, James Stuart Mackenzie, who was the king's envoy in Turin. Mackenzie's Anglo-French secretary, Louis Dutens (1730–1812, fig. 36), organised the chain of communication with Choiseul, something Dutens proudly describes in his *Mémoires*.[17] As Bute ambled along the Loire, he probably did not know that Choiseul's financial difficulties were becoming pressing and that selling his paintings would relieve some of the pressure. Choiseul's pictures were few in number, compared to the collection that Bute was building, but the commercial device of having the collection engraved as the *Cabinet Choiseul* (1771, fig. 31) was extremely successful in creating high prices when the collection was auctioned in 1772.[18]

In addition to his paintings, Bute assembled a collection of prints and drawings, which he kept in beautiful "Russia leather" portfolios at his cliff-top retreat at Highcliffe House, in Hampshire, overlooking the Isle of Wight. Bute left instructions for these to be sold after his death. However, the descriptions given in Hutchins's 1794 auction catalogue reveal how useful his print collection would have been for study, containing important groups of original prints by etchers such as Rembrandt (fig. 32) and Ostade, as well as "documentary" engravings after paintings by artists represented in the collection, such as Dou, Hobbema and Van Herp.[19] Because his prints were not stamped with a collector's mark, only a few exceptional works can now be identified, as well as one or two print albums which have Bute's coat of arms on the binding. Fine works went immediately to other collectors, such as William Esdaile (1758–1837), Richard,

33 Pieter de Molijn (1595–1661), *Landscape with Cattle and Figures on a Road, by a River*, 1654, black chalk and grey wash, 17.1 × 28.3 cm, Fitzwilliam Museum, PD.474-1963. Bute's collection of drawings was sold at auction in 1794 and 1809. This very characteristic dune landscape near the artist's native town of Haarlem is one of the few works that can be securely linked to Bute's collection; it was engraved in 1774 by William Baillie.

32 opposite page: Rembrandt (1606–1669), *Christ Before Pilate*, large plate, 1635, etching, touched with brown oil paint, 55.2 × 45.0 cm, Trustees of the British Museum F,4.181. One of the extraordinary works from Bute's collection of drawings and prints, which were sold after his death.

Viscount Fitzwilliam (1745–1816, fig. 33) and Daniel Daulby, author of the 1796 *Descriptive Catalogue of the Works of Rembrandt*, from whom they later passed into museums, having in the meantime lost their connection with Bute. The quality and range can be gleaned from the catalogue's title page which declared that the prints were, "In Fine Condition, and of the Best Impressions, more particularly in the works of Rubens, Van Dyck, Poussin, Visscher, Drevet, Edelinck, and Rembrandt, Many of them being Proofs before the Letters, and with curious variations. Likewise several excellent Books of Prints and Portfolios, Elegantly bound in Morocco, Russia, &c." Among the albums was, not surprisingly, the *Cabinet Choiseul*, which would have served as a reminder to Bute that his opposite number was also primarily a collector of Dutch and Flemish paintings.[20]

Bute clearly shared Choiseul's taste for small, highly finished paintings, such as works by the Leiden *fijnschilders* and artists who worked in the same vein such as Metsu (cat. 16) and Ter Borch (cat. 5–6). This is further manifested in the largest group of works by a single artist in Bute's collection, Jan Brueghel the Elder, who was represented by thirteen works (Choiseul had seven). Brueghel's usually small landscapes with many figures, flowers, animals and other beautiful details painted with an impressive, miniaturist accuracy, were highly sought after. Brueghel's commercial success inspired others including the landscape painters Jan Griffier I, Herman Saftleven and Jan van der Heyden to work in a similar manner, and these artists were also well represented in the Bute collection.[21] The painting of *The Valkhof at Nijmegen*, by Jan van der Heyden (cat. 14), is a serene evening scene, inspired by the beautiful, old citadel which rises above the boats moored on the River Waal. The acquisition by Bute is not documented, but the similarity of this painting to a work sold by Dr Robert Bragge (1700–1777, fig. 34), a pioneer dealer in Dutch paintings known to both Bute and Baillie, may indicate that it was an early acquisition.[22] The old attribution inscribed on the frame, to "A Van der Heyden and W. van der Velde", matches that given in the detailed catalogue of works in the collection of Willem Lormier, from whom Bragge bought the work in 1758.[23] But it is difficult to be confident about the provenance of a similar sounding work, when such paintings often existed in several versions. The records of Bragge's dealings show that in 1759 his painting of Nijmegen, from the Lormier sale, was sold to Bute's close associate Sir Richard Grosvenor, and thus it may be the same work.[24]

Numerically speaking, we could say that Jan Brueghel the Elder was Bute's favourite, but this would not have been obvious to visitors to the impressive rooms on the ground floor of Luton Hoo. In the grander and taller spaces of the hall, library, saloon and with-drawing room, small Brueghel paintings would not have made an impression. These spaces were hung with the largest and most impressive works, such as the monumental *Landscape Representing a Cold Autumn Windy Day* by Nicolaes Berchem which hung in the library where the two largest of Bute's ten Zuccarellis were also hanging as pendants.[25] This section of the library was dominated by landscapes, including two major works by Cuyp, both of which were pioneering acquisitions of an artist who was soon to become the darling of British collectors: the *River Landscape with Horseman and Peasants* (fig. 35), now in the National Gallery, London, and the painting of *Orpheus Charming the Animals*, which remains at Mount Stuart.[26] The landscapes were interspersed with other large works such as the Rubens (and workshop) and Snyders painting of *Fruit and Vegetables with a Maid and a Boy* (cat. 28), or the huge altarpiece by Guercino, the *Assumption of the Virgin; Two Angels Supporting Her*, 1650, now in Detroit, but then hanging in the saloon.[27]

Public recognition of the excellence of the Bute collection came in 1838, in the important survey of English collections written by Gustav Waagen, Director of the Berlin Gemäldegalerie. It is worth quoting at length because Waagen gives a brief visual impression of the collection and an analysis of its principal strengths:

"On the following morning I drove from my excellent inn, the George, to Luton House, the seat of the Marquis of Bute, to see the very great collection of pictures which it contains. The house, situated on an eminence, is very extensive. A considerable portico of six Ionic columns, and a large hall, have very lately been added. The rather bare and desolate appearance of the hall will, it is to be hoped, be soon removed by the ornament of sculptures. Lord Howe had had the goodness to give me a letter to Lord Bute, which, though the marquis was in Scotland, had the desired effect, that the housekeeper allowed me to examine at my ease the collection, of about 400 pictures. When she perceived how leisurely I proceeded, she, to my great satisfaction, fetched some work, and sat down with it in every room, till I asked her to show me another. In this manner six hours passed before I left Luton House.

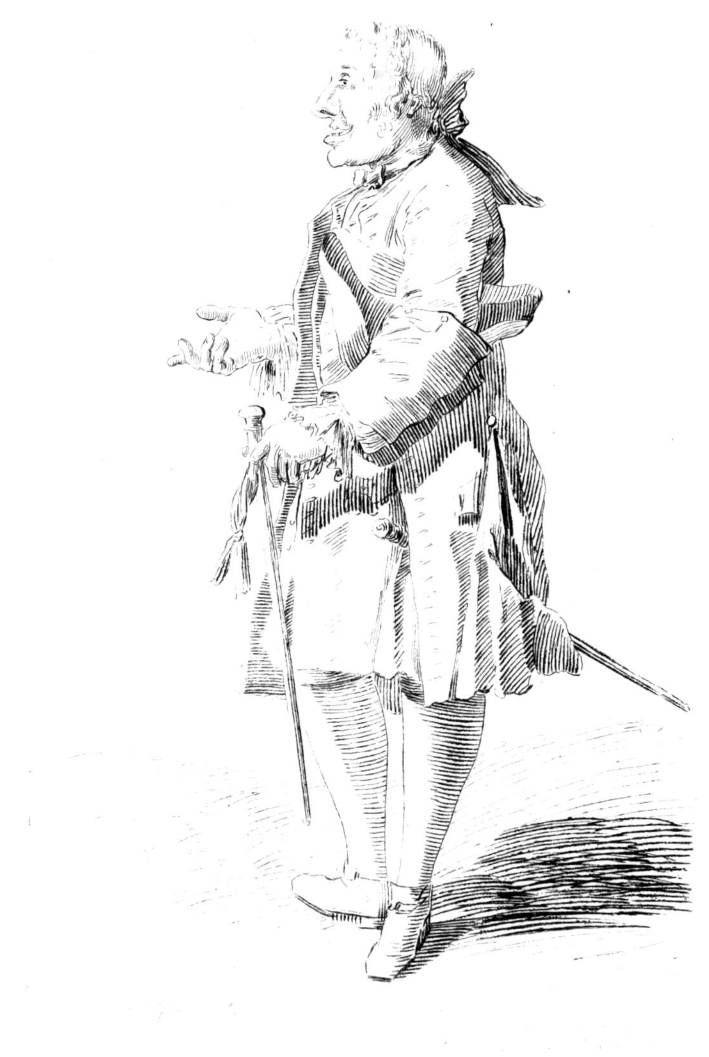

34 *Dr Bragg*, ca. 1745, etching by Arthur Pond (1701–1758), after Pier Leone Ghezzi (1674–1755) 32.9 × 21.3 cm, Trustees of the British Museum 2006,U.2125. "Gentleman art dealer," Robert Bragge (1700–1777) was an early specialist in Dutch paintings.

"With the exception of several late purchases, this collection was formed by the great-grandfather of the present marquis, John Stuart Earl of Bute, the celebrated favourite and for many years prime minister of King George III. Its greatest treasure is a number of excellent pictures of the Dutch and Flemish schools. Of all the collections formed in England before the Revolution, it is the most important in works of this class; so that for productions of many of the first masters it may vie even with the finest collections formed since the Revolution: such as those of Sir Robert Peel, Lord Ashburton, and the Marquis [sic] of Westminster; nay, it contains very fine works of several good masters of whom there are no specimens in those collections."[28]

Waagen knew that the collection at Luton had been subject to changes since the time of the Third Earl, but he was nevertheless clear about the taste of the man who had been its principal creator. That he emphasises, above all, the strength of its Dutch and Flemish works is indicative of the rising status of these works. Waagen mentions the collection formed by another prime

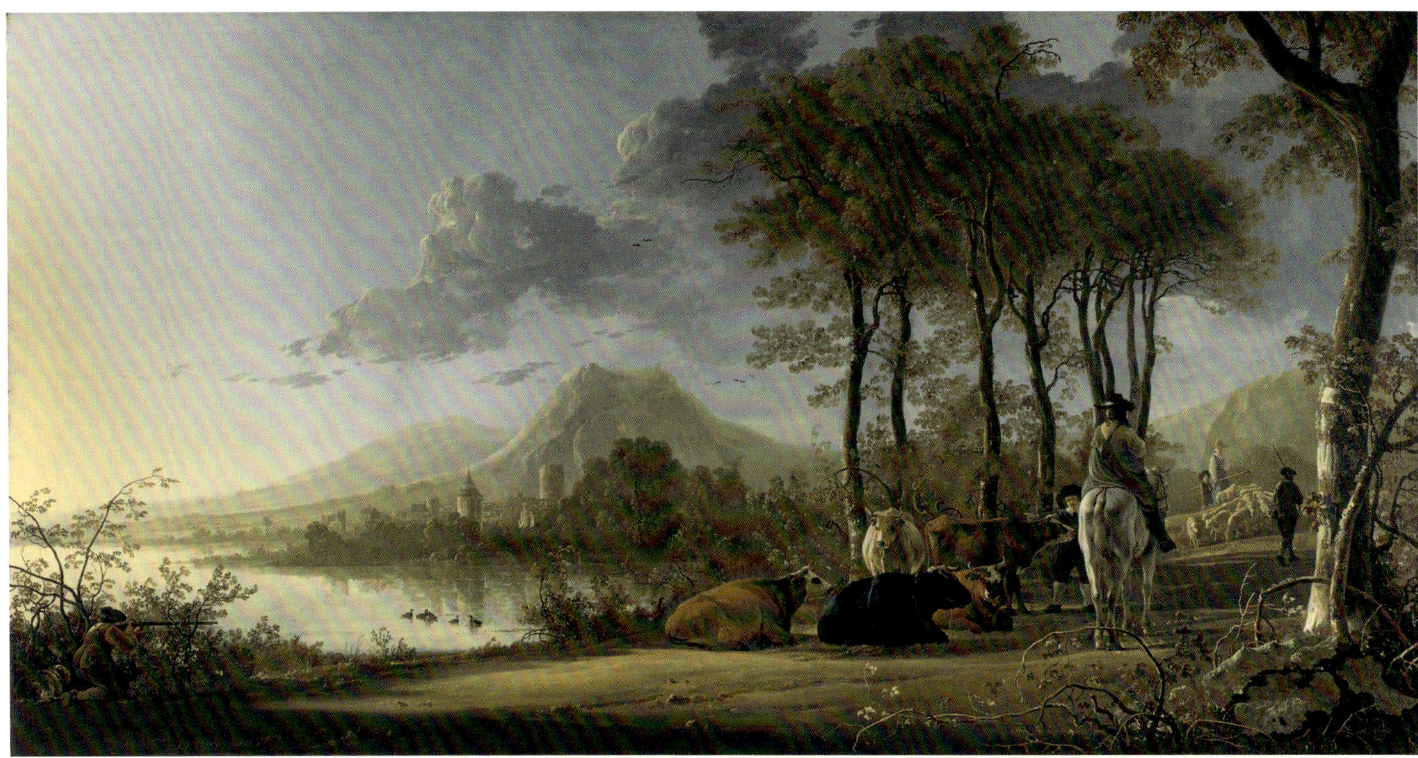

35 Aelbert Cuyp (1620–1691), *River Landscape with Horseman and Peasants*, ca. 1658–1660, oil on canvas, 123 × 241 cm, National Gallery, bought with the assistance of the National Heritage Memorial Fund and the Art Fund, 1989. Regarded as "one of the greatest 17th-century Dutch landscapes," this very large painting was one of the jewels of the collection at Luton.

minister, Sir Robert Peel, which was small by comparison with Bute's, but was still regarded as of such importance that a group including sixty-eight Dutch and Flemish pictures was rescued from sale in 1871 for the National Gallery. The Bute collection, reduced somewhat in scale by the auction of 1822, lived on in other family houses after the fire at Luton of 1843, and could still furnish an impressive 294 paintings for exhibition at Bethnal Green in 1882, and similar numbers at Glasgow (1884) and Manchester (1885). Mostly it remained out of sight, and recent writers on Dutch collections have emphasised more accessible ones: the Royal Collection, especially the works purchased by George IV; that of the Duke of Wellington at Apsley House and the Wallace Collection, at the core of which we might note were pictures bought by the Earl of Hertford, who was dispatched to Paris as ambassador following the Peace of Paris negotiated by Bute in 1763.[29]

Artists and connoisseurs had inherited from Renaissance thinkers the idea that art should aspire to the qualities and forms of ancient painting. However, the focus of Enlightenment thought was, in general, towards an understanding of the world in all its physical aspects and life on the planet in all its forms. In a word: nature. The science of understanding how everything worked, which we call physics, was known as natural philosophy. A serious natural historian, as Bute called himself, would unquestionably have favoured nature over art. In addition to Bute's stance as a man of science, his position as first Lord of the Bedchamber to Prince Frederick and, after his death in 1751, as Groom of the Stole to Prince George, gave him a role in shaping the Royal Collection, which had been rich in Dutch and Flemish paintings since the early seventeenth century. Although it has been rightly said that Bute studiously avoided collecting Italian paintings himself in order not to enter into conflict with young King George's collecting, Dutch and Flemish paintings dominated that collection.[30]

Britain and Holland were closely linked both economically and socially at the end of the seventeenth century, the period known as the Dutch "Golden Age", and collecting Dutch pictures went with the Royal Family's political allegiances. A. G. H. Bachrach wrote in his introduction to an exhibition of Dutch art at the Victoria and Albert Museum in 1964 of the close dynastic links between Holland and Britain, naming "the historical fact that, in succession, the Princes William II of Orange, William III, and William IV married the Princess Mary, daughter of Charles I, Mary, daughter of James II, and Anne, daughter of George II." He continues, "As professor Charles Wilson has said, defining succinctly the relationship from the British point of view: Of all the foreign influences which have been brought to bear on English life, few have been more powerful, more profound or more lasting than that of the Dutch who ... between 1600 and 1750 helped to shape not only our economic institutions, but our ideas on architecture, art, science, agriculture, to say nothing of our conceptions of philosophy, theology and law."[31]

Although George III is remembered more for his purchases of Italian art, including the Consul Smith collection, the acquisition of which Bute organised in 1762, his greatest contribution to collecting was, arguably, not paintings but the magnificent library at Buckingham House, which his son George IV would later give to the British Museum, where the King's Library formed the core of what would become the British Library. Demonstrably the idea of specialisation played an important role in both Bute's and the king's collections; collectors have in every age found it wise to focus. In the context of the current exhibition a comparison can be made which might not otherwise seem relevant. However, the anatomist and collector William Hunter received from Bute his appointment as Physician in extraordinary to Queen Charlotte in 1762. And in collecting for his encyclopaedic museum (later The Hunterian, University of Glasgow) he certainly aimed for completeness and, through his own networks of dealers, was probably aware of Bute's purchases. With completeness in mind, Hunter bought collections *en-bloc*, including Matthew Duane's coin collection for £2,300 in 1776 and Dr John Fothergill's shell collection for £1,100 in 1780. Hunter had the advantage over Bute in being directly involved in the world of painting, as Professor of Anatomy to the artists at the St Martin's Lane Academy and from 1768 at the Royal Academy. If his collection of paintings was tiny (sixty-five) compared with Bute's, it was at least comparable in the significant proportion of Dutch works it contained. Yet, if collecting Dutch and Flemish paintings was of central importance to Bute, the same cannot be said of Hunter, whose correspondence reveals, in the prevalence of letters to numismatists, that he was dedicated above all to forming a great coin collection and indeed, at the time of his death in 1783, Hunter's coin collection was the greatest in Britain. But coins and medals are no longer consulted by historians as they once were, and other Enlightenment fashions such as collecting ancient engraved gems have suffered a similar fate of incomprehension in our time. Yet, for Hunter, there was perhaps – even if he did not express it thus – a determination to leave behind one collection from the ancient world which would complement, for example, the unrivalled vase collections formed by his friend Sir William Hamilton and sold to the British Museum.

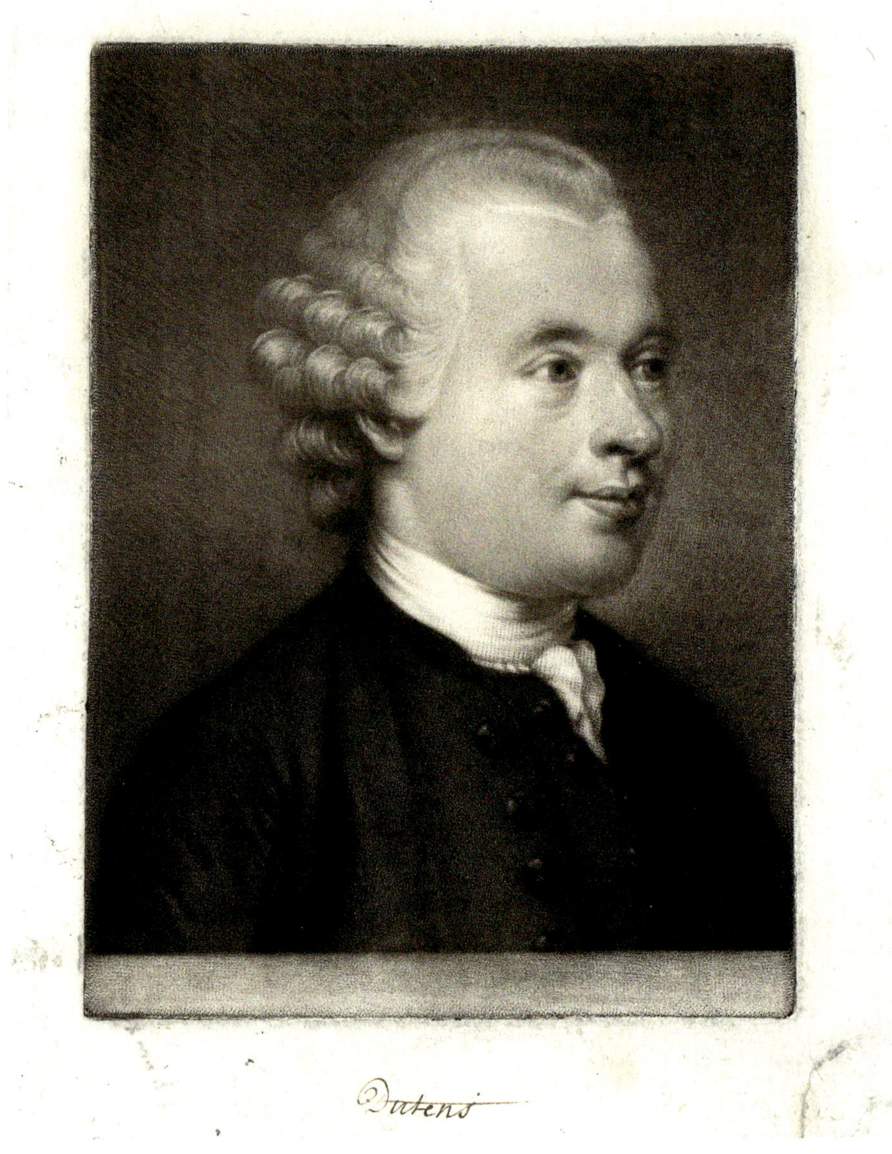

36 Edward Fisher (1722–1821), *Louis Dutens* (1730–1812), 1777, mezzotint, 15.0 × 11.5 cm, Trustees of the British Museum, Q,3.38. Dutens was secretary to Bute's brother James Stuart Mackenzie in Turin, from where he passed communications from Bute to the French government. Dutens was one of the recipients of Bute's *Botanical Tables*.

The idea that each collector might achieve something for the common good can be found, even if not voiced by a Bute, a Hunter or a King George III, in one of the conversations diligently recorded by James Boswell in his *Life of Samuel Johnson*. Boswell noted something that was on people's lips, and which touched Hunter's interests very closely, telling us that "He [Johnson] approved the famous collection of editions of Horace by Douglas, mentioned by Pope, who is said to have had a closet filled with them; and he added, 'every man should try to collect one book in that manner, and present it to a publick [sic] library.'"[32]

If the Duc de Choiseul was, like Bute, a collector with a strong leaning towards Dutch pictures, there were significant figures elsewhere in Europe whose collections or writings show a similar approach, counterbalancing the conservative promoters of Italian culture. Germany, where an understanding of the importance of the "Idea" in art was as strong as anywhere, produced in Johann Wolfgang von Goethe (1749–1832), a poet, novelist and playwright, whose experience and writings demonstrate conclusively the vanity of the project to separate "art and nature." Whereas British writers such as Sterne and Smollett could suggest the absurdity of any debate about taste, for Goethe it was a serious question how to harness both art and nature in pursuit of literary or scientific goals. The comparison is instructive, for both Bute and Goethe surrounded themselves with art, and for both, botanical science was a route to helping their fellow men and women, Bute with his *Botanical Tables* (1785) and Goethe his *Metamorphose der Pflanzen* (1790). Goethe's education, like Bute's, gave him an abiding love of Italy and ancient culture, while his upbringing in Protestant Frankfurt strongly influenced his liking for Dutch pictures. Perhaps the most magisterial image of Goethe, is that created by one of the poet's many painter friends, Johann Heinrich Wilhelm Tischbein (1751–1829), in which he reclines under a toga in the Campagna, surrounded by sculpture and with the tombs of the Via Appia in the background. It was in Italy, which was the source of so many of his ideas, literary and scientific, that Goethe hoped also to locate what he called the *Urpflanze*, or archetype plant. Yet, in his autobiography, *Dichtung und Wahrheit*, or Poetry and Truth, we learn that as a young man Goethe, "took the excellence of the Italian masters more on trust and in faith, than by pretending to any insight into them. What I could not look upon as nature, put in the place of nature, and compare with a known object, was without effect upon me. It is the material impression which makes the beginning even to every more elevated amateurship."

Goethe tells the story of his visit as a young man to the great art collections in Dresden, which were particularly rich in Dutch and Flemish works. He uses the image of a genre painting more than once to reveal how closely he identified with Golden Age artists. It is a *topos*, and he is playing very appropriately with the idea, borrowed from the Roman author Pliny's famous anecdote about the competition between the Greek painters Zeuxis and Parrhasius, that for a moment he did not know if he was looking at art or nature:

"When I returned to my cobbler's house to eat the midday meal, I could scarcely believe my eyes; I thought I was beholding a picture by Ostade, perfect enough to be hung in the gallery as it was. Everything I had admired in his pictures: placement of objects, light, shadow, the brownish tint over everything, the magical harmony of parts – I here saw in reality."[33]

Goethe's affection for Dutch painting deeply affected the German philosopher and writer on aesthetics, G. W. F. Hegel (1770–1831), who produced this remarkably perceptive formulation of what Dutch seventeenth-century painting has to offer:

"While classical art essentially gave shape in its ideal figures only to what is substantial, here we have, riveted and brought before our eyes, changing nature in its fleeting expressions, a burn, a waterfall, the foaming waves of the ocean, still-life with casual flashes of glass, cutlery etc., the external shape of spiritual reality in the most detailed situations, a woman threading a needle by candlelight, a halt of robbers in a casual foray, the most momentary aspect of a look which quickly changes again, the laughing and jeering of a peasant, in all this Ostade, Teniers and Steen are masters. It is a triumph of art over the transitory, a triumph in which the substantial is as it were cheated of its power over the contingent and the fleeting."[34]

Dutch painting, which Bute collected with passion, was a branch of art which, because its subject matter was independent of history or mythology, was hard to accommodate in the Enlightenment period because it was not rooted in ideas from the classical world. At Luton, Bute achieved magnificently what other enlightened European collectors, including nobles and crowned heads, were also setting out to do: the creation of a reference collection that allowed judgements of Dutch painting – such as Hegel's – to be measured against the evidence. Luton may have faded away, but in the very time that it was emptied and destroyed by fire, other institutions were coming into being such as the National Gallery, the Wallace Collection, and Dulwich Picture Gallery, where Constable was able to study by copying his favourite Dutch and Flemish painters and make his contribution to an art that was becoming increasingly focused on the observation of nature, which had been the goal of such men as Goethe and Bute.

1 Julia Lloyd Williams in exhib. cat. Edinburgh, 1992, p. 160.

2 Russell, 2004, p. 14: "If I could guess what you wanted here my dear lord I would willingly help you, I mean in Virtu. I am making a small collection of prints and books ..."

3 Bute's text is part of a collection of his manuscripts (Cambridge University Library MS Add. 8826) which were possibly bound together by his family in the early nineteenth century. The label on the spine, "Vol. 1" suggests that the volume was part of a larger series. The standard works were, for Italy, Maximilien Misson, *Nouveau voyage d'Italie* (The Hague, 1691), and for central Europe, Johann Georg Keyßler's *Neüeste Reise durch Teütschland, Böhmen, Ungarn, die Schweitz, Italien und Lothringen* (Hannover, 1740–1742).

4 The conclusion that Bute's collection was formed with the idea of contributing to an understanding of the history of art follows from the admittedly limited knowledge we have of his substantial libraries as well as his impressive collections of prints and drawings. Of the latter there are rudimentary lists in the auction catalogues which facilitated their dispersal after Bute's death. The prints were sold by Hutchins, 31 March–19 April 1794, in 1654 lots (Lugt, *Répertoire* 5179). Sales of drawings were held by Leigh and Sotheby, 8–19 May 1794, Paintings drawings 16, Drawings 230, Manuscripts 13, Books 1018, Various 4 (Lugt, *Répertoire* 5202); and 20–26 April 1809, Drawings prints 432, Books 369, Various 24 (Lugt, *Répertoire* 7569).

5 See "Sir Joshua Reynolds' Collection of Pictures," *The Burlington Magazine*: Part I, 86:507 (1945), pp. 133–34; Part II, 87:510 (1945), pp. 211–17; Part III, 87:512 (1945), pp. 263–73. Christopher Brown in exhib. cat. Hull, 1981, p. 7, noted that Reynolds's affection for Rembrandt was inspired by his master, Hudson.

6 For a contemporary use of the phrase "Age of Observation," see the review of Sir William Hamilton's study of Volcanoes, the *Campi Phlegraei*, in *Monthly Review, or Literary Journal*, LVI (January–June 1777), p. 380: "In this age of observation and experimental researches, there are few philosophers who have examined Nature with such profound attention, and expressed her phenomena with such truth and energy as Sir William Hamilton." "With a Sincere Hand and a Faithful Eye," the title of chapter 3 of the excellent book on Dutch painting by Svetlana Alpers, *The Art of Describing* (Chicago, 1983), is taken from Robert Hooke's *Micrographia*, 1664. Hooke called for a more careful observation and recording of phenomena as a route to reforming science.

7 Walpole, 1747, x-xi.

8 Russell, 2004, p. 189, comments that "Alas, no comments on potential purchases submitted to Bute by Baillie have survived." Russell's analysis of Bute's taste, pp. 198–199, is convincing: "If his years at Leyden influenced Bute's tastes in pictures, his delayed experience of Italy unveiled new horizons."

9 Canvas, 63.5 × 51 cm, Bute Inventory No. B00520.

10 *Rembrandt Corpus*, vol. 1, A 10. Panel 31.9 × 42.5 cm. The painting was sold in The Hague from the collection of M. D. Eversdijck on 28 May 1766, Lot 77, bought by Lemmens for f.20. In this period, Bute was using agents in Holland such as William Baillie, or Baillie's associate, the Amsterdam dealer Pieter Fouquet. Lemmens is not known to have acted for Bute but may have been part of the same network. The location of the painting is recorded again in 1881 when it was sold from the collection of Sir Francis Ferdinand Maurice Cook (Fourth Baronet), Doughty House. I am very grateful to Christian T. Seifert for the suggestion that the "Usurer Examining Gold ..." painting might be the panel in Berlin.

11 7–8 June 1822 (Lugt, *Répertoire* 10271). The painting was lot 15, "Eckhout, A Miser: Candlelight" and was bought by Adams for the surprisingly low price of £2.7.0d. The "Catalogue of a Valuable Selection of About Two Hundred Italian, French, Flemish & Dutch Pictures From the Very Noble and Extensive Collection of the Marquess of Bute, at Luton Park in Bedfordshire" contained among the 173 lots, the paintings on copper of *The Four Times of the Day* by Lancret, Lot 60, £33.12.0, now in the National Gallery, London. See above, p. 29.

12 The Luton inventory of ca. 1799 lists three paintings by Dou and six by Ostade.

13 The collection was sold by Greenwood, Leicester Square 29–31 May 1794 (Lugt, *Répertoire* 5215).

14 William Baillie's letter to Sir James Lowther, referring to the Murillo, is quoted by Russell, 2004, p. 186.

15 CUL, MS Add. 8826, p. 22.

16 Bute MSS, quoted by Russell, 2004, p. 82.

17 Dutens, 1806, pp. 172–173, my translation: "This is how this great affair unfolded; My Lord Bute took the instructions of the king, and communicated them to his brother; Mr Mackenzie passed them on to the Conte de Viry, Minister of the King of Sardinia, who was a man of the utmost discretion; The Conte de Viry wrote about the matter to Bailli de Solar in Paris, and he discussed it with the Duc de Choiseul; and when there was

agreement about an article this was communicated through the ministerial channel by Lord Egremont. If there were important differences, My Lord Bute and the Duc de Choiseul would write to one another."

18 The full title of the "Cabinet" is, *Recueil d'éstampes gravées d'après les tableaux du Cabinet de Monseigneur le duc de Choiseul par les soins du Sr. Basan, MDCCLXXI. À Paris chez l'auteur, rue et hotel Serpente.*

19 See note 4.

20 The *Cabinet Choiseul* was Lot 58 on the final day. On Choiseul, see Scott, 1973: "Out of the 138 pictures sold, 107 were of the Dutch and Flemish school. They included ten Wouwermans, eight Rembrandts, seven Tenierses, six Berchems, five Ter Borchs, five Metsus and paintings by Ruisdael, Mieris, Steen, Van der Werff and Gerard Dou ..."

21 The interest in paintings of this type is referred to as a "Brueghel Renaissance" by Korthals Altes, 2000, p. 281, note 112.

22 Russell, 2004, p. 183. For a rounded picture of Bragge, see Russell, 2016.

23 Russell, 2004, p. 190 names Berckheyde's *View of the Groote Kerk, Haarlem* as a work acquired by Bute from the Lormier collection. Bute's *Cock Fight* by Jan Steen (cat. 29) also came from the Lormier collection; see Korthals Altes, 2015, p. 276.

24 Korthals Altes, 2000, Appendix B, List of paintings sold by Willem Lormier (1748–1758), no. 60. The sale to Grosvenor is noted by Simpson, 1953, pp. 39–42, cat. 47; see also Russell, 2004, p. 191.

25 Luton, 1799, Library, no. 6; Russell, 2004, plate 139.

26 The National Gallery painting measures 123 × 241 cm, NG6522. For *Orpheus* see Russell, 2004, plate 131.

27 1650, 308.0 × 219.7 cm, Detroit Institute of Arts.

28 Waagen, 1838, vol. 3, pp. 358–359.

29 On the Peel collection see Roberts, 1971.

30 Russell, 2004, pp. 198–199. See above, note 8.

31 Exhib. cat. London, 1964, p. 10. The introduction was titled "Holland and Britain in the Age of Observation." Charles Wilson was author of *Holland and Britain* (London: Collins, 1946), p. 12.

32 Boswell, 1985, p. 1281. Dr James Douglas FRS (1665–1742), anatomist and "physician in extraordinary" to Queen Caroline, was Hunter's master and mentor in London from 1741 until his death, and from that brief period of study, Hunter possibly learned the need for focused collecting. Like Douglas, Hunter went on to collect early printed classical texts.

33 Goethe, 1987, p. 241; see also Pliny the Elder, *Natural History* XXXV, XXXVI, 65–66.

34 Hegel, 1975, p. 599; quoted by Haskell, 1993, p. 3.

PETER BLACK

AND CAITLIN BLACKWELL

CATALOGUE

1 LEMUEL FRANCIS ABBOTT
(Leicestershire ca. 1760–1802 London)
PORTRAIT OF CAPTAIN WILLIAM BAILLIE

date unknown
oil on canvas
76.2 × 63.3 cm
inventory no. B00174
lit: Luton, 1799, Green With-Drawing Room, no. 14
exhib: Glasgow, 1884, cat. 1
(displayed at the Hunterian)

Captain Baillie (1723–1810) was an Irish soldier, artist and art dealer. His distinguished career in the British army ended in the early 1760s after which he focused on art dealing, becoming one of Bute's principal buyers of Dutch art. Baillie made accomplished engravings which reproduced paintings and drawings. This allowed him to publicise fine works, some already placed in collections. Bute owned an impressive album of prints presented by Baillie (Paris, Fondation Custodia), which includes Rembrandt's *Hundred Guilder Print*, the plate of which Baillie owned and "restored."

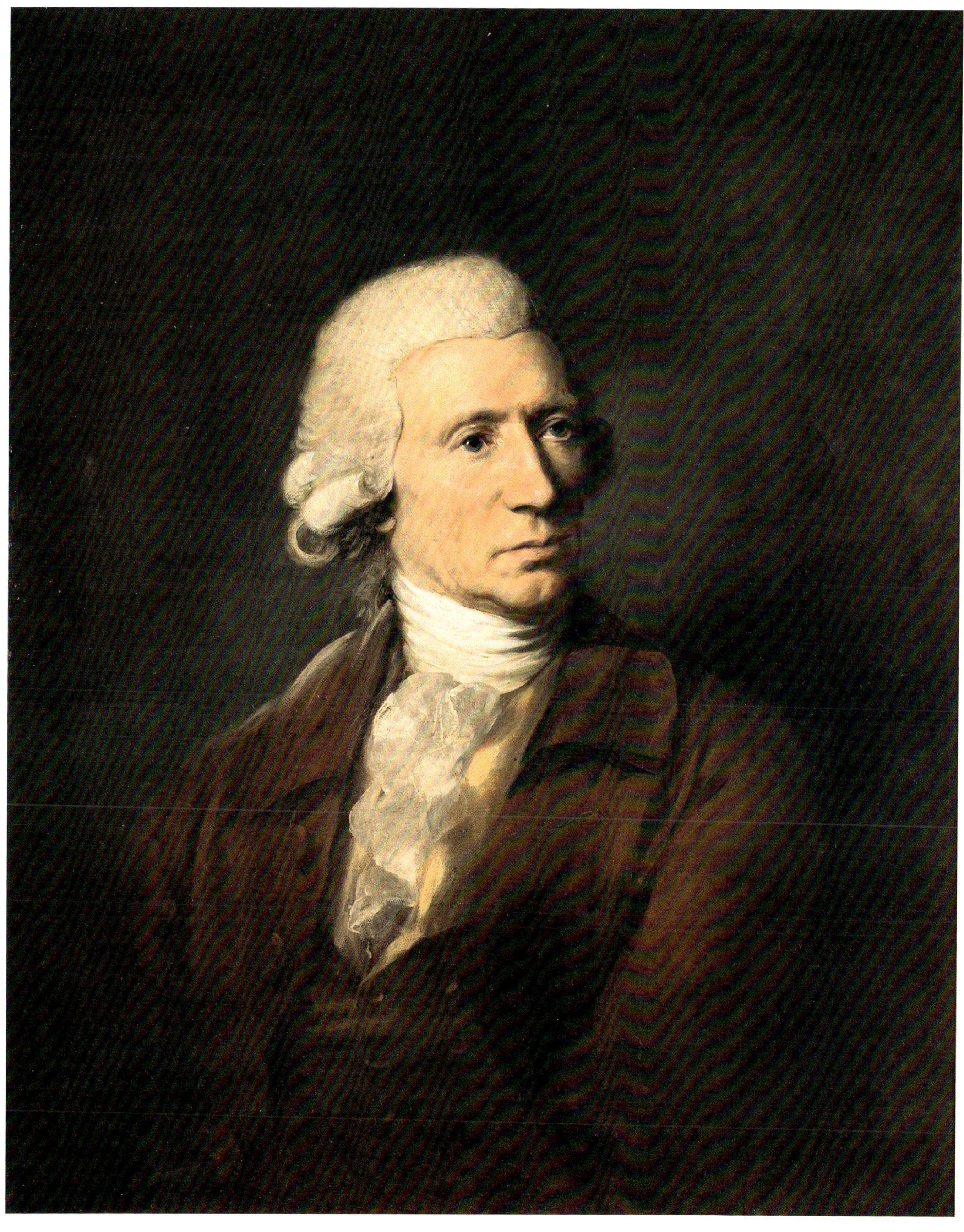

2 CORNELIS BEGA
(Haarlem ca. 1631/32–1664)
A BOOR DRINKING

1664
oil on canvas
40.3 × 35.4 cm
signed and dated bottom left, "C.Bega A.° 1664"
inventory no. B00256
(displayed at the Hunterian)

lit: Luton, 1799, North Red Dressing Room, no. 27, 28; Waagen, 1838, vol. 3, p. 366; Russell, 2004, p. 197
exhib: Glasgow, 1884, cat. 3, 4; Edinburgh, 2012, cat. 1, 2

Bega was the outstanding pupil of the famous genre painter, Adriaen van Ostade (1610–1685). These two very similar paintings (not formally a pair) are examples of one of the artist's favourite subjects: a couple in an interior, with love in the air. In the *Boor Drinking*, the woman's head is framed by an Old Testament engraving, pinned to the wall. The *Girl Singing* provides a virtuoso treatment of the different silks of her clothing, which are as disorderly as the musical instruments and books piled to the left. They may be emblematic warnings about the danger of loose morals.

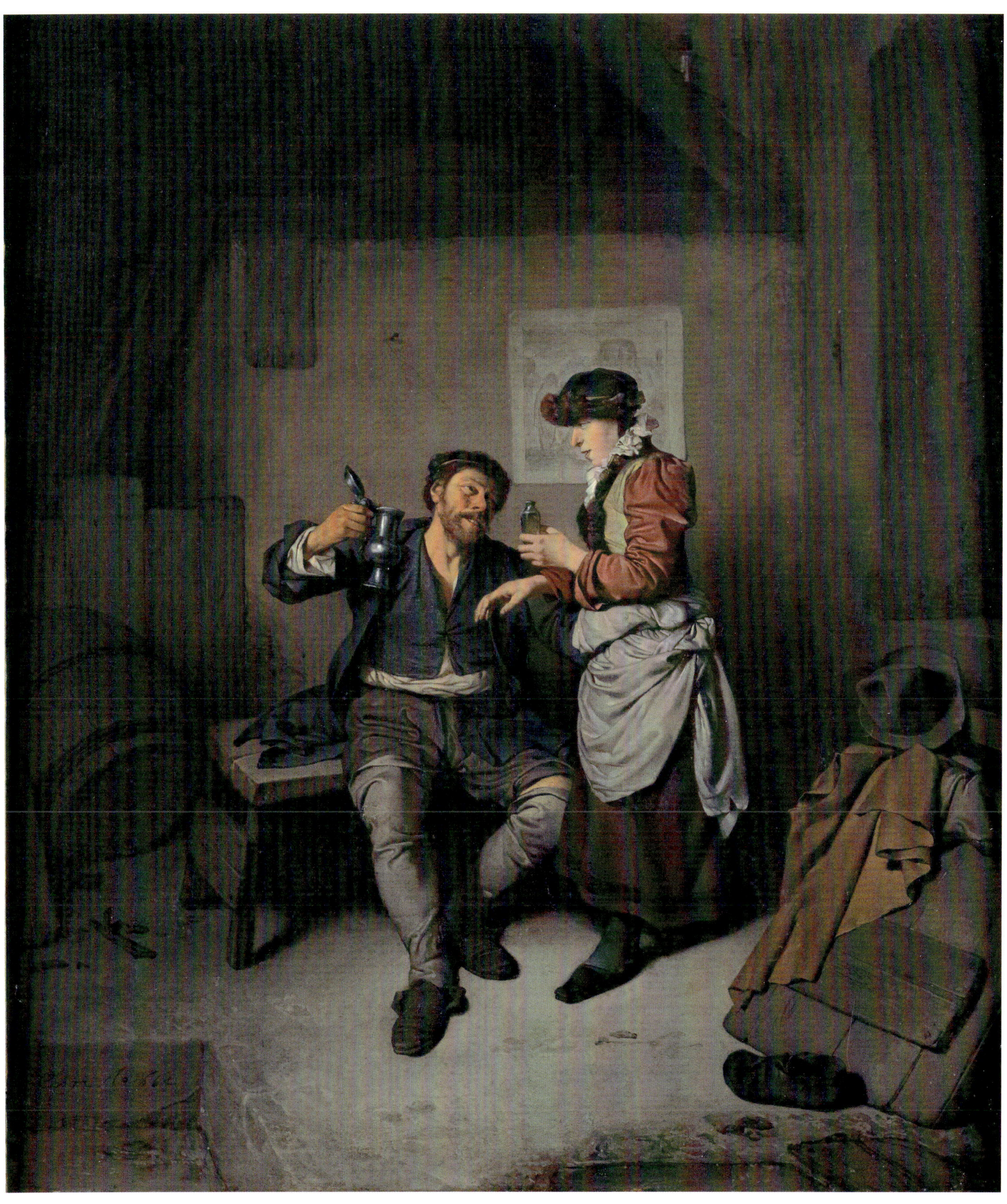

3 CORNELIS BEGA
(Haarlem ca. 1631/32–1664)
A GIRL SINGING

1663
oil on canvas
39.5 × 34.4 cm
signed and dated bottom right, "C. Bega, A.º 1663"
inventory no. B00253
(displayed at the Hunterian)

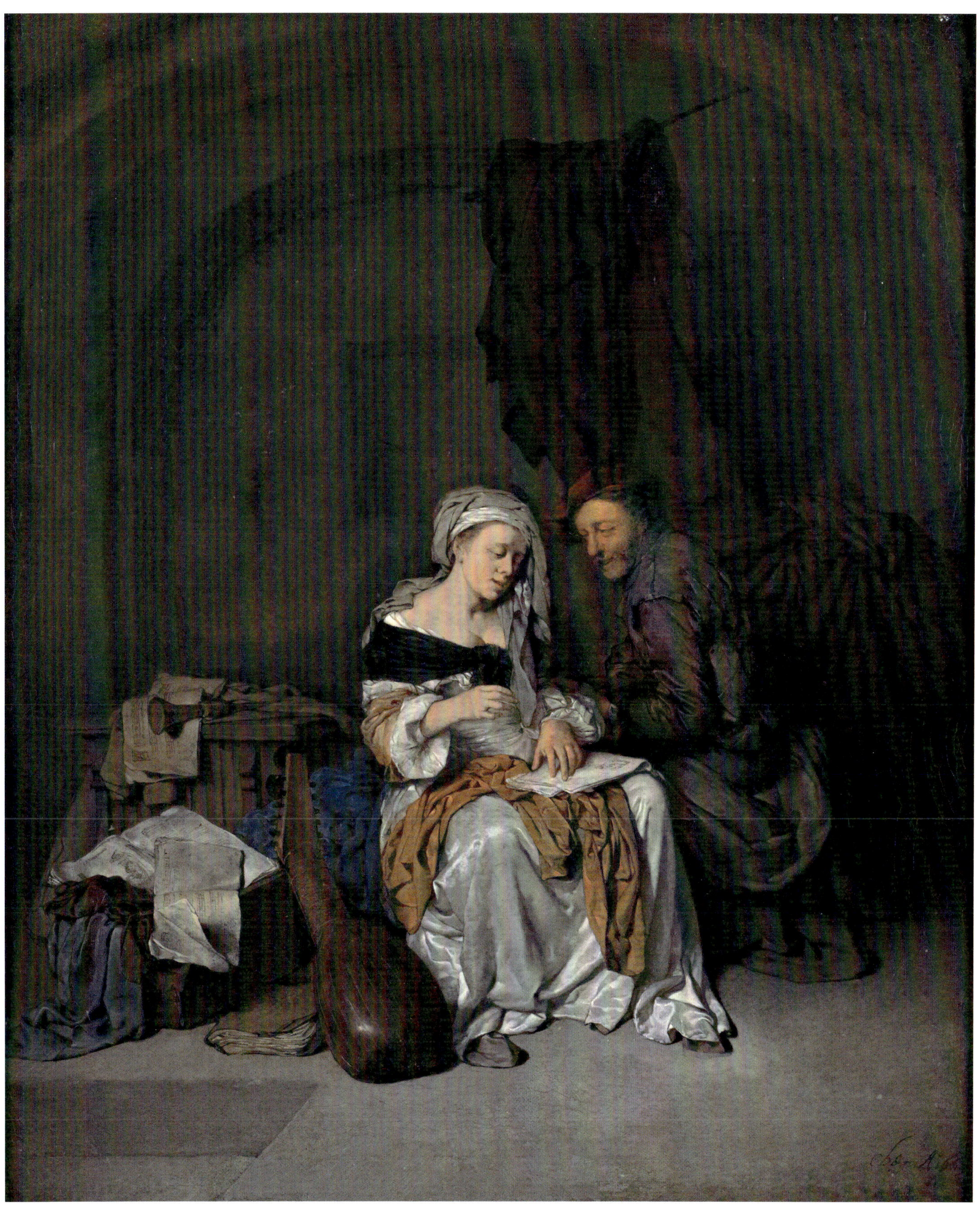

4 NICOLAES BERCHEM
(Haarlem 1621/2–1683 Amsterdam)
A WINTER LANDSCAPE

ca. 1665–1670
oil on panel
39.4 × 52.0 cm
signed bottom right, "C Berchem f"
inventory no. B00344
lit: Luton, 1799, West Bow Window Dressing Room, no. 14
exhib: Glasgow, 1884, cat. 8
(displayed at the Hunterian)

The Italianate landscape painter, Nicolaes Berchem was one of the Third Earl's favourite painters. He owned six works by him, including the masterpiece, the *Landscape representing a cold autumn windy day*, which hung with other major works in the library at Luton. The distinctive footbridge was of a kind known as a *kwakel*, which was built high above the water to allow boats to pass. The same bridge appears in another slightly smaller painting, the *Winter Landscape with Lime Kiln*, of the late 1660s (24.7 × 37.0 cm), in Karlsruhe, Staatliche Kunsthalle (inv. no. 297).

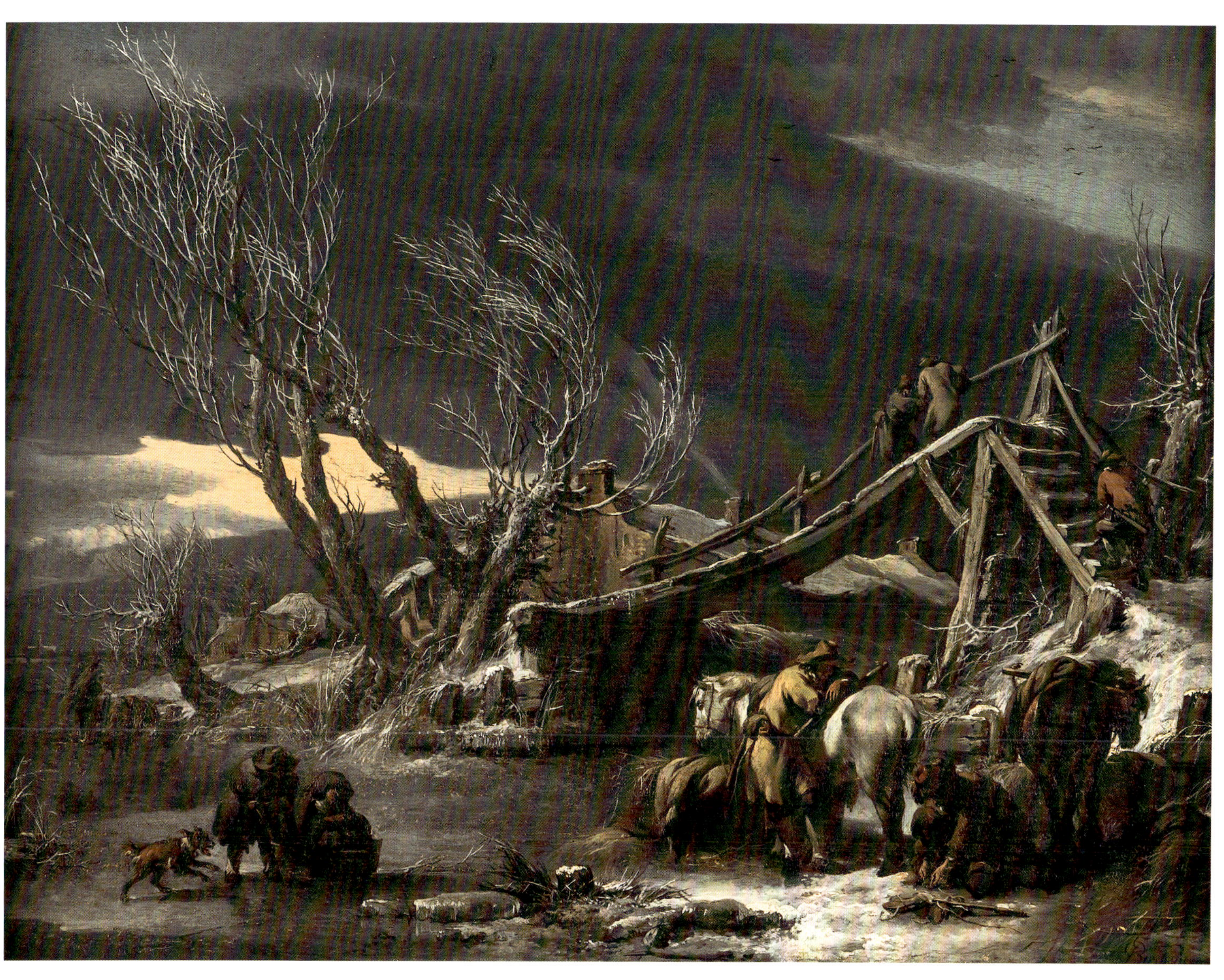

5 GERARD TER BORCH
(Zwolle 1617–1681 Deventer)
PORTRAIT OF GOSEWIJN HOGERS

ca. 1663–1668
oil on canvas
71 × 58.5 cm
signed with monogram
inventory no. B00304
(displayed at the Hunterian)

lit: Luton, 1799, East Bow Window Dressing Room, no. 17, 19;
Russell, 2004, p. 197; Waagen, 1838, p. 1854;
Kettering, 1999, pp. 60–62
exhib: London, 1883, cat. 232, 235; Glasgow, 1884, cat. 172, 173;
Edinburgh, 1949, cat. 32, 33; London, 1976, cat. 14

Ter Borch is famous for his sober genre scenes, often depicting well-to-do ladies in satin dresses. He also made portraits for the Deventer elite, which followed this very characteristic, small full-length format. His sitters are often unidentified, but these two portraits are known to represent a prominent couple, probably painted at the time of their marriage. Hogers (1636–1676) served as Burgomaster 1668–1674, but he was also Professor of History and Rhetoric at the High School in Deventer, which explains the numerous books surrounding him.

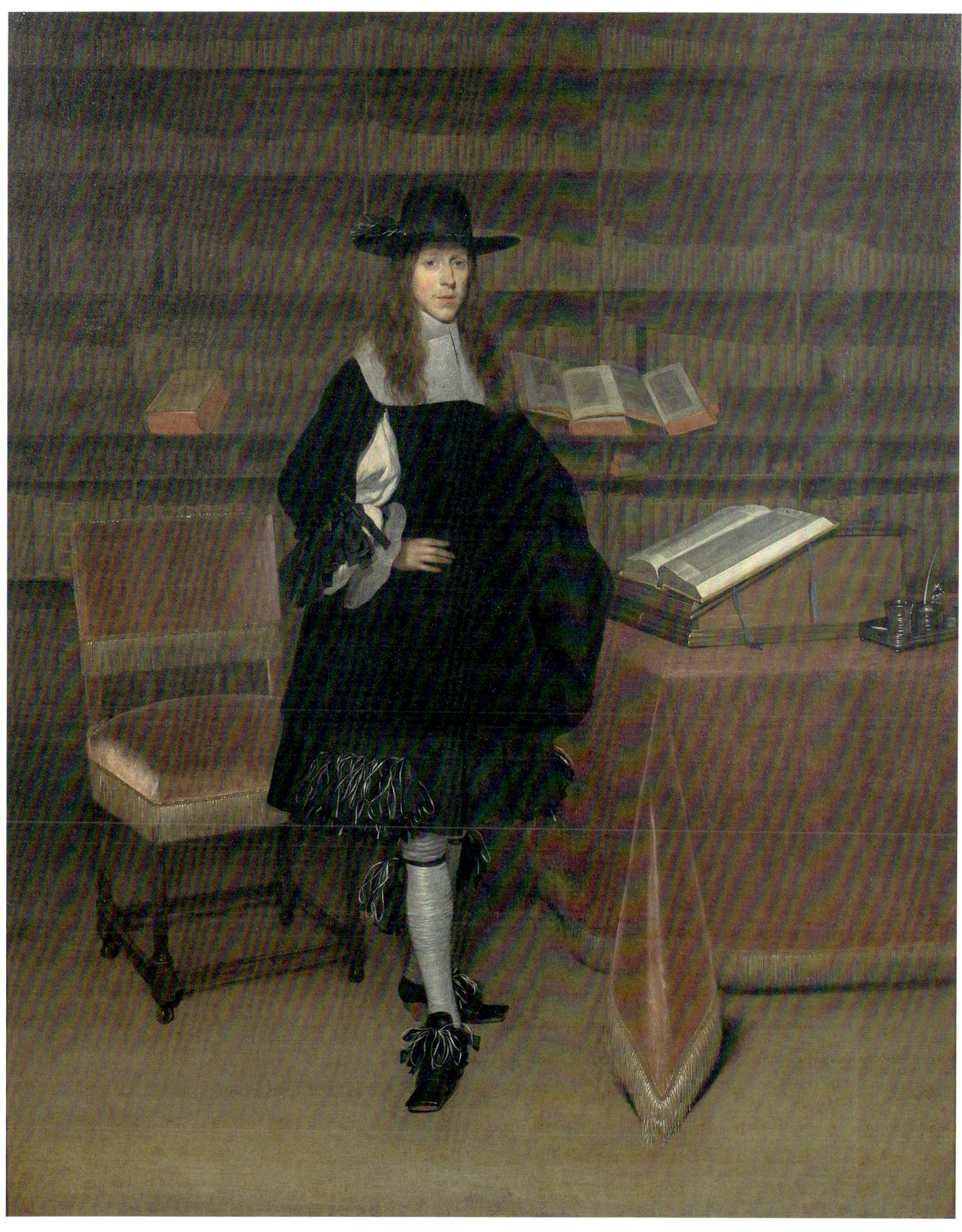

6 GERARD TER BORCH
(Zwolle 1617–1681 Deventer)
PORTRAIT OF FREDA QUADACKER,
WIFE OF GOSEWIJN HOGERS

ca. 1663–1668
oil on canvas
71 × 58.5 cm
inventory no. B00307
(displayed at the Hunterian)

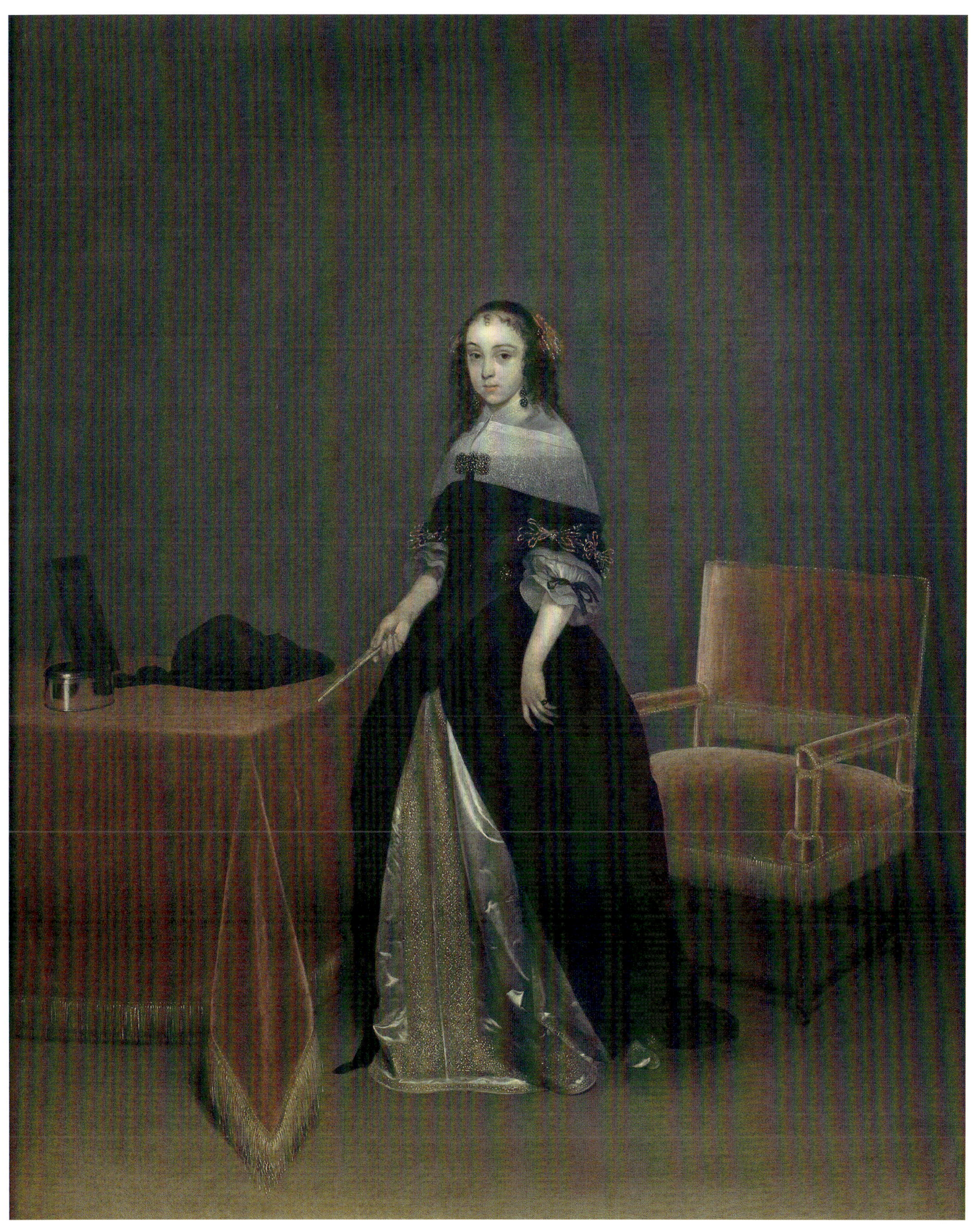

7 AELBERT CUYP
(Dordrecht 1620–1691)
CATTLE WATERING BY AN ESTUARY

ca. 1650
oil on panel
59.7 × 72.4 cm
signed right, "A.cúÿp"
inventory no. B00331
lit: Luton, 1799, North Green Dressing Room, no. 14, 15
exhib: London, 1883, cat. 79; Glasgow, 1884, cat. 36;
Edinburgh, 2012, cat. 7
(displayed at the Hunterian)

No fewer than eight landscapes with cattle by Cuyp were hung at Luton, and these included what is possibly the artist's greatest work of all, the *Landscape with Horsemen and Peasants*, now in the National Gallery, London (fig. 35). Bute's desire to include Cuyp in his collection was as influential as it was adventurous. It is said that the artist was hardly known outside his native Dordrecht until the eighteenth century. According to the painter Benjamin West, it was Bute's interest that created the rage for his work.

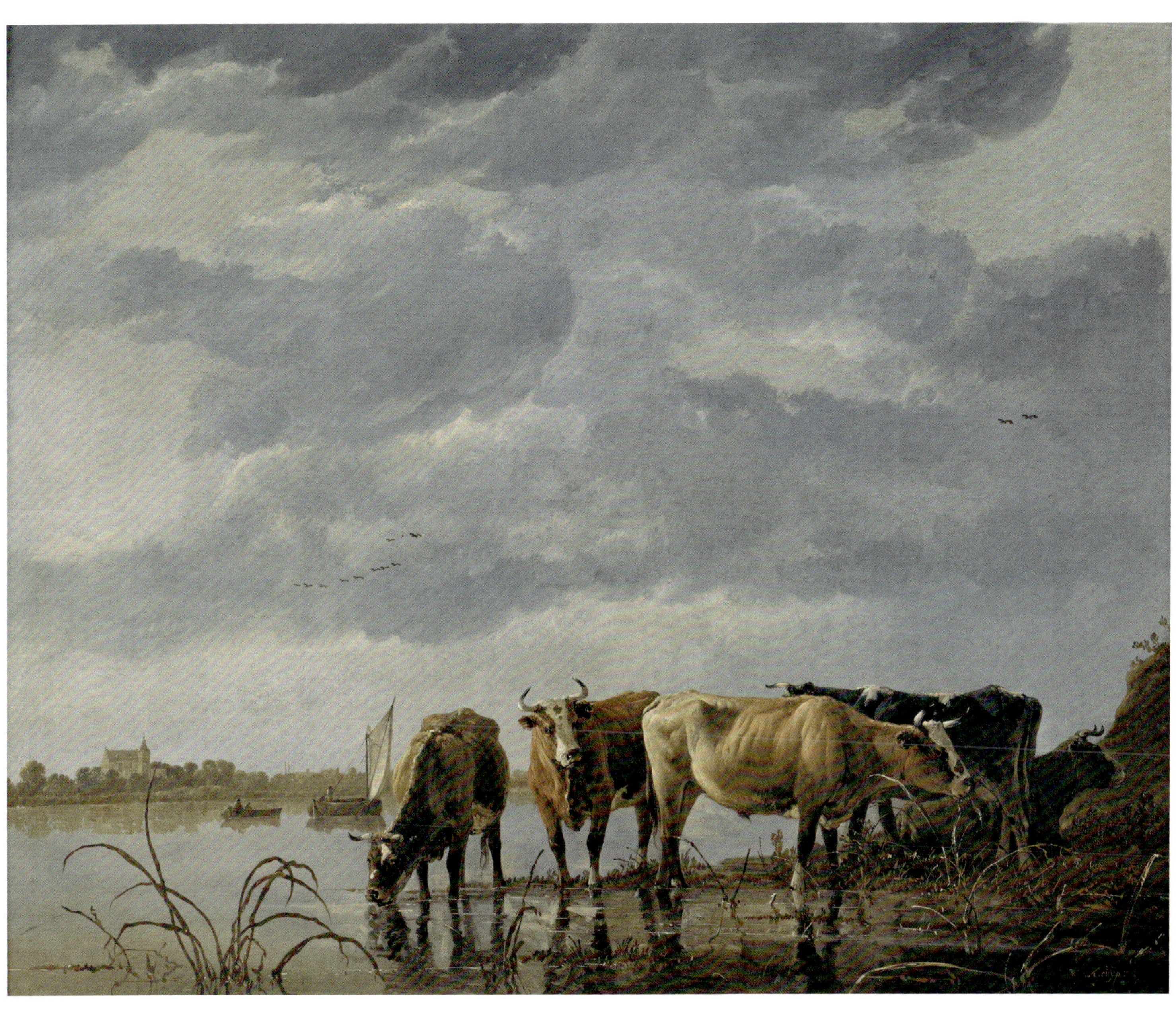

8 SIR ANTHONY VAN DYCK
(Antwerp 1599–1641 London)
WILLIAM HOWARD, VISCOUNT STAFFORD

ca. 1638–1640
oil on canvas
91.0 × 80.0 cm
inventory no. B00353
lit: Luton, 1799, Antiroom to the With-Drawing Room, no. 1;
Russell, 2004, p. 195, plate 114; Barnes, 2004, cat. 212
exhib: London, 1883, cat. 103; Glasgow, 1884, cat. 178
(displayed at the Hunterian)

The sitter in this vigorous half-length portrait, Viscount Stafford (1612–1680), was the fifth son of the great art collector, Thomas Howard, Earl of Arundel, who was painted by both Rubens and Van Dyck. Like his father, Stafford was himself a collector as a young man. He was brought up as a Catholic and fell victim to the accusation of being involved in the "Popish Plot" and was beheaded after the Restoration of Charles II.

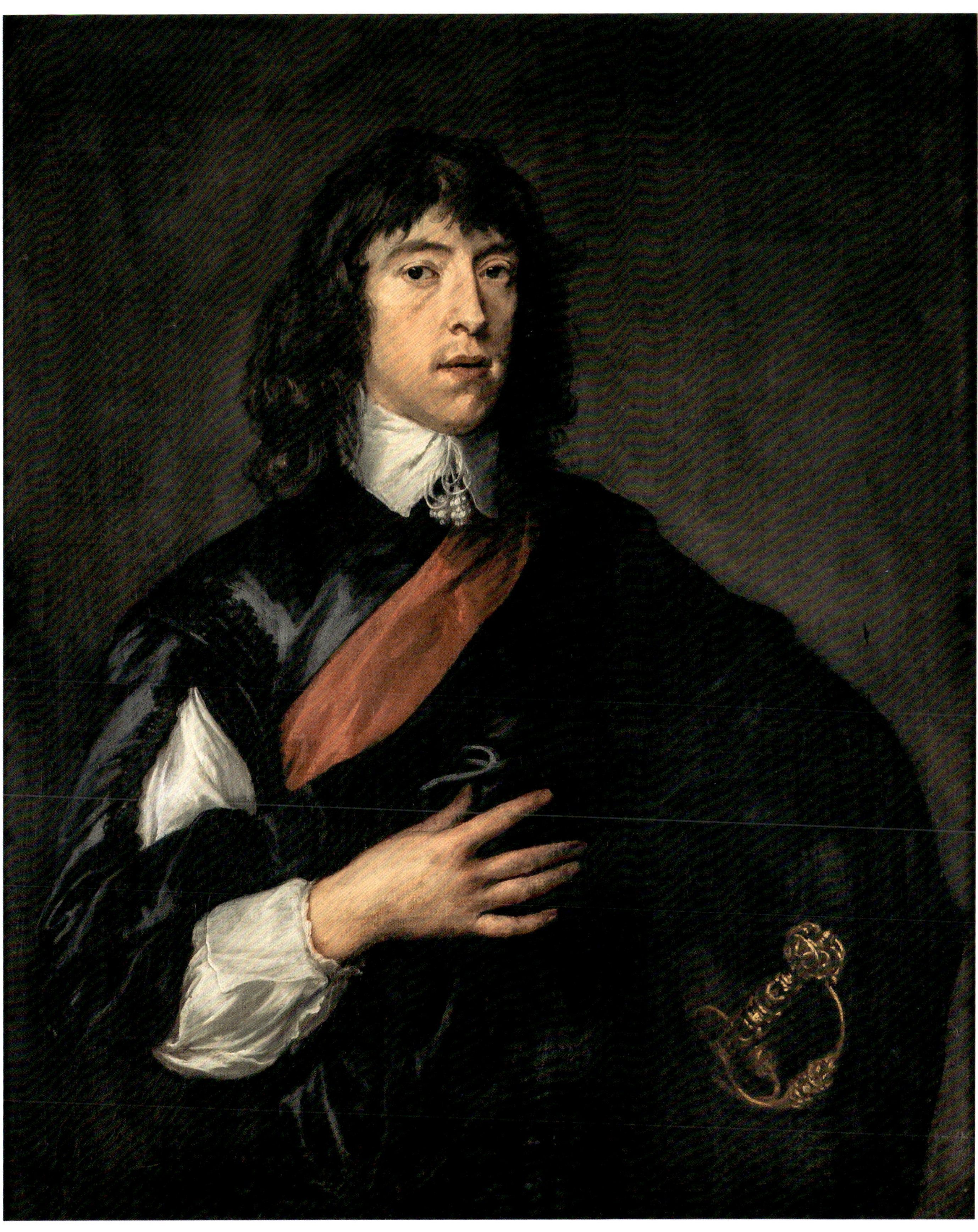

9 FRANS FRANCKEN II
(Antwerp 1581–1642)
A COLLECTOR'S GALLERY

ca. 1630
oil on panel
66.6 × 91.4 cm
inventory no. B00301
lit: Luton, 1799, Antiroom to the Library, no. 9;
Russell, 2004, p. 196
exhib: London, 1883, cat. 248; Glasgow, 1884, cat. 58
(displayed at the Hunterian)

Francken the Younger was the inventor of the imaginary gallery interior, a type of painting with a strong appeal to collectors. The fictive paintings in the foreground, being examined by connoisseurs, resemble works by famous Antwerp artists: a still life by Snyders, a landscape by De Momper and a history painting by Rubens. Portraits of the two greatest Antwerp masters, Rubens and Van Dyck, appear on the wall to the right. At Luton, this work was hung in the anteroom to the library, where some of the greatest works in the Bute collection were placed.

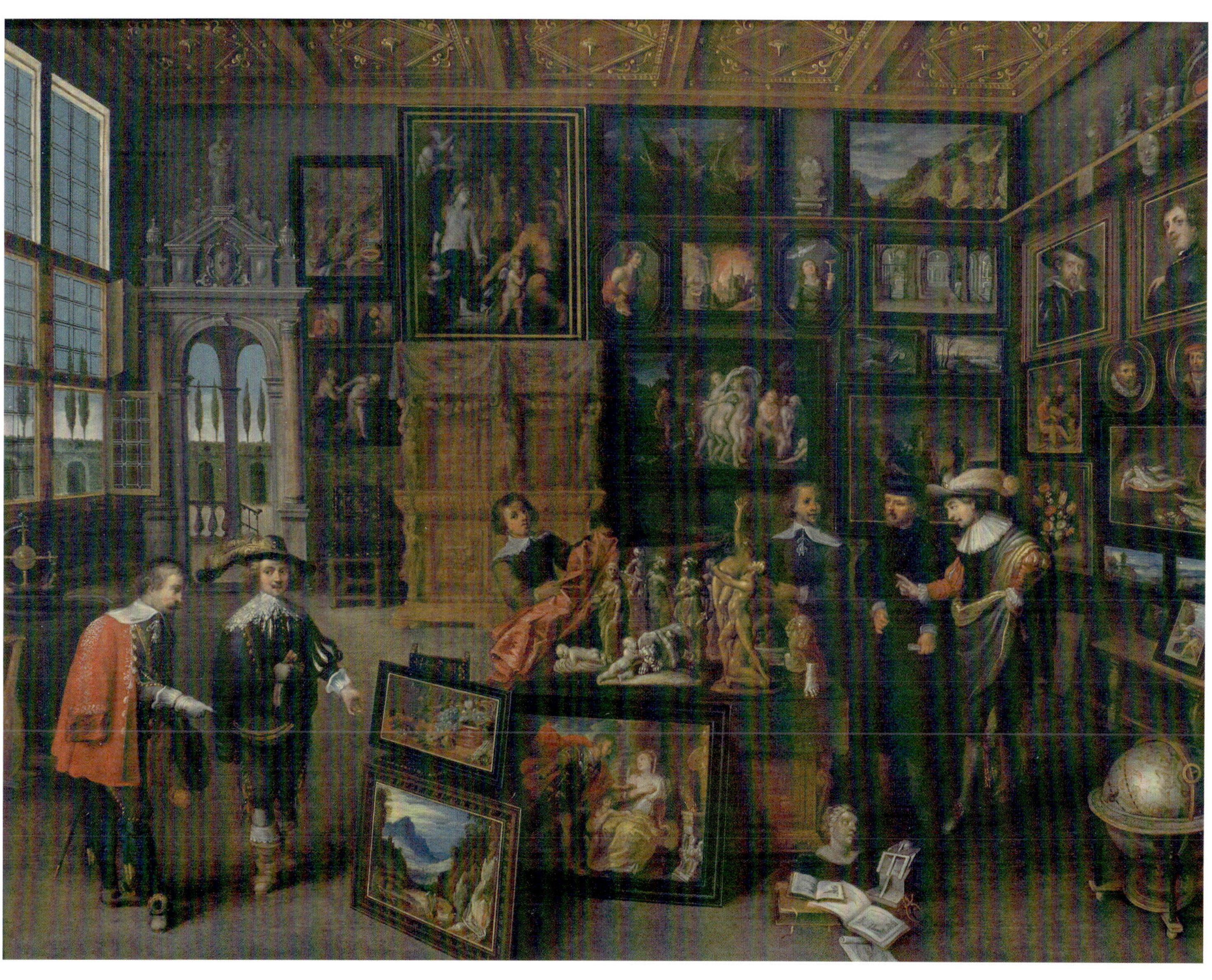

10 CLAUDE GELLÉE, KNOWN AS CLAUDE LORRAIN
(Chamagne, Vosges ca. 1604/5–1682 Rome)
EVENING: A SEAPORT AT SUNSET

1638
oil on canvas
73.0 × 96.0 cm
signed "Claudio ...Romae" and dated "1638"
inventory no. B00337
lit: Luton, 1799, East Bow Window Dressing Room, no. 7, 8;
Röthlisberger 1961, 31, 203; Russell, 2004, p. 197
exhib: London, 1883, cat. 1, 3; Glasgow, 1884, cat. 27, 28
(displayed at the Hunterian)

Bute's two Claudes were among his most important acquisitions. Claude was the father of classical landscape painting, and his work had a very broad influence, especially on Dutch Italianate painters. These idyllic landscapes stem from a group of eight commissioned by one of the artist's most important patrons, Angelo Giorio (1585–1662), who was a friend of Pope Urban VIII (Barberini). From Giorio they apparently passed to the Barberini family (Luton catalogue) later passing to the Third Earl. Their complementary vistas indicate that they were painted as a pair.

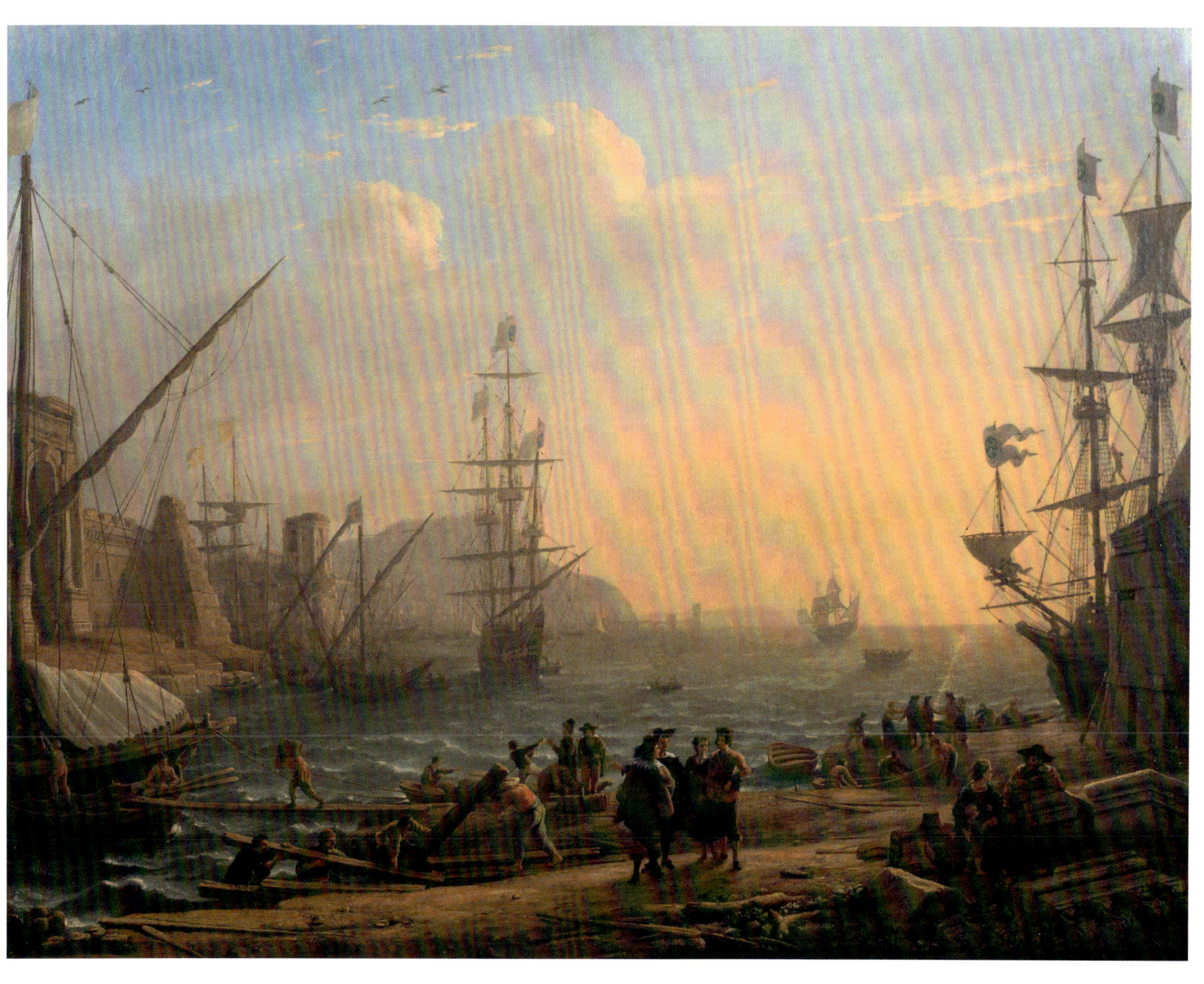

11 CLAUDE GELLÉE, KNOWN AS CLAUDE LORRAIN
(Chamagne, Vosges ca. 1604/5–1682 Rome)
MORNING: A WOODED LANDSCAPE

ca. 1638
oil on canvas
73.7 × 96.5 cm
inventory no. B00340
lit: Luton, 1799, East Bow Window Dressing Room, no. 7, 8;
Röthlisberger 1961, 31, 203; Russell, 2004, p. 197
exhib: London, 1883, cat. 1, 3; Glasgow, 1884, cat. 27, 28
(displayed at the Hunterian)

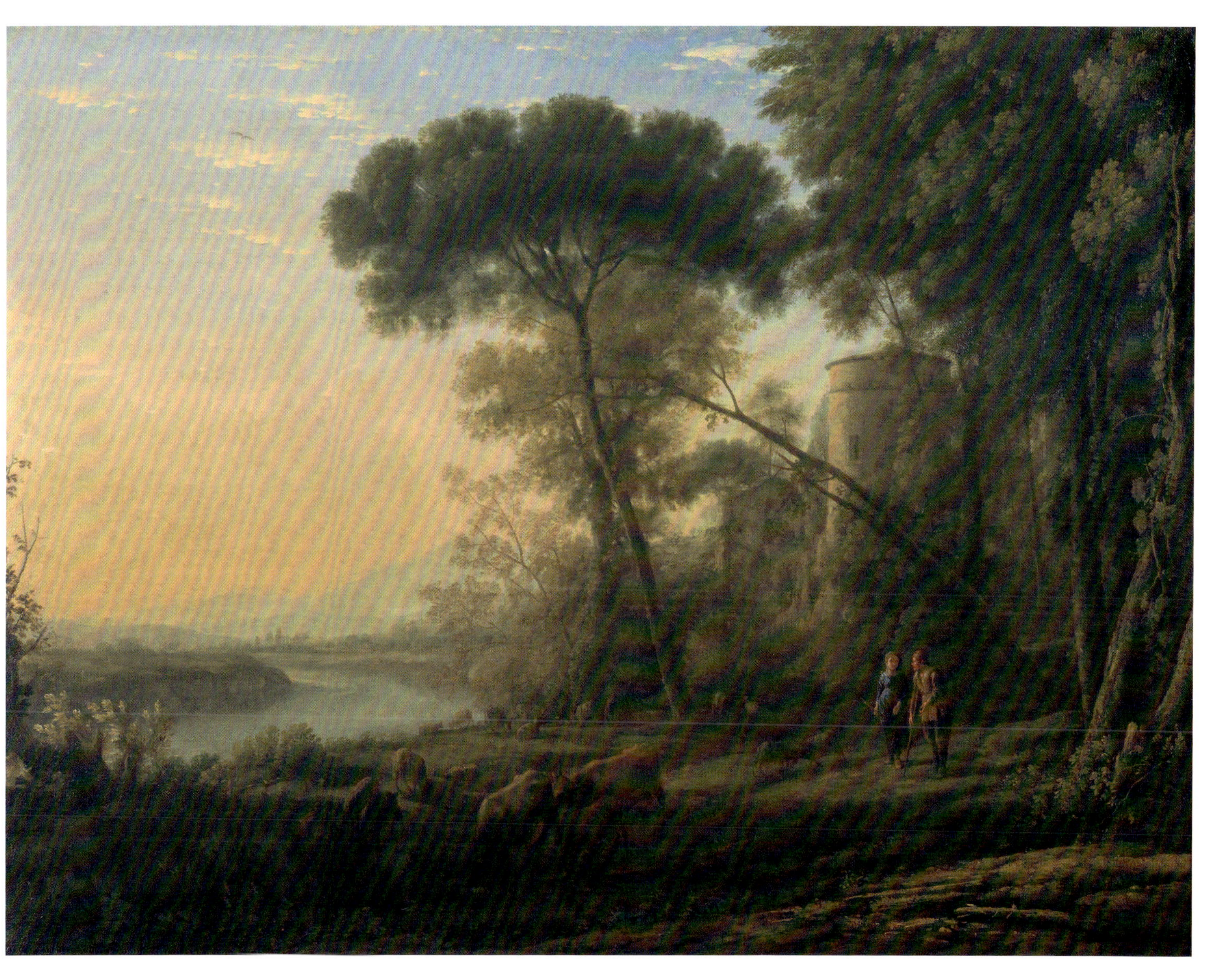

12 WILLEM VAN HERP
(Antwerp 1613/14–1677)
INTERIOR WITH FIGURES (A FLEMISH COLLATION)

date unknown
oil on copper
96.5 × 114.3 cm
inventory no. B00345
(displayed at Mount Stuart)

13 INTERIOR WITH GROUPS FEASTING
(A FLEMISH ENTERTAINMENT)

date unknown
oil on copper
96.5 × 114.3 cm
inventory no. B00345
(displayed at Mount Stuart)

lit: Luton, 1799, North Red Dressing Room, no. 20, 21
exhib: London, 1883, cat. 61, 56

Van Herp is not such a familiar figure now, but he enjoyed success in Antwerp with religious subjects in addition to his merry companies, of which these are important examples acquired by 1765. There are several versions of both images, and for the *Flemish Entertainment* there is a preparatory drawing in brown ink and blue-grey wash (18.0 × 26.3 cm), in Osnabrück, Kultur-geschichtliches Museum (inv. A. 2433). Both works were selected to be engraved for Boydell's *Collection of Prints, Engraved after the Most Capital Paintings in England.*

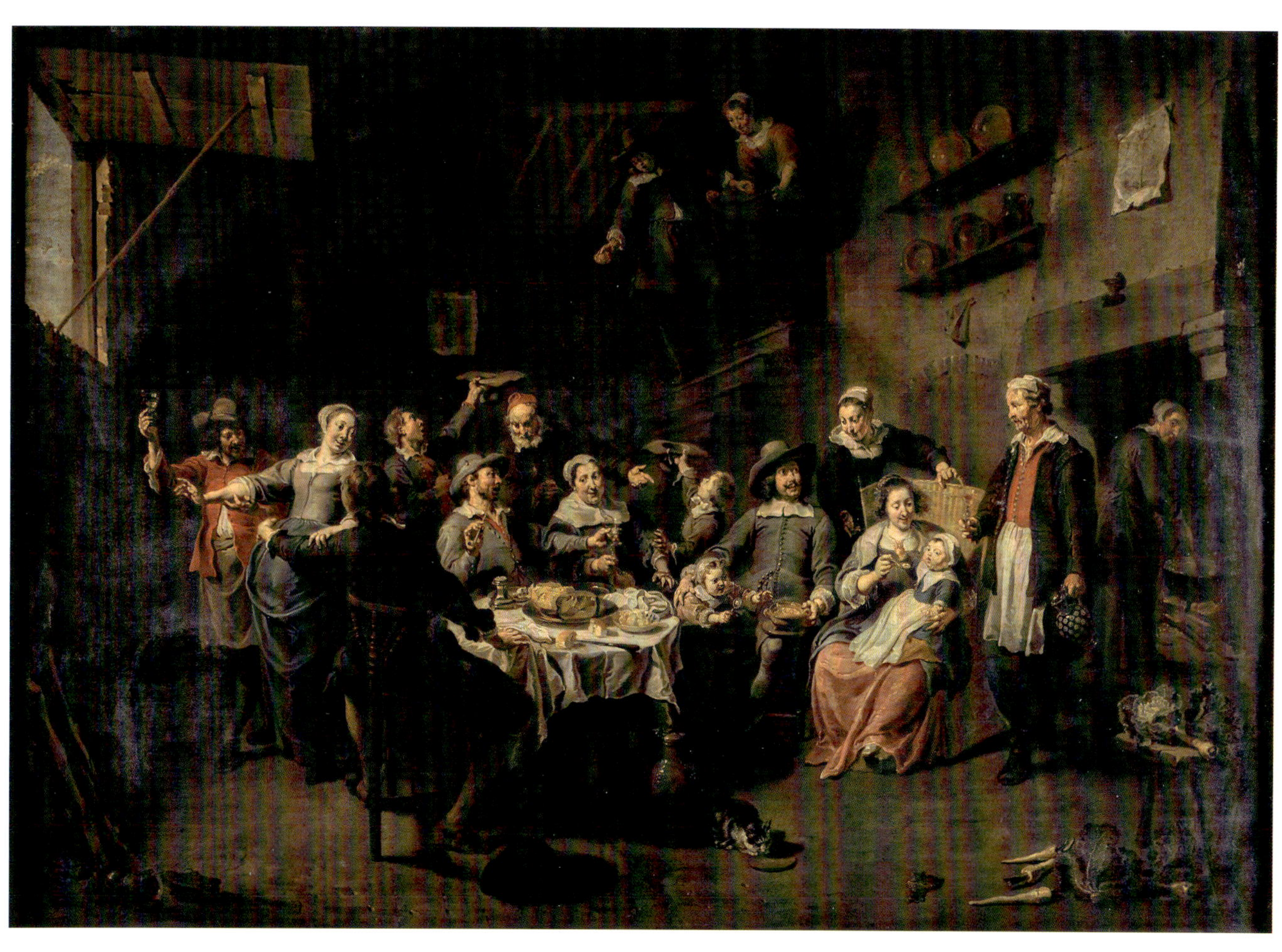

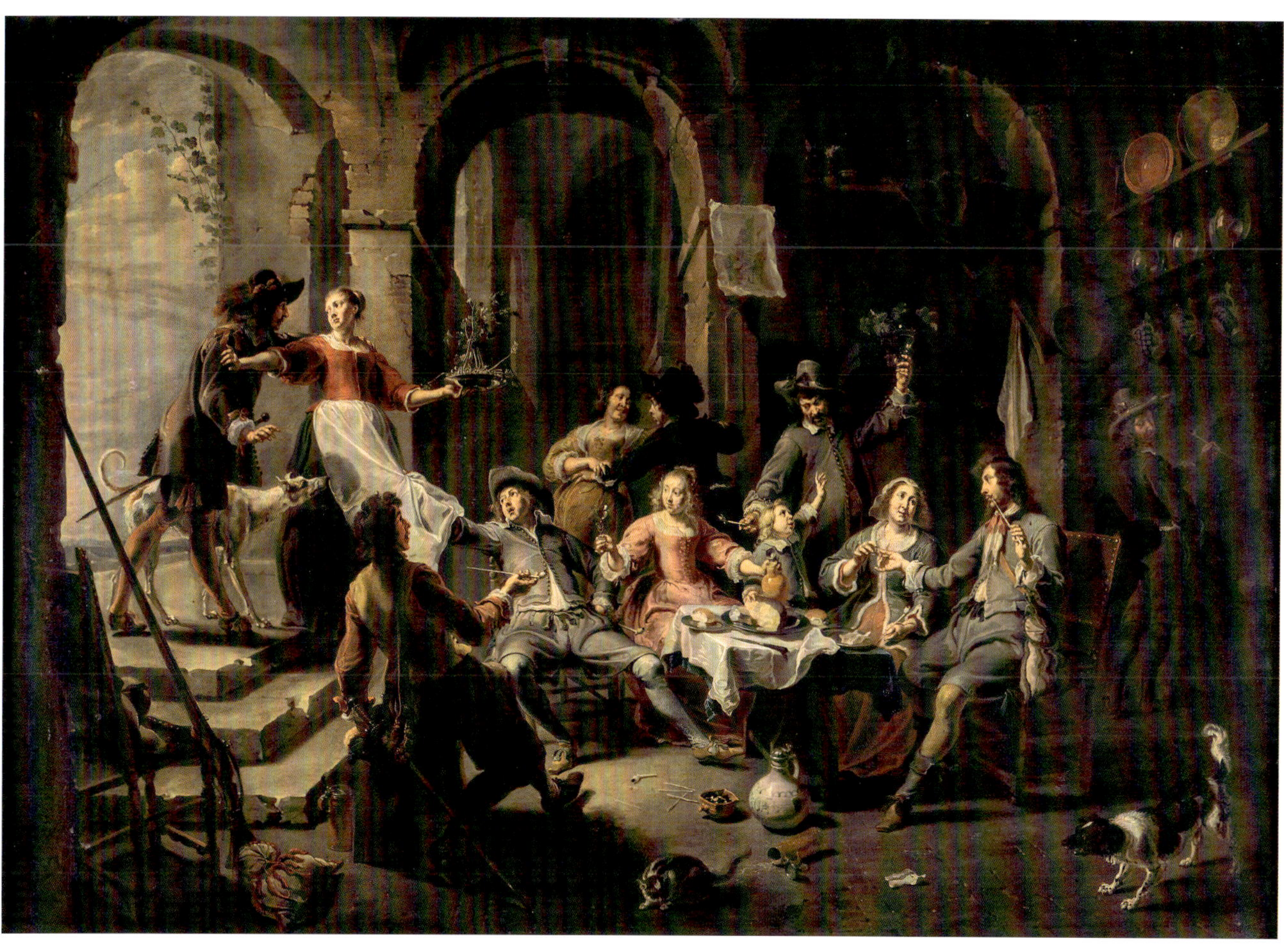

14 JAN VAN DER HEYDEN
(Gorinchem 1637–1712 Amsterdam)
THE VALKHOF AT NIJMEGEN

date unknown
oil on canvas, laid down on panel
38.8 × 47.5 cm
inventory no. B00290
lit: Luton, 1799, West Bow Window Dressing Room, no. 10;
Russell, 2004, plate 146
exhib: Glasgow, 1884, cat. 79
(displayed at the Hunterian)

Van der Heyden was inspired by the commercial success of Jan Brueghel the Elder to work in a similar miniaturist technique, a style which clearly appealed to Bute, who owned 13 works by Brueghel alone. This evening scene shows boats on the river Waal, above which rises the Valkhof citadel, a landmark that appears in many paintings by artists who ventured east along the river trade route. Nijmegen is close to the border with Germany and was an important staging post for travellers going south into Europe.

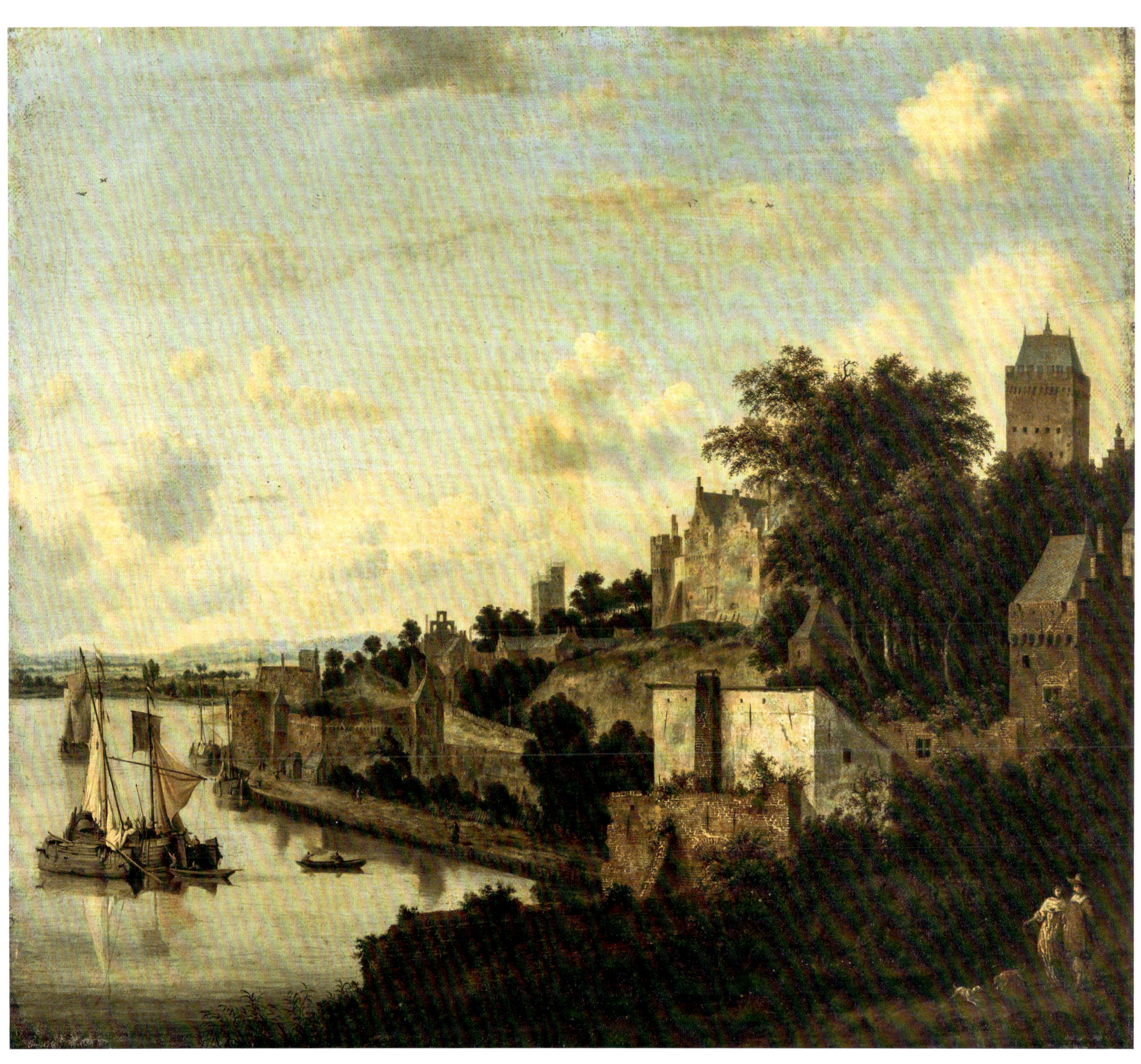

15 MEINDERT HOBBEMA
(Amsterdam 1638–1709)
WOODED LANDSCAPE WITH A WATERMILL

date unknown
oil on canvas
67.8 × 81.4 cm
inventory no. B00252
lit: Luton, 1799, North Red Dressing Room, no. 29
exhib: London, 1883, cat. 231
(displayed at Mount Stuart)

As with his interest in landscapes by Cuyp, in acquiring works by Hobbema Bute was choosing to represent an artist with little or no reputation in the seventeenth century. Hobbema was a pupil of his uncle, Jacob van Ruisdael from ca. 1655 and travelled with him to the Veluwe and over the border into Germany in 1661. The journey introduced Hobbema to a different kind of landscape, and evidence of a delight in remote farmhouses, tucked among woods and streams, appears in paintings from this point on. The watermill is one of Hobbema's favourite motifs.

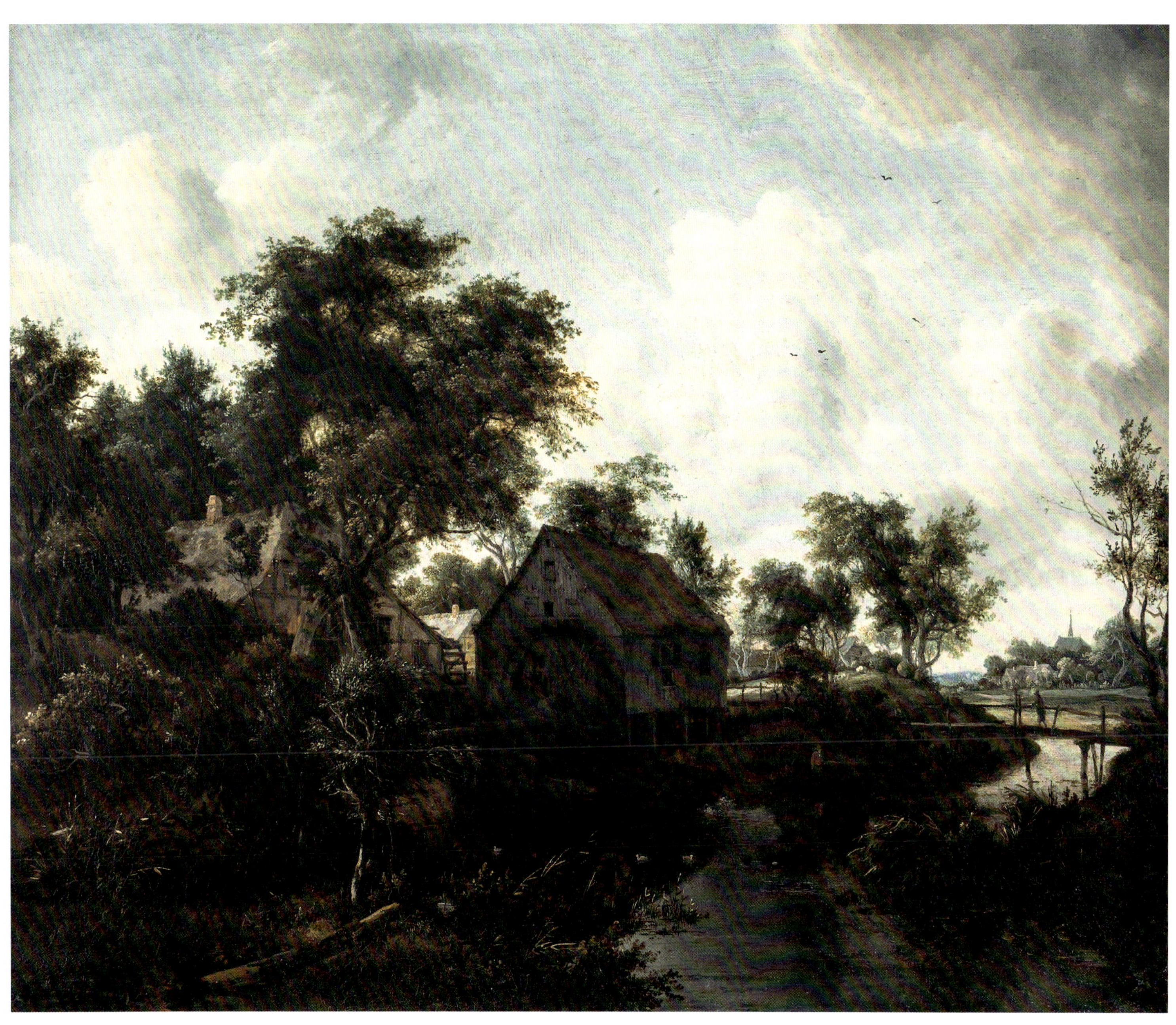

16 GABRIËL METSU
(Leiden 1629–1667 Amsterdam)
AN OLD WOMAN FEEDING A DOG

ca. 1654–1657
oil on canvas
41.7 × 30.5 cm
signed on the bottle on the widow sill, "GMetsu"
and on the grindstone bottom right, "GMetsú"
inventory no. B00296
provenance: Johannes Coops, Amsterdam;
Gerrit Braamcamp sale, Amsterdam 31 July 1771
(Lugt, 1938–1987, 1950), bought by Fouquet for Bute, f.1,200
lit: Luton, 1799, North Red Dressing Room, no. 23;
Russell, 2004, p. 197; Waiboer 2012, p. 38, cat. A-25
exhib: Glasgow, 1884, cat. 107; Edinburgh, 1949, cat. 24;
Edinburgh, 2012, cat. 12
(displayed at the Hunterian)

In the text of his catalogue raisonné, Adriaan Waiboer singled out this painting as an example of the tranquil atmosphere often sought by Metsu, saying, "The attraction of this painting lies in the charming way the couple cares for their poised pet. This subject is unique in Dutch art and constitutes Metsu's variation of paintings of old couples by Dou and Van Mieris, although neither of these artists depicted a mundane task with such tenderness." Metsu painted in a refined and meticulous manner, similar to that of the Leiden *fijnschilders* whose work, judging from their prominence in the collection, was admired by Bute.

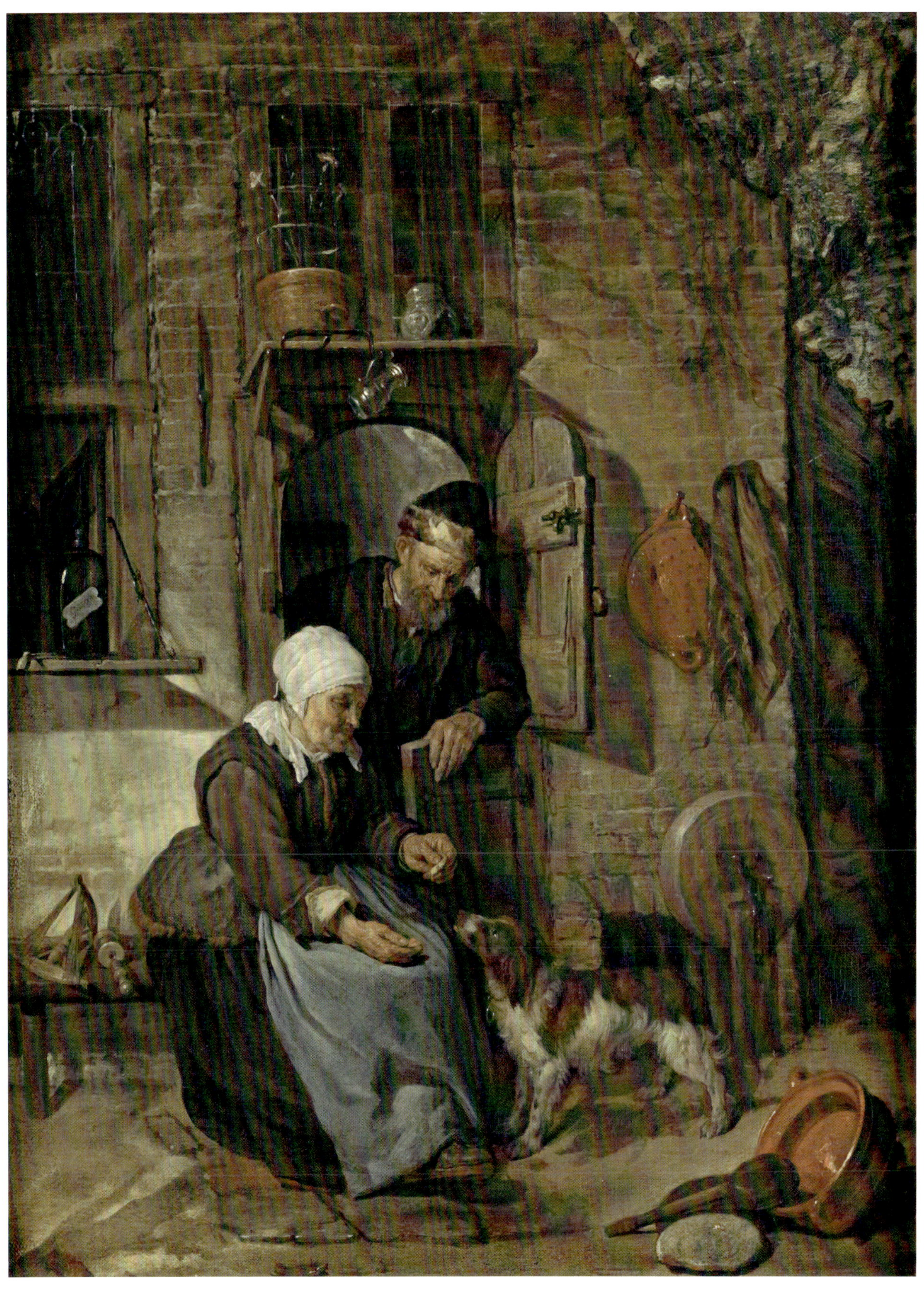

17 WILLEM VAN MIERIS
(Leiden 1662–1747)
WOMAN AND BOY AT A WINDOW WITH VEGETABLES

1726
oil on panel
22.7 × 20.2 cm
signed and dated, "W. van Mieris F. 1726"
inventory no. B00310
(displayed at the Hunterian)

Willem van Mieris came from a family of Leiden *fijnschilders*. His more talented father was the famous Frans van Mieris (1635–1681), whose meticulously painted figures in interiors were much sought after, expensive works. Willem's son, Frans II (1689–1763), continued this tradition well into the eighteenth century. This work was added to the collection by a later generation, who clearly shared the Third Earl's affection for the minutely accurate style of painting.

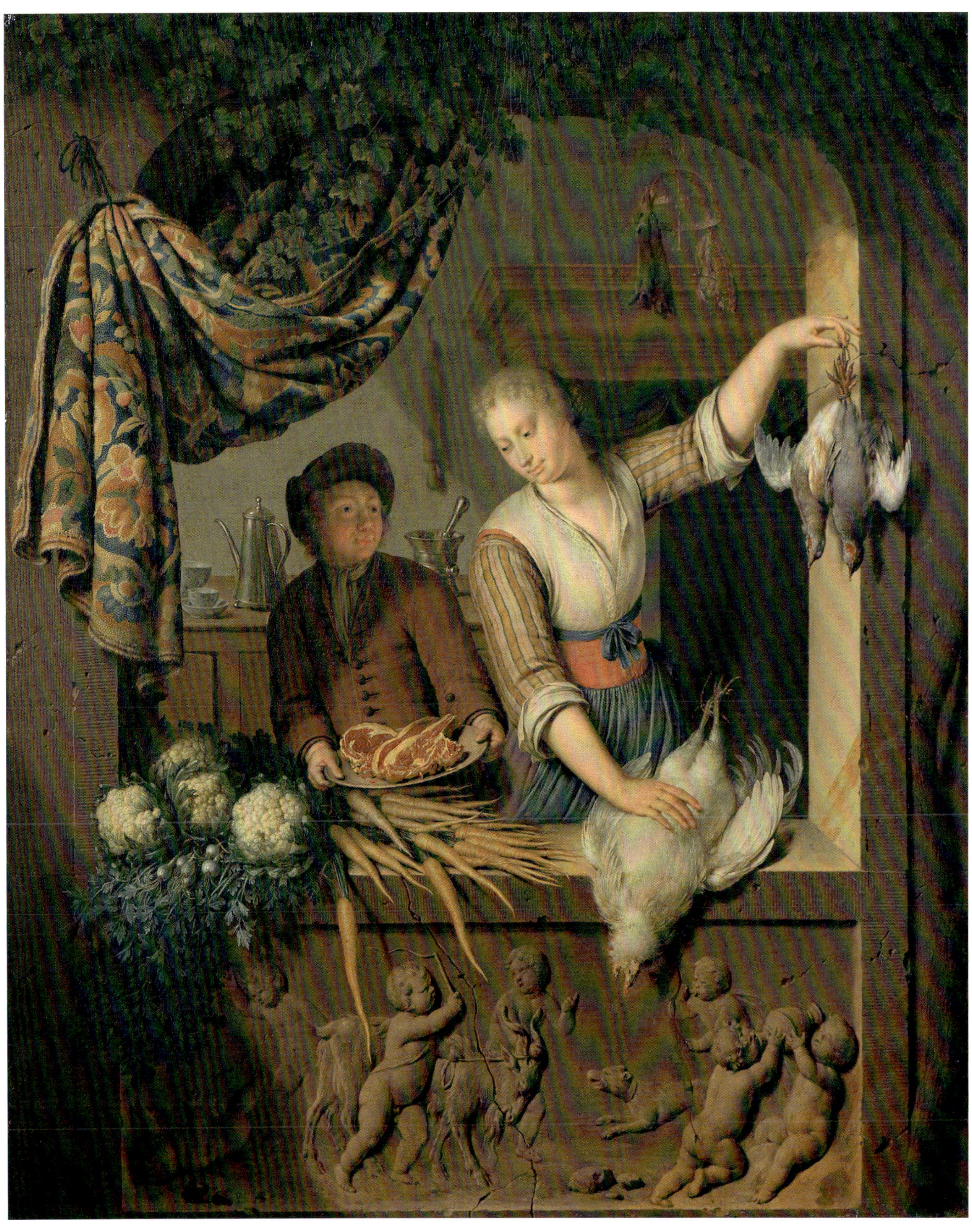

18 ABRAHAM MIGNON
(Frankfurt am Main 1640–1679 Utrecht)
FESTOON OF FLOWERS

date unknown
oil on canvas
31.5 × 43.0 cm
signed bottom left, "A. Mignon fec"
inventory no. B00242
lit: Luton, 1799, South Green Dressing Room, no. 5
exhib: London, 1883, cat. 138
(displayed at the Hunterian)

Flower painting became popular in the Low Countries in the early seventeenth century, mirroring the rising importance of horticulture and botany. Bute's collection of drawings was rich in works by celebrated flower painters such as Van Huysum and Maria Sibylla Merian, but such works were rare among the paintings displayed at Luton. Mignon was a highly accomplished flower painter, adapting a similar style to Jan Davidsz. de Heem (1606–1684), with whom he shared a studio in Utrecht from 1664. Both excelled at the representation of luminous and transparent, life-like flowers and insects against a very dark background.

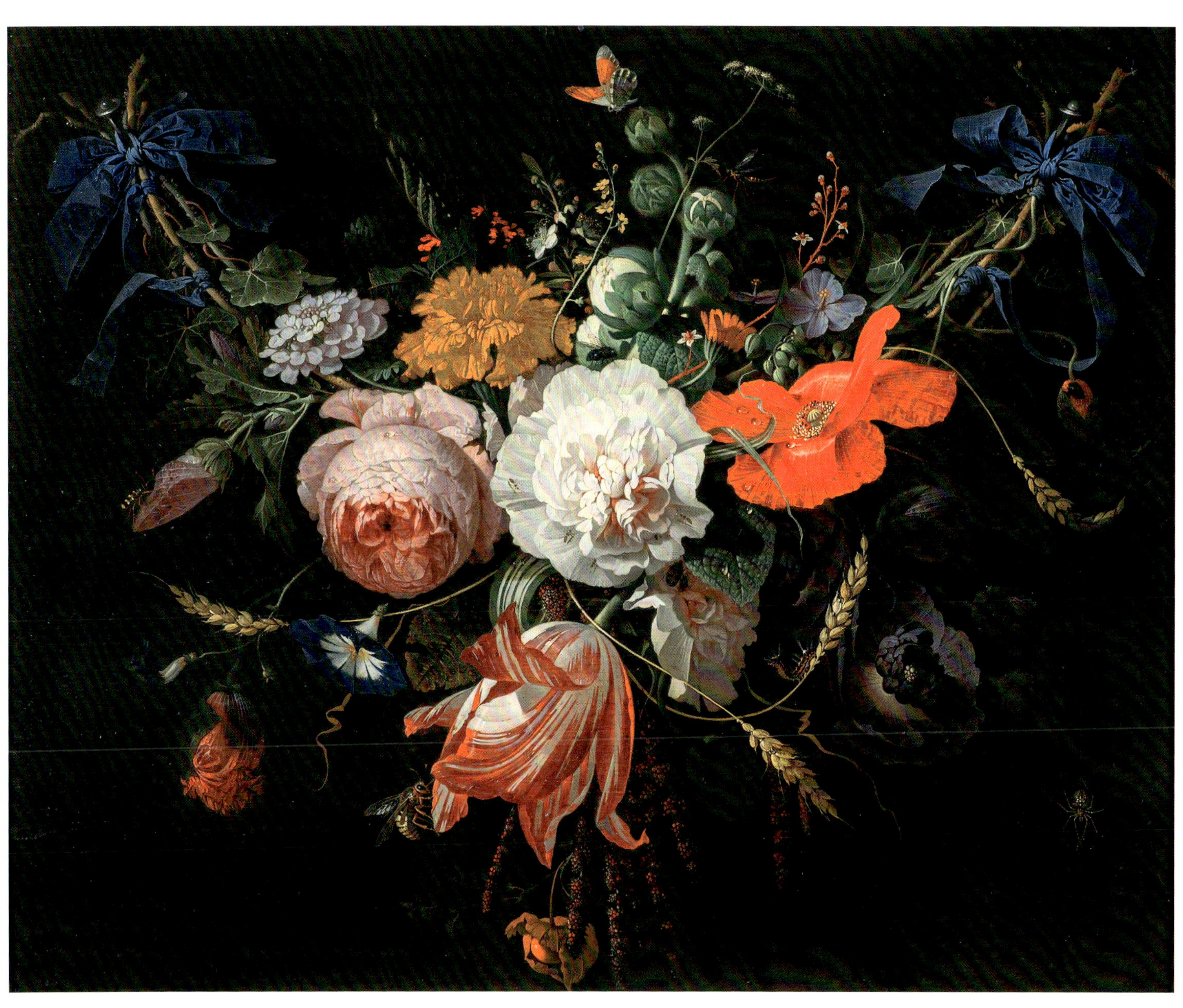

19 JOOS DE MOMPER II (Antwerp 1564–Paris 1635) and JAN BRUEGHEL I (Antwerp 1568–1625) VILLAGE WITH A BLEACHING FIELD (SPRING)

ca. 1620–1623
oil on canvas
82.5 × 147.4 cm
inventory no. B00017
provenance: bought for Bute by Fouquet at the Braamcamp sale, Amsterdam 31 July 1771 (Lugt, 1938–1987, 1950)
lit: Luton, 1799, North Green Dressing Room, no. 7
exhib: London, 1883, cat. 238; Glasgow, 1884, cat. 113 (displayed at the Hunterian)

De Momper created landscapes together with his contemporary Jan Brueghel the Elder, who painted the small, colourful figures. Theirs was one of several partnerships in Antwerp, where there was a strong demand for special paintings by more than one master. This is an autograph version of a larger work with different proportions, the *Market and Bleaching Ground*, ca. 1620–1623 (Madrid Prado, lit: Ertz 1986, 375). In Flemish landscape painting, taking linen out to bleach it in the sun was an annual ritual and it implies that this landscape was once part of a set of *Four Seasons*.

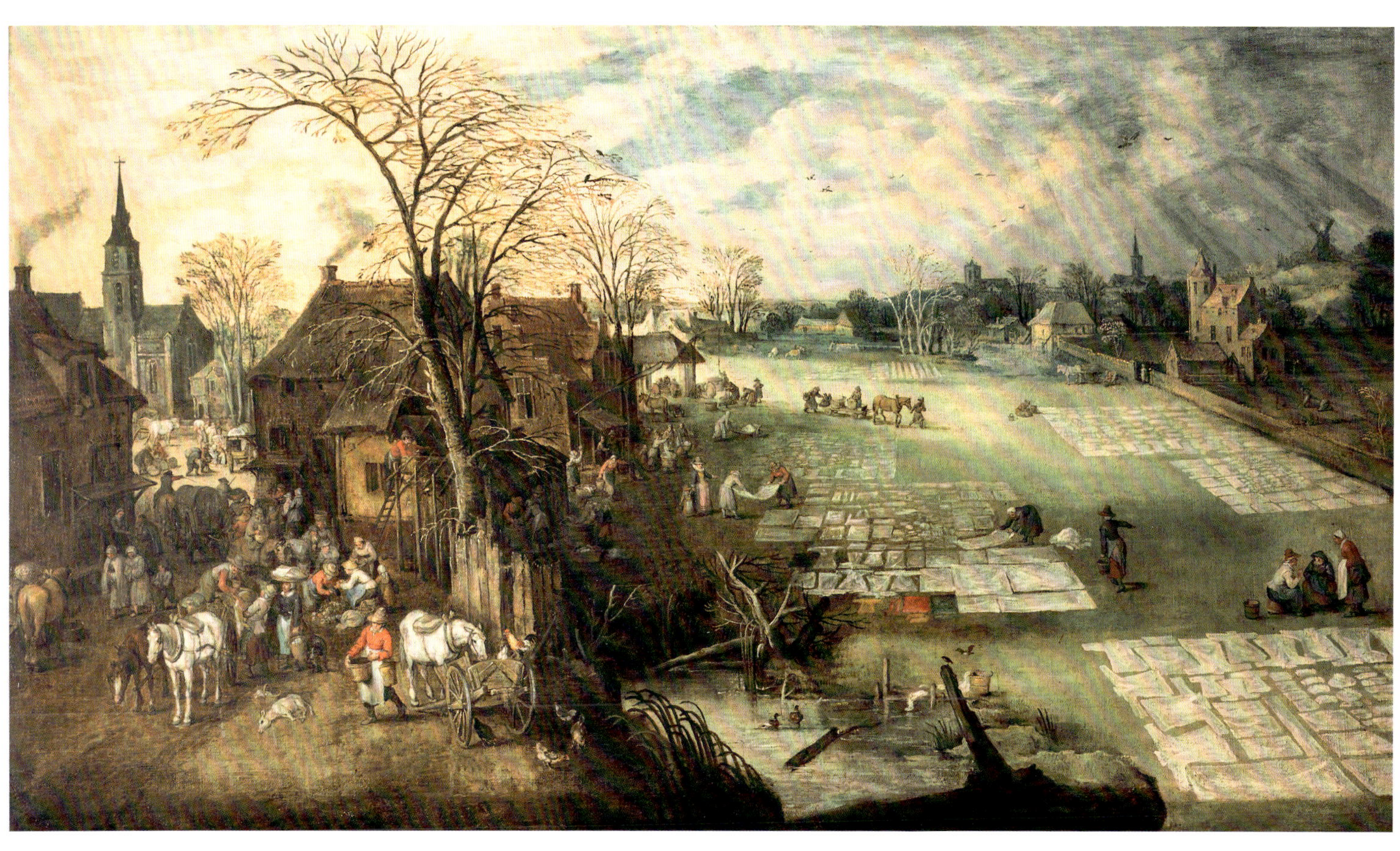

20 JOOS DE MOMPER II
(Antwerp 1564–Paris 1635)
and JAN BRUEGHEL I (Antwerp 1568–1625)
SUMMER

ca. 1620
oil on panel
54.6 × 81.3 cm
inventory no. B00014
lit: Luton, 1799, North Green Dressing Room, no. 24
(as Kierings and Brueghel)
(displayed at the Hunterian)

Jan Brueghel the Elder seems to have been one of Bute's favourite painters. This painting is one of thirteen works by Brueghel recorded in the Third Earl's collection, several of them painted in partnership with other Antwerp painters, a category aimed specially at more refined collectors. The landscape was painted by De Momper and the brightly coloured figures were added by Brueghel. They are city dwellers from Brussels enjoying a coach trip to the country-side in order to see the beautiful view of the lake and castle. A similar composition appears in a set of *Four Seasons* in Braunschweig, Herzog Anton Ulrich Museum (inv. 65).

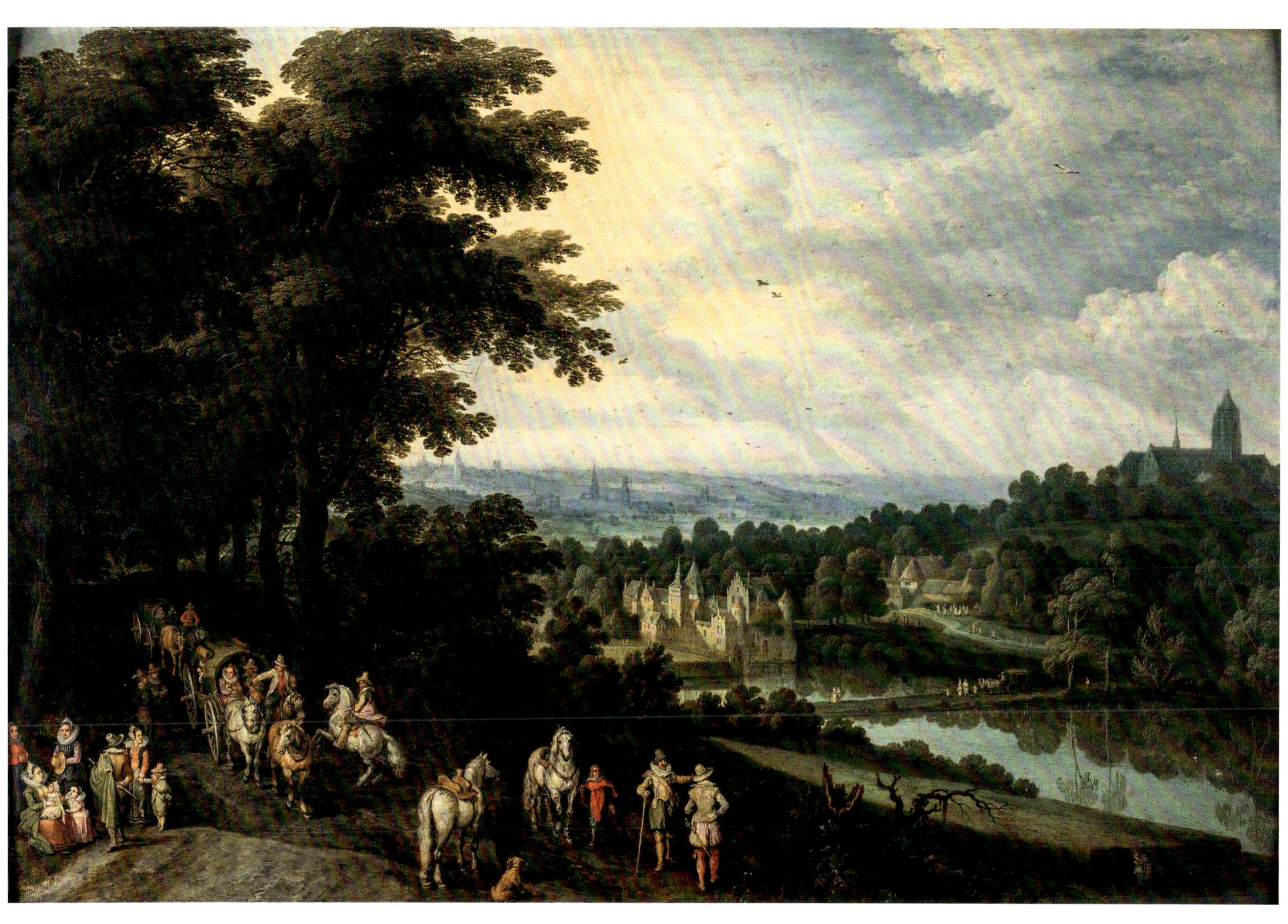

21 EGLON HENDRIK VAN DER NEER
(Amsterdam ca. 1635/6–1703 Düsseldorf)
LADY FEEDING PARROT

date unknown
oil on canvas
31.8 × 28.0 cm
signed "E. van der Neer"
inventory no. B00325
lit: Luton, 1799, Cabinet, no. 18
exhib: Glasgow, 1884, cat. 121.
(displayed at the Hunterian)

Judging from the paintings he bought, sometimes for large sums, Bute clearly appreciated the Leiden *fijnschilders* – artists such as Gerard Dou (1613–1675) and his followers, who achieved commercial success with a perfectionist painting technique, representing materials and surfaces with astonishing accuracy. Van der Neer was the son of the landscape painter, Aert van der Neer. Eglon took a different path, attracted perhaps by the success of the *fijnschilders*. Here he appropriated the figure of a prosperous woman feeding her parrot, her hair decorated with bundles of tiny silk ribbons, from Gabriël Metsu, a celebrated painter also represented in the Bute collection.

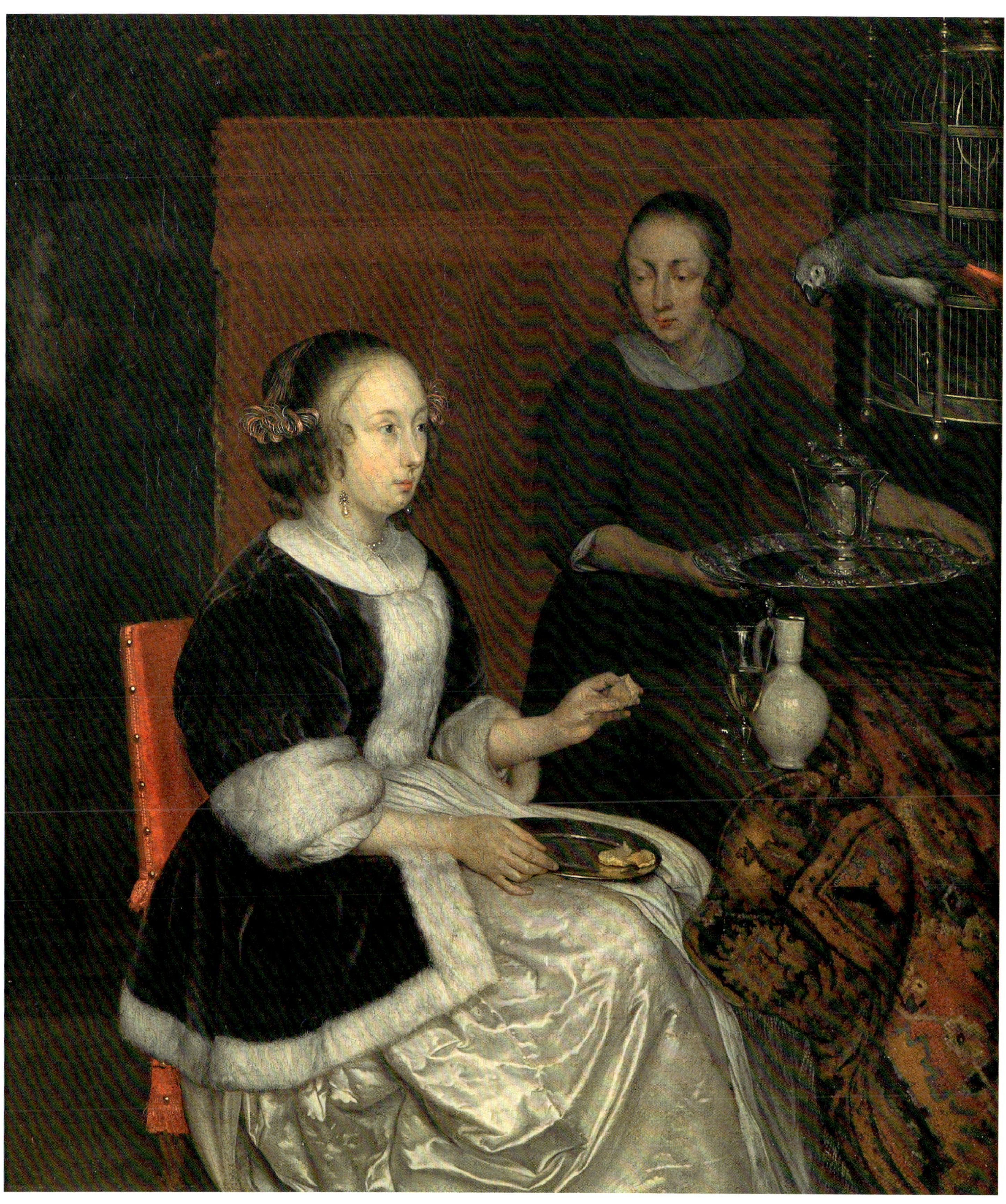

22 ALLAN RAMSAY
(Edinburgh 1713–1784 Dover)
PORTRAIT OF GEORGE III

ca. 1760
oil on canvas
74.9 × 61.0 cm
inventory no. B00172
lit: Luton, 1799, East Library, no. 20; Russell, 2004, p. 196;
Smart and Ingamells, 1999, cat. 193
(displayed, in a temporary frame, at the Hunterian)

In 1761, the Scottish portraitist Allan Ramsay (1713–1784) was appointed Painter in Ordinary to the new king, George III. That same year, in addition to the full-length portrait of the King in his coronation robes, Ramsay painted this half-length likeness, in profile, dressed in a red silk coat and adorned with the sash and star of the Order of the Garter. According to the artist, this profile portrait was intended as the model "for coinage." The work was probably commissioned by Bute, soon after the coronation in 1760.

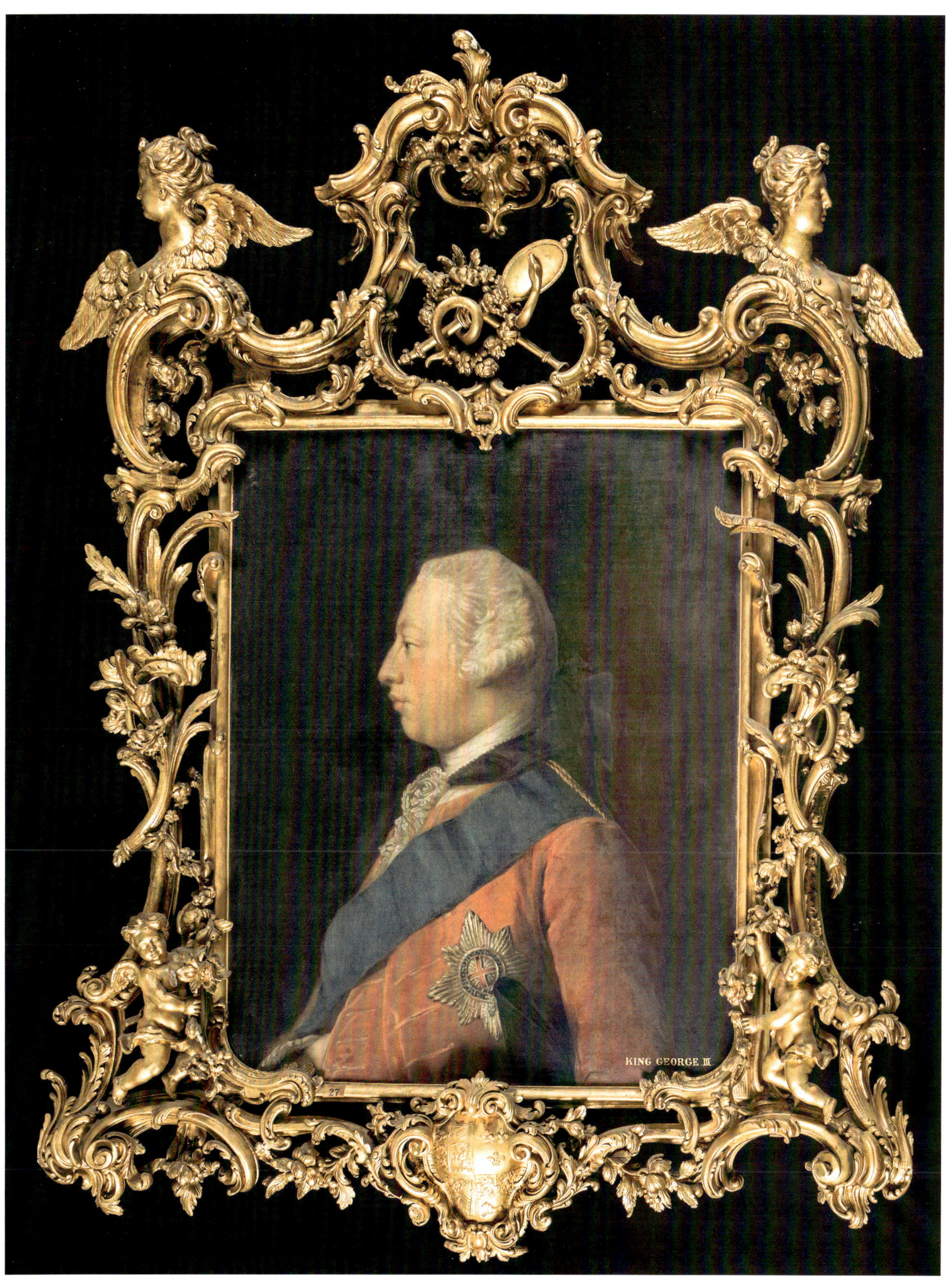
KING GEORGE III

23 SIR JOSHUA REYNOLDS
(Plympton 1723–1792 Richmond)
JOHN STUART, THIRD EARL OF BUTE

1773
oil on canvas
233.7 × 144.8 cm
inventory no. B00213
lit: Luton, 1799, Saloon, no. 2; Waagen, 1838, p. 485; Mannings, 2000, cat. 1719; Russell, 2004, pp. 103–104, 195, plate 10
exhib: BI 1823, cat. 51 (probably); London 1883, cat. 191
(displayed at Mount Stuart)

Though commissioned in 1773, ten years after Bute's retirement from office, this portrait presents the earl in his public capacity, dressed in the robes of the Order of the Garter. This stately work was one of two autograph versions, this one presumably designed to hang at Luton Hoo, the earl's country seat in Bedfordshire. The other (National Portrait Gallery, London, NPG 3938) was probably for his London townhouse on South Audley Street. At the advanced age of sixty, in spite of ill health, the Earl appears virile, graceful and confident, perhaps even haughty. He would seem to be a man very much at the height of his powers.

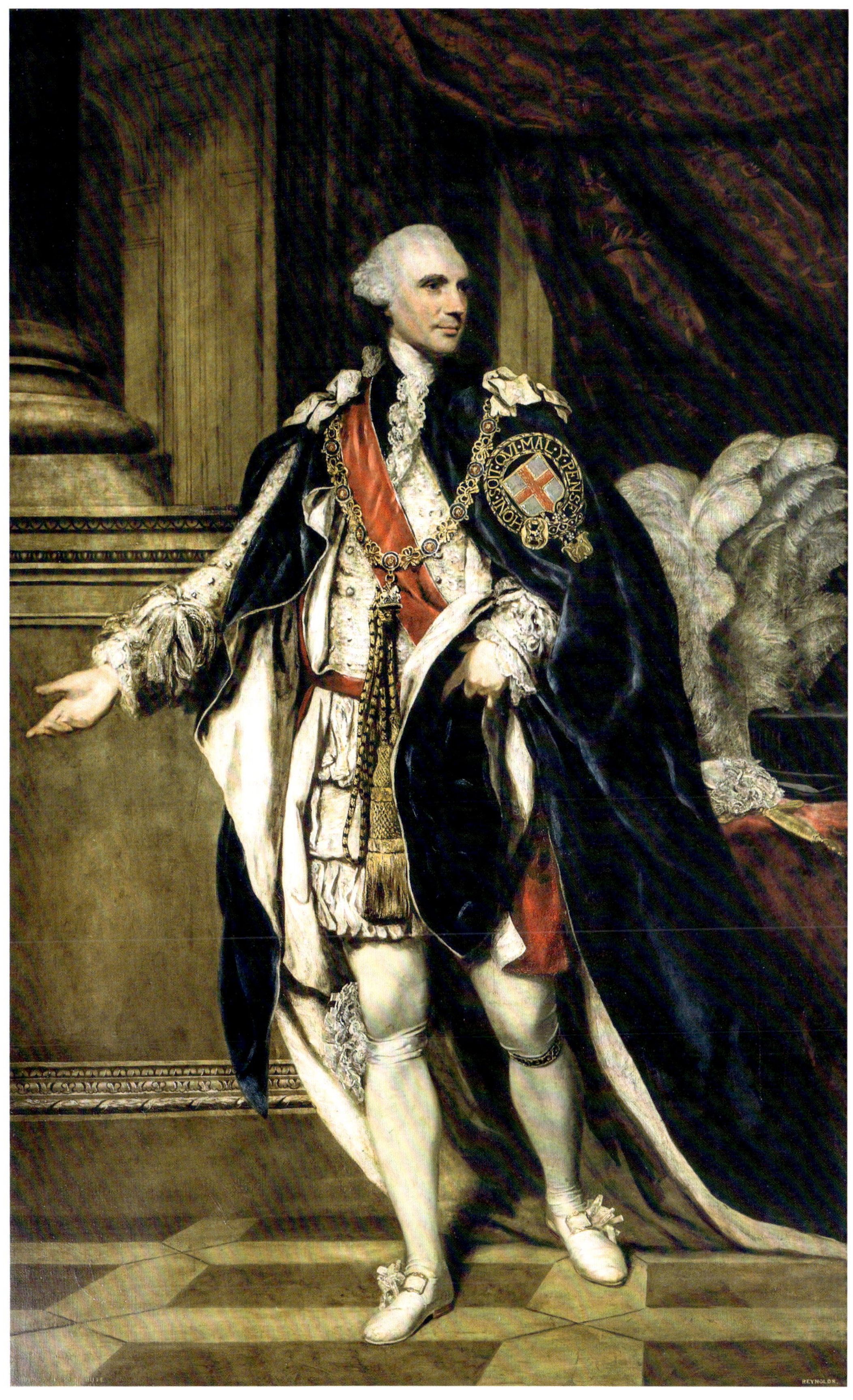
HONI SOIT QUI MAL Y PENSE
REYNOLDS.

24 PETER PAUL RUBENS (Siegen 1577–1640 Antwerp)
(and workshop)
and FRANS SNYDERS (Antwerp 1579–1657)
KITCHEN STILL LIFE WITH MAID AND CHILD

ca. 1630–1635
oil on canvas
167.7 × 170.2 cm
inventory no. B00339
lit: Luton, 1799, East Library, no. 13;
Sutton and Wieseman 2004, pp. 202–203
exhib: London, 1883, cat. 217
(displayed at Mount Stuart)

The monumental *Kitchen Still Life* painting, which Bute acquired as by Rubens, has a pendant in another large work in the Hermitage Museum, St Petersburg, in which the still life is again by Snyders, and the figure has been attributed to Boeckhorst (inv. GE 608). The starting point for both was an oil sketch by Rubens (Antwerp, Koninklijk Museum voor Schone Kunsten, inv. 5146), outlining the figures and leaving the table blank for Snyders to execute what he did best: fruit, vegetables and game. A head study for the woman (Birmingham, Barber Institute, no. 50.1) reveals how Rubens's design was taken a stage further by an assistant, probably Jan Boeckhorst (1604-1668), as he worked in collaboration with the great still-life painter Snyders.

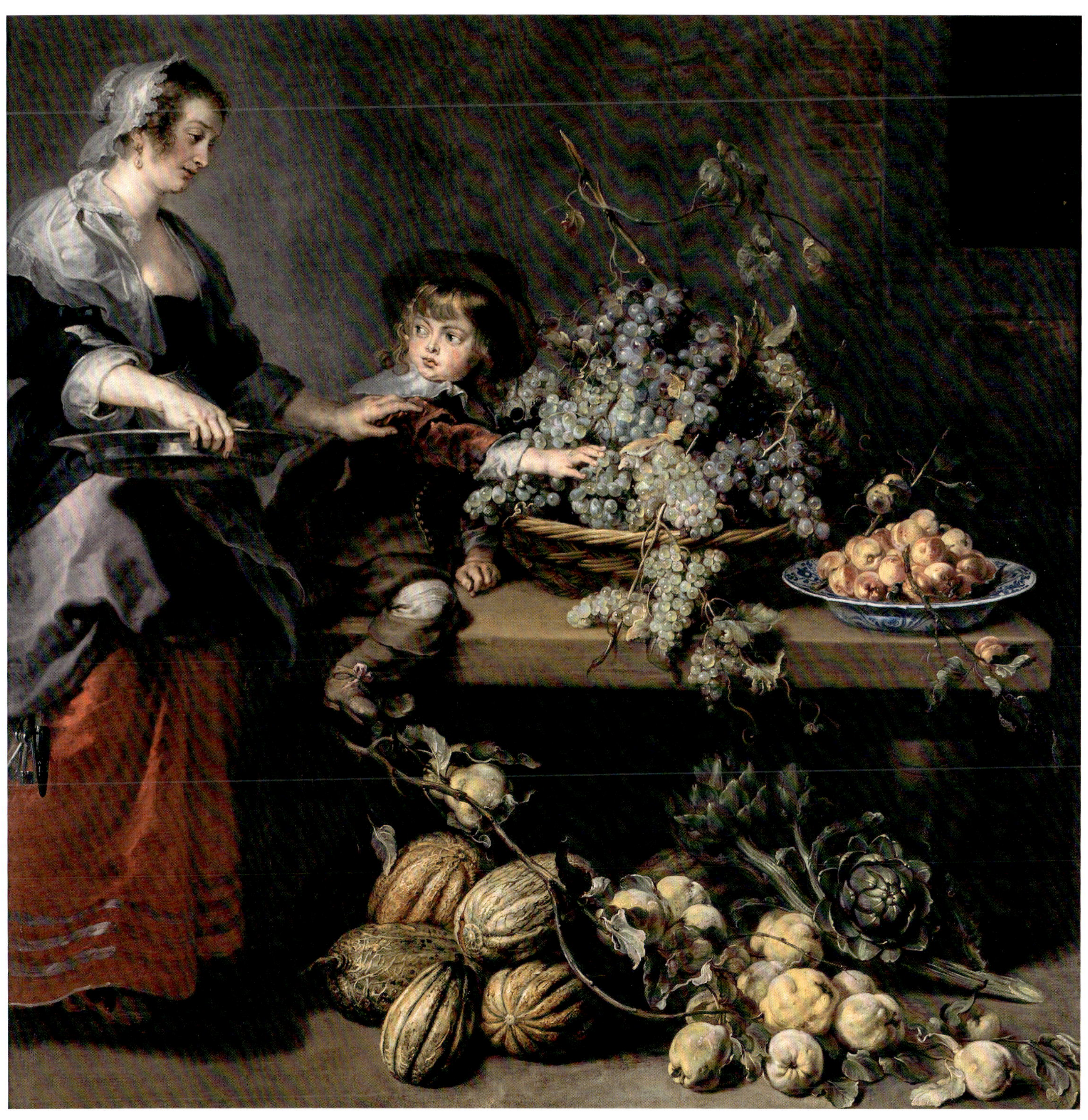

25 JACOB VAN RUISDAEL
(Haarlem ca. 1628/9–1682 Amsterdam)
DISTANT VIEW OF HAARLEM

ca. 1670
oil on canvas
50.8 × 66.0 cm
signed right, "I. van Ruisdael"
inventory no. B00257
lit: Luton, 1799, North Blue Dressing Room, no. 29 or 30
exhib: London, 1883, cat. 136; Glasgow, 1884, cat. 146
(displayed at the Hunterian)

Haarlem was a major trading city but also an important centre for artists. Ruisdael was one of the most original Dutch landscape painters, and this is an example of one of his trademark subjects. It is a *Haarlempje*, or "little Haarlem," in which the flat dune and farm landscape is transformed into an upright study of a cloudy sky, against which the tall nave of St Bavo's Cathedral forms a familiar landmark.

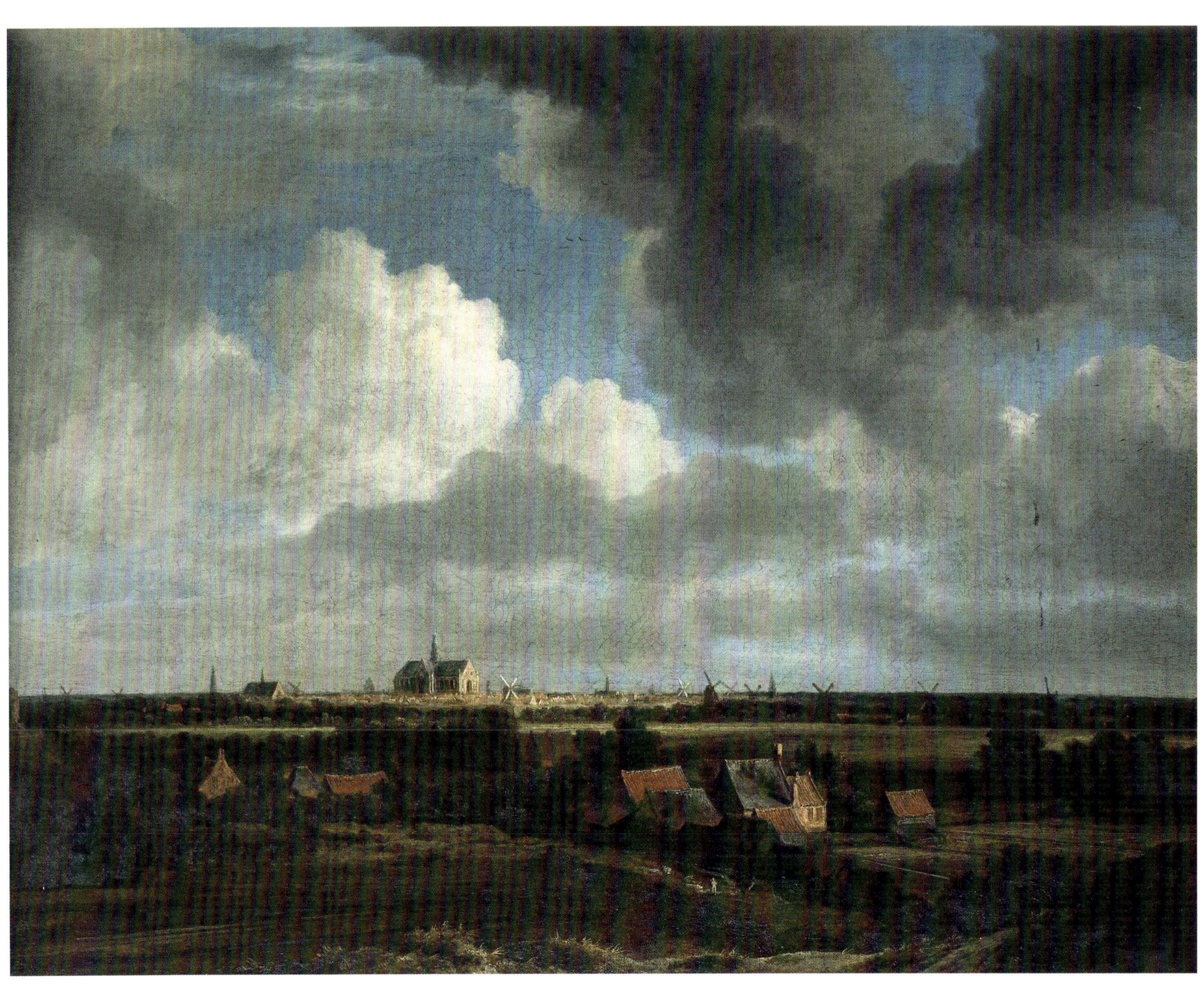

26 ROELANDT SAVERY
(Courtrai 1576–1639 Utrecht)
WOODED LANDSCAPE WITH NATURAL ARCH

ca. 1616–1620
oil on panel
25.9 × 33.8 cm
inventory no. B00285
(displayed at the Hunterian)

27 WOODED LANDSCAPE WITH RUINS AND FIGURES

ca. 1616–1620
oil on panel
25.9 × 33.8 cm
signed in centre on stone, "R.SAVERY"
inventory no. B00291
(displayed at the Hunterian)

lit: Luton, 1799, Cabinet, no. 27, 28; Russell, 2004, p. 197
exhib: London, 1883, cat. 75, 87; Glasgow, 1884, cat. 152, 153

The Flemish-born Savery was an influential landscape painter in the first decades of the seventeenth century. These are fine examples of his mountain landscapes, inspired by travel in Bohemia and the Tyrol (1606–1608), and incorporating such motifs as ruins and the rock arch, which he studied in drawings made on the spot. Both are based on signed drawings in the Staatliche Kunstsammlungen Dresden, of the rock arch (C 1945-17) and the ruins (C 930). They were probably painted on the artist's return to Holland 1614–1616.

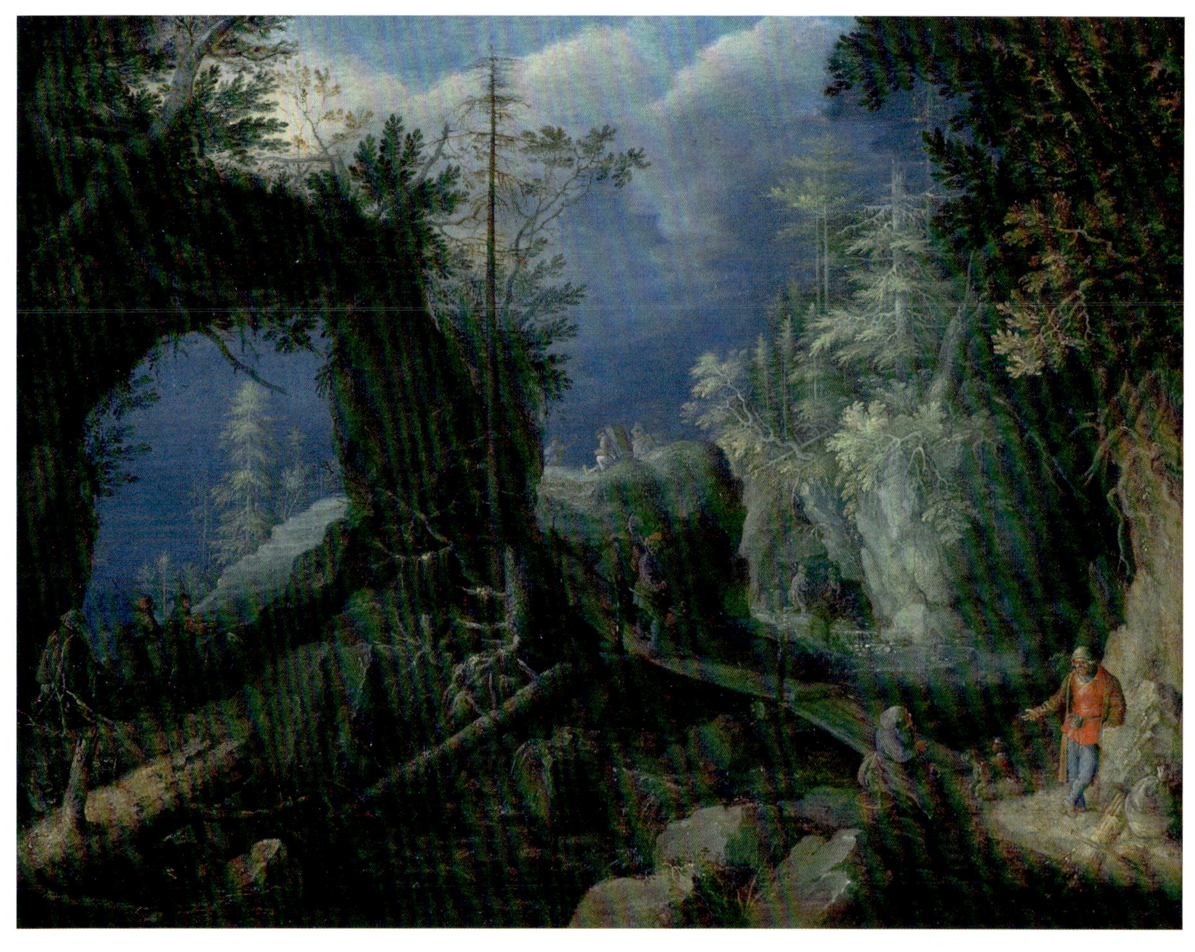

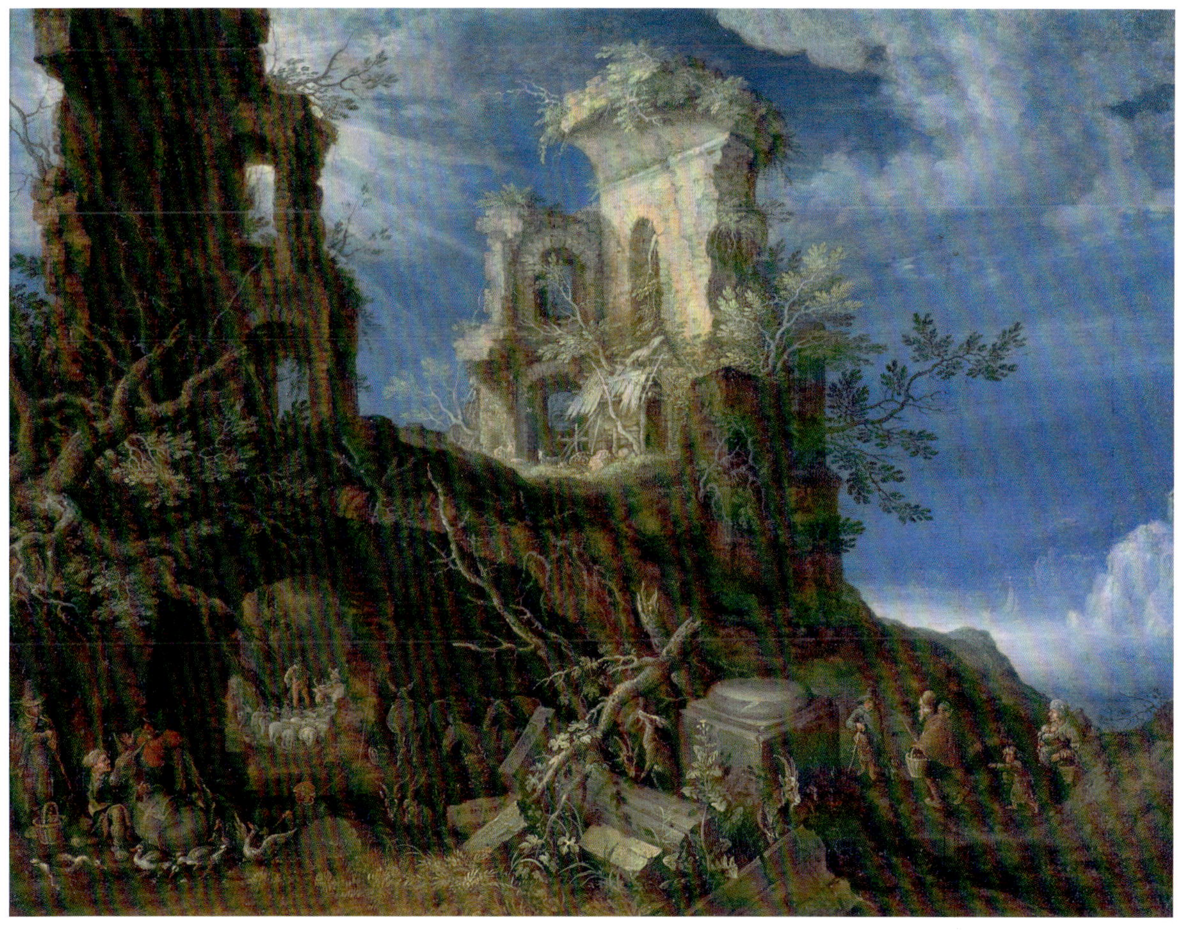

28 PIETER CORNELISZ. VAN SLINGELANDT
(Leiden 1640–1691)
A KITCHEN MAID

date unknown
oil on canvas
20.3 × 17.8 cm
inventory no. B00318
lit: Luton 1799, South Blue Dressing Room, no. 20
(displayed at Mount Stuart)

Van Slingelandt was one of the many pupils of Gerard Dou, founder of the school of Leiden *fijnschilders*. In this sunlit interior, in which a maid pauses for thought mid-task, the artist has created a still life in the manner of his master, with a lamp and basket placed bottom right to provide a demonstration of his skills in meticulously representing different materials. Dou, Frans van Mieris and Metsu especially were the artists who commanded collectors' attention, but Bute seems also to have collected works by less well-known Dou pupils, including Van Slingelandt, Domenicus van Tol, Pieter Verelst (cat. 32) and Abraham de Pape.

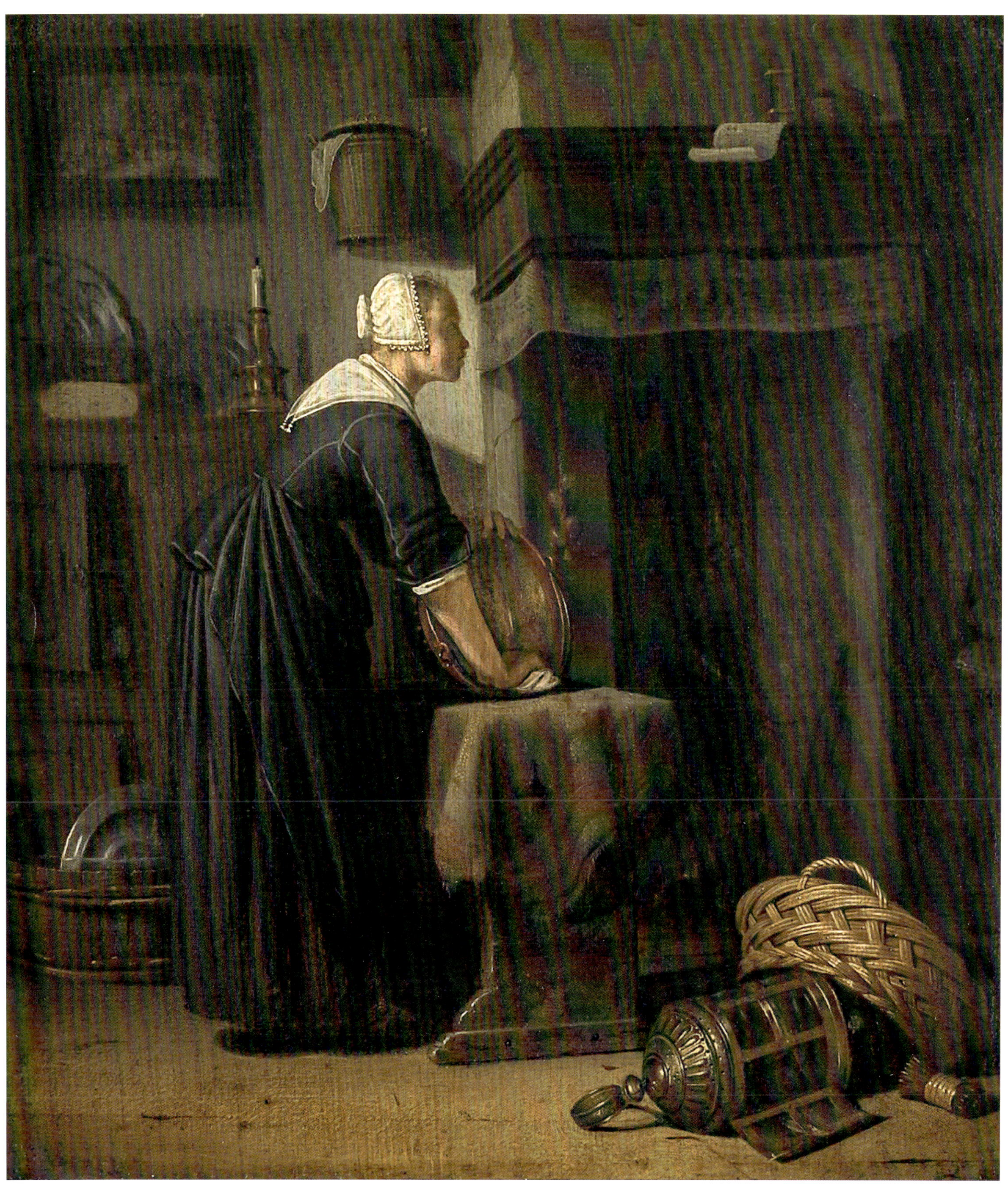

29 JAN STEEN
(Leiden 1626–1679)
A COCK FIGHT

date unknown
oil on canvas
91.4 × 110.7 cm
signed "JSteen"
inventory no. B00312
lit: Luton, 1799, East Bow Window Dressing Room, no. 6;
Korthals Altes, 2015, p. 276
exhib: London, 1883, cat. 121; Glasgow, 1884, cat. 160;
Edinburgh, 1949, cat. 30
(displayed at the Hunterian)

At Luton, Steen's *Cock Fight* was hung between the two Claude landscapes. It was acquired from the Lormier collection, which was sold in Amsterdam in 1763. This menacing scene, as often in Steen's work, involves careful observation of human behaviour. The cocks are present to provide an image from the animal kingdom which symbolises the intense, soon to be violent, struggle between two men. The older man in the hat and cloak, next to whom the victorious cock stands, is demanding the attention of the woman to the right who is flirting with another man.

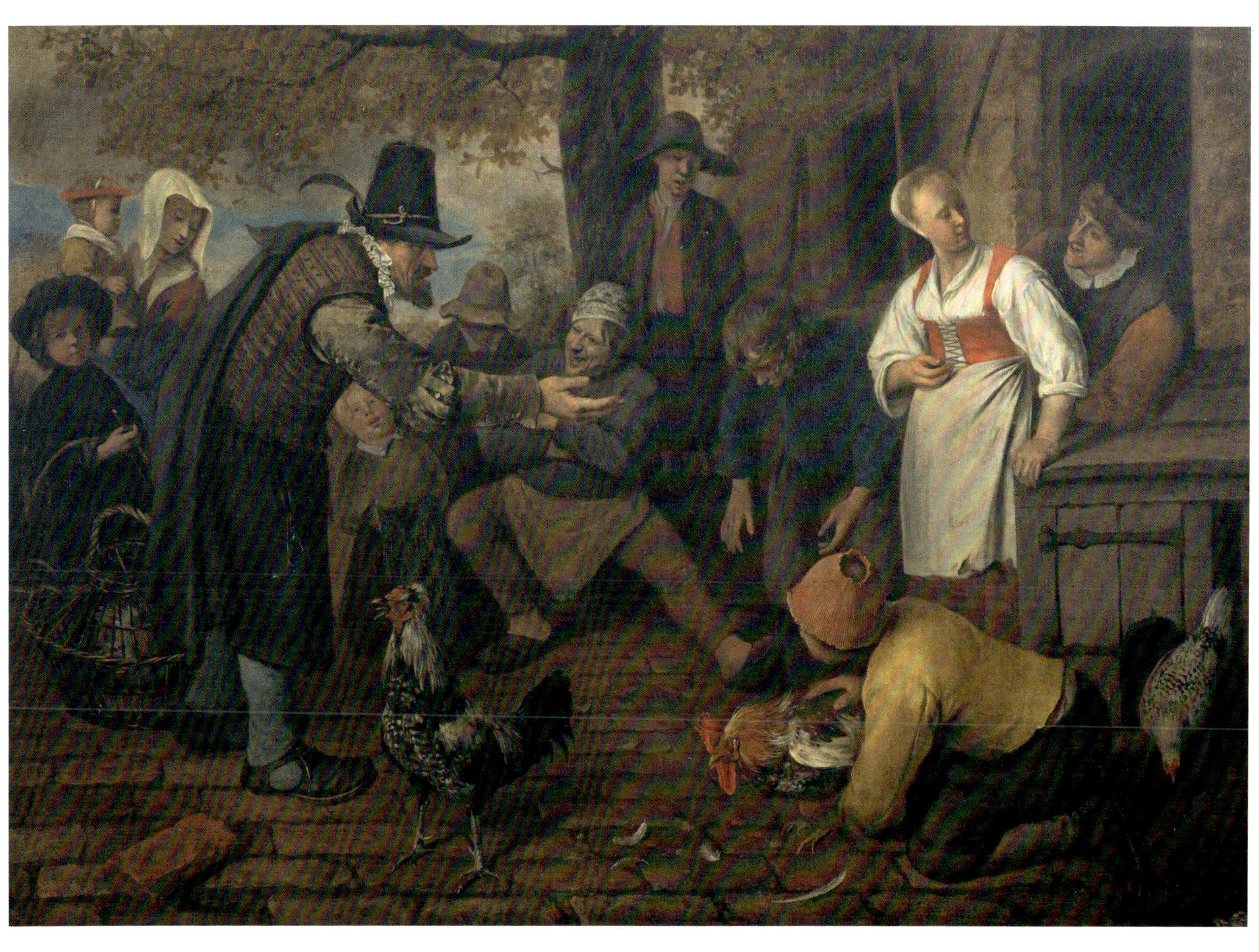

30 JAN STEEN
(Leiden 1626–1679)
ROBBERS PLUNDERING A FARMHOUSE

date unknown
oil on canvas
44.0 × 52.1 cm
signed "JSteen"
inventory no. B00283
lit: Luton, 1799, South Blue Dressing Room, no. 30
(displayed at Mount Stuart)

Brawls in country inns were one of Steen's stock subjects. In times of war, the peasants often suffered violent treatment from the many mercenary soldiers who lived among them. The Third Earl's collection contained several works which reflected the unpleasant realities of war in the Low Countries, including land and sea battle scenes, and a *Guardroom Interior* by Eeckhout (Edinburgh, 2012, 8).

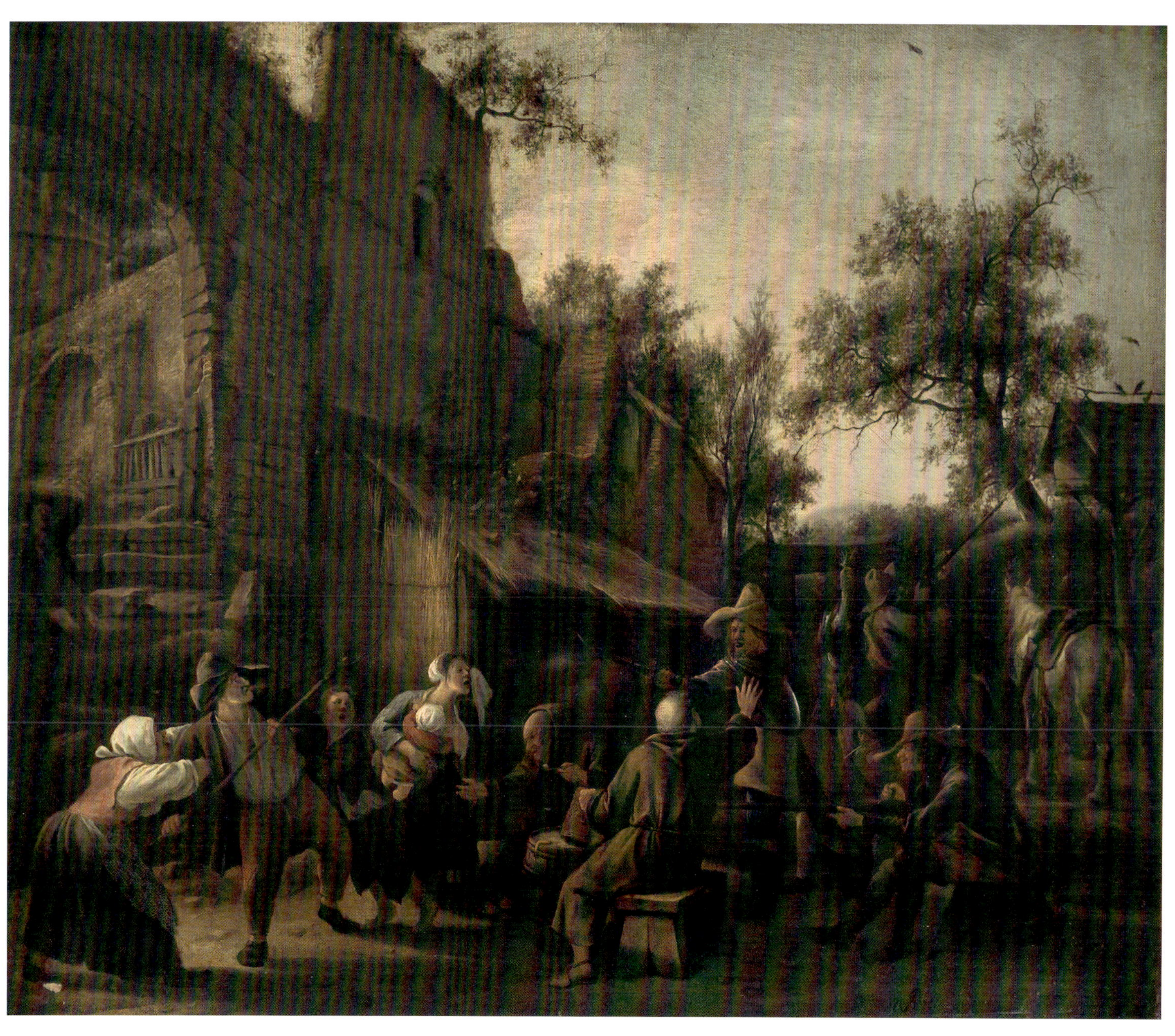

31 DAVID TENIERS II
(Antwerp 1610–1690 Brussels)
THE CARD PLAYERS

ca. 1640–1650
oil on panel
55.3 × 68.8 cm
signed bottom right, "D.TENIERS.Fec."
inventory no. B00018
lit: Luton, 1799, West Bow Window Dressing Room, no. 4
exhib: London, 1883, cat. 82; Glasgow, 1884, cat. 168;
Edinburgh, 2012, cat. 19
(displayed at the Hunterian)

Teniers was born in Antwerp, but he moved to Brussels in 1651 when he was appointed court painter. He was a prolific painter, and in the eighteenth century, his small-scale genre scenes became very popular and commanded high prices. There were seven paintings by him on display at Luton. The taste for his sometimes dramatic and always beautifully painted works was controversial. Collectors happily paid high prices, but critics, unaware of the cultural context for which they were created, were universally hostile to the representation of "low" company.

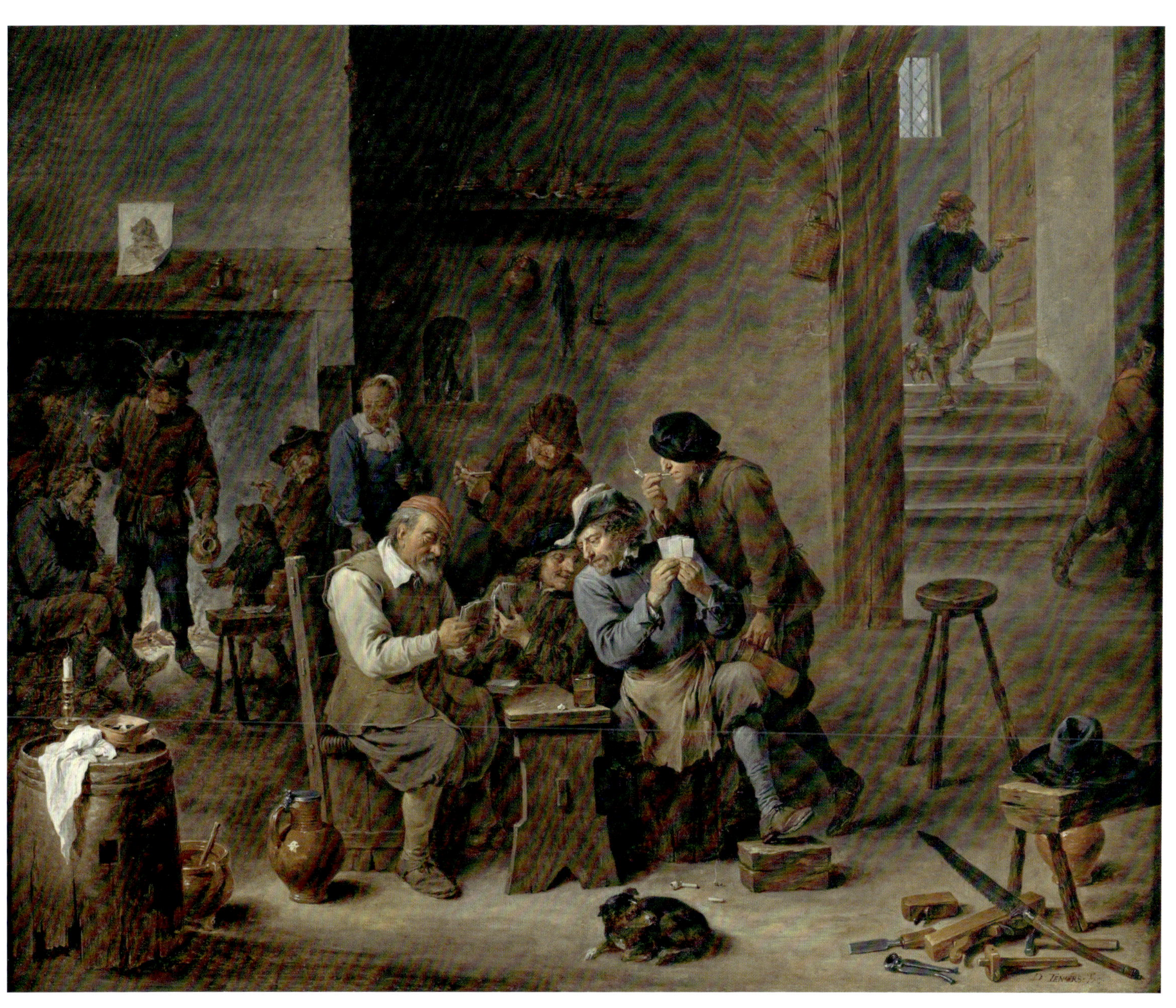

32 PIETER HERMANSZ. VERELST
(Dordrecht ca. 1618–1678)
AN INTERIOR WITH A LADY AND GENTLEMAN

ca. 1655
oil on canvas
35.2 × 43.4 cm
signed top right, "P.Verelst 165[...]"
inventory no. B00297
lit: Luton, 1799, Dining Room, no. 33; Russell, 2004, plate 164
(displayed at the Hunterian)

It was perhaps characteristic of Bute that he chose to acquire this signed and dated work by a less well-known genre painter. Working in The Hague, Verelst followed the manner of his master, Gerard Dou, who was founder of the tradition of *fijnschilders*, and was among the artists most highly prized by eighteenth-century collectors. Like Dou, Verelst delighted in the meticulous rendition of materials and surfaces. Here, Verelst focuses on a fleeting moment as a man and a woman, under the influence of music and wine, exchange a glance as they prepare to sing together.

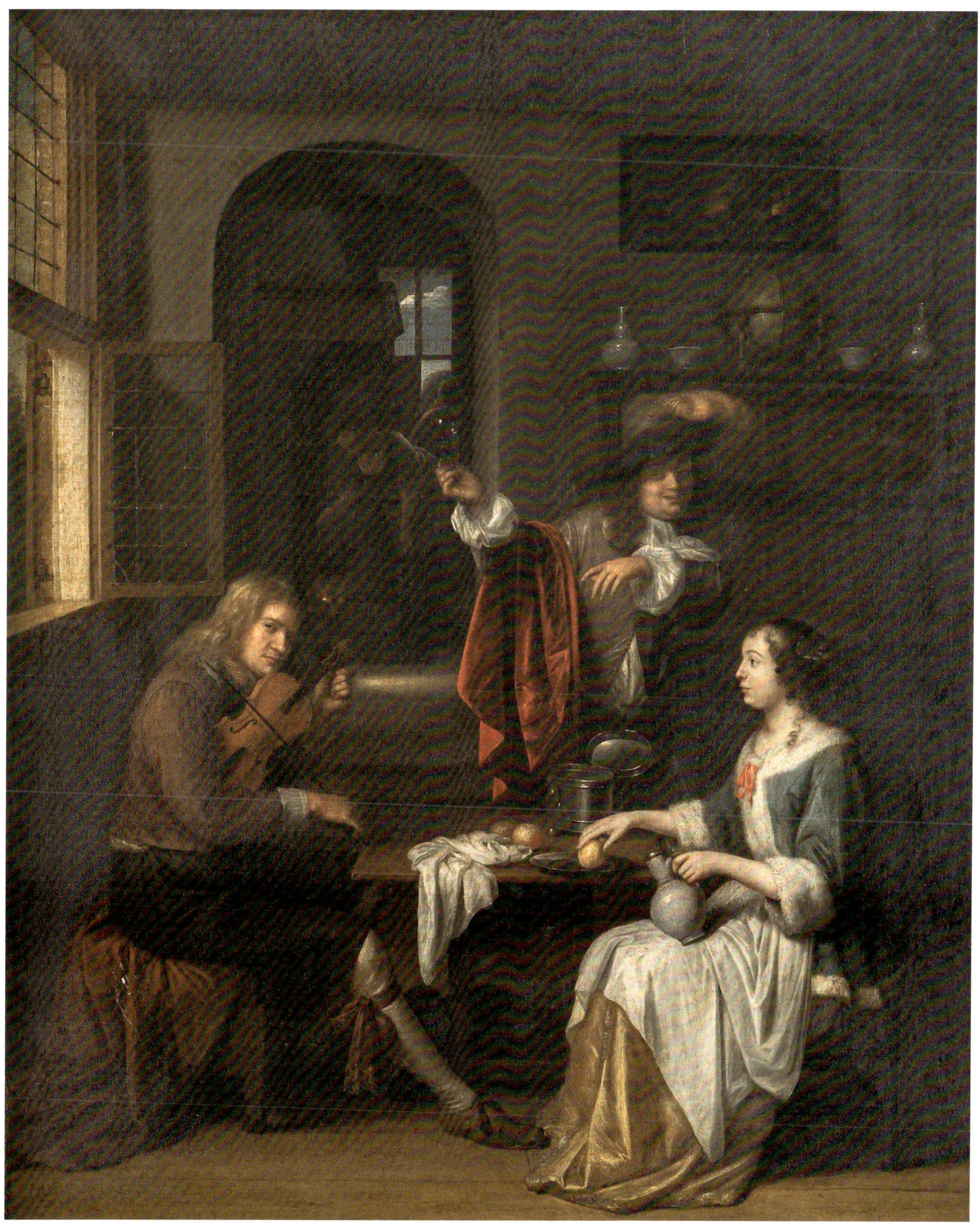

33 PAOLO VERONESE
(Verona 1528–1588 Venice)
THE MYSTIC MARRIAGE OF ST CATHERINE

ca. 1555
oil on canvas
97.7 × 161.2 cm
inventory no. B00107
lit: Luton, 1799, With-Drawing Room, no. 3
exhib: London, 1883, cat. 14; Glasgow, 1884, cat. 190; Edinburgh, 2004, cat. 57
(displayed at Mount Stuart)

Images of the legendary Saint Catherine of Alexandria provided a model of Christian faith and chastity. She was a popular saint, not least in Venice where Bute purchased several important paintings in 1770–1771, including several works by Tintoretto and Veronese. In her legend, Catherine's mystical marriage took place in the dream that she recounted to the Emperor Maxentius before she was put to death. Veronese presents a colourful and opulent vision of the saint, richly clad in coloured silks, as she is honoured by Christ and the Holy Family.

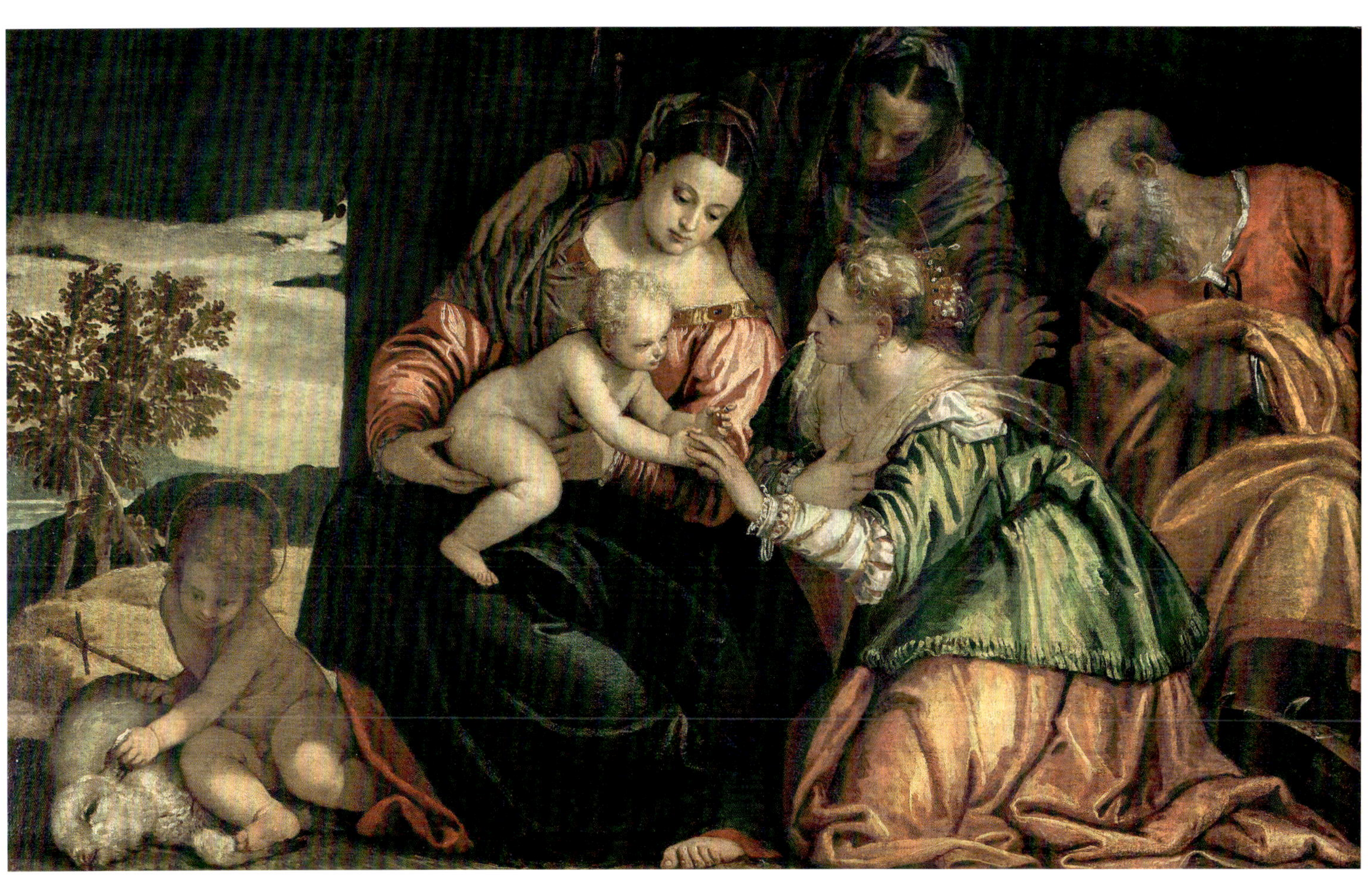

34 JOHAN ZOFFANY
(Frankfurt am Main 1733–1810 Strand-on-the-Green)
THE LADIES ANNE, CAROLINE AND LOUISA STUART

ca. 1763
oil on canvas
101.2 × 126.5 cm
Tate Collection, T07864. Accepted by HM Government in lieu of tax and acquired by Tate Britain in 2002.
lit: Manners and Williams 1920, p. 186; Russell, 2004, pp. 63, 175, plate 7
exhib: London, 1977, cat. 21
(displayed at the Hunterian)

Johan Zoffany arrived in Britain in 1761. Bute was among his earliest patrons, also commissioning a pendant of his three sons (Tate T07863) and a full-length portrait of his heir, Lord Mountstuart (Private Collection). Bute's patronage helped Zoffany to establish an impressive roster of elite clients in his adopted country. It was likely through Bute that Zoffany gained royal attention and patronage, inspiring portraits of *Queen Charlotte with her Two Eldest Sons*, and *The Prince of Wales and Prince Frederick* (Royal Collection). Bute's daughters are shown in the grounds of Luton Hoo, the Bedfordshire estate that was purchased in 1763.

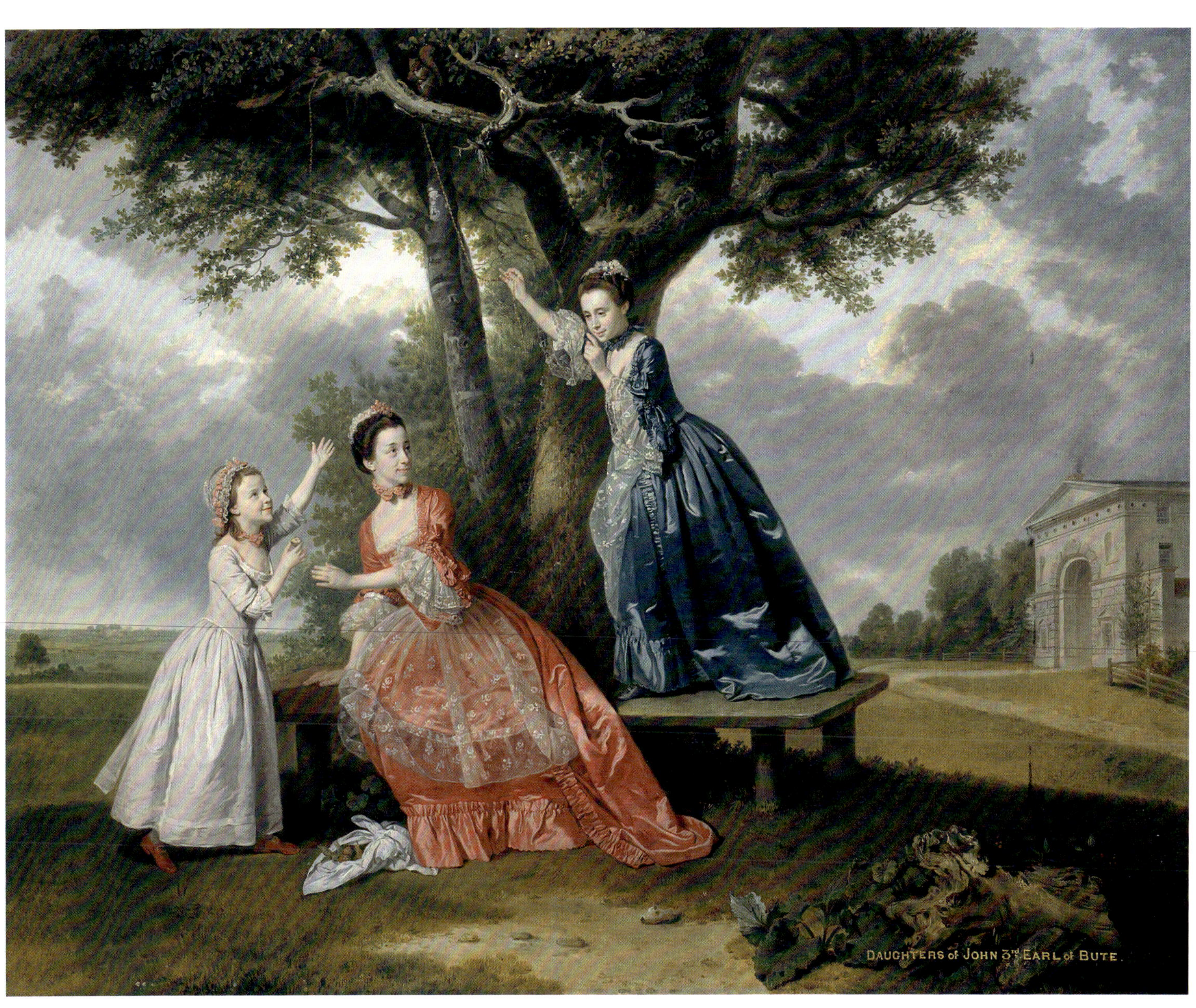
DAUGHTERS of JOHN 3rd EARL of BUTE.

BIBLIOGRAPHY

Adam 1773–1778
Robert Adam and James Adam, *The Works in Architecture of Robert and James Adam*, 2 vols., London 1773–1778.

Alpers 1983
Svetlana Alpers, *The Art of Describing: Dutch Art in the Seventeenth Century*, Chicago (University of Chicago Press) 1983.

Anon 1783
"Luton Hoo, The Seat of the Earl of Bute," *General Evening Post* (18 November 1783).

Atherton 1974
Herbert M. Atherton, *Political Prints in the Age of Hogarth: A Study of the Ideographic Representation of Politics*, Oxford (Oxford University Press) 1974.

Barnes 2004
Susan J. Barnes et al., *Van Dyck: A Complete Catalogue of the Paintings*, London and New Haven (Yale University Press) 2004.

Bedford 1846
Correspondence of John, Fourth Duke of Bedford, selected by Lord John Russell, 3 vols., London (Longman, Brown, Green and Longman) 1846.

Berridge 2015
Vanessa Berridge, *The Princess's Garden: Royal Intrigue and the Untold Story of Kew*, Stroud (Amberley) 2015.

Blackburne 1780
Francis Blackburne, *Memoirs of Thomas Hollis, Esq. F.R. and A.S.S*, London (J. Nichols) 1780.

Blunt 1966
Anthony Blunt, *The Paintings of Nicolas Poussin. Critical Catalogue*, London (Phaidon) 1966.

Boswell 1885
James Boswell, *The Life of Samuel Johnson, LL. D., and the Journal of his Tour to the Hebrides*, London and New York (G. Routledge and Sons) 1885.

Boswell 1985
James Boswell, *Life of Johnson*, R. W. Chapman (ed.), Pat Rogers (intr.), Oxford (Oxford University Press) 1985.

Brewer 1972
John Brewer, "The Faces of Lord Bute: A Visual Contribution to Anglo-American Political Ideology," *American History*, 6 (1972), pp. 95–116.

Brewer 1973
John Brewer. "The Misfortunes of Lord Bute: A Case-Study in Eighteenth-Century Political Argument and Public Opinion," *The Historical Journal*, 16:1 (1973), pp. 3–43.

Brewer 1981
John Brewer, *Party Ideology and Popular Politics at the Accession of George III*, 2nd edition, Cambridge (Cambridge University Press) 1981.

Brooke 1974
John Brooke, *King George III*, London (Panther) 1974.

Bullion 1989
John L. Bullion, "The Prince's Mentor: A New Perspective on the Friendship between George III and Lord Bute during the 1750s," *Albion: A Quarterly Journal Concerned with British Studies*, 21:1 (1989), pp. 34–55.

Bullion 1992
John L. Bullion, "The Origins and Significance of Gossip about Princess Augusta and Lord Bute, 1755–1756," *Studies in Eighteenth-Century Culture*, 21 (1992), pp. 245–265.

Bullion 2013
John L. Bullion, *George III, National Reform and North America: "The True Essential Business of a King,"* Lewiston, NY (Edwin Mellen Press) 2013.

Burlington Magazine 1945
Editorial, "Sir Joshua Reynolds' Collection of Pictures." *The Burlington Magazine:* Part I, 86:507 (1945), pp. 133–134. Part II, 87:510 (1945), pp. 211–217. Part III, 87:512 (1945), pp. 263–273.

Campbell-Orr 2002
Clarissa Campbell-Orr (ed.), *Queenship in Britain, 1660–1837: Royal Patronage, Court, Culture and Dynastic Politics*, Manchester (Manchester University Press) 2002.

Christie 2000
Christopher Christie, *The British Country House in the Eighteenth Century*, Manchester (Manchester University Press) 2000.

Coke 1896
Lady Mary Coke, *The Letters and Journals of Lady Mary Coke*, James Home (ed.), vol. 4, Edinburgh (David Douglas) 1896.

Connell 1957
Brian Connell, *Portrait of a Whig Peer: Compiled from the Papers of the Second Viscount Palmerston, 1739–1802*, London (André Deutsch) 1957.

Conway 2001
Stephen Conway, "War and National Identity in the Mid-Eighteenth-Century British Isles," *English Historical Review*, 116:468 (2001), pp. 863–893.

Cox 2013
Oliver J. W. Cox, "Frederick, Prince of Wales and the First Performance of 'Rule, Britannia!'," *Historical Journal*, 56:4 (2013), pp. 931–954.

De-la-Noy 1996
Michael De-la-Noy, *The King Who Never Was. The Story of Frederick, Prince of Wales*, London (Peter Owen) 1996.

Delany 1862
Mary Delany, *The Autobiography and Correspondence of Mary Granville, Mrs. Delany, with Interesting Reminiscences of King George the Third and Queen Charlotte*, 2 vols., London 1862.

Dickinson 2011
H. T. Dickinson, "George III and Parliament," *Parliamentary History*, 30:3 (2011), pp. 395–413.

Dukelskaya and Moore 2002
Larissa Dukelskaya and Andrew W. Moore, *A Capital Collection: Houghton Hall and the Hermitage: With a Modern Edition of "Aedes Walpolianae," Horace Walpole's Catalogue of Sir Robert Walpole's Collection*, New Haven and London (Yale University Press) 2002.

Dutens 1806
Louis Dutens, *Mémoires d'un voyageur qui se repose: contenant des anecdotes...*, Paris (Chez Bossange, Masson et Besson) 1806.

Eagles 2014
Robin Eagles, "Loyal Opposition? Prince Frederick and Parliament (1729–1751)," *Parliamentary History*, 33:1 (2014), pp. 223–242.

Eagles 2016
Robin Eagles, "Frederick, Prince of Wales, the 'Court' of Leicester House and the 'Patriot' Opposition to Walpole, c. 1733–1742," *The Court Historian*, 21:2 (2016), pp. 140–156.

Emerson 2002
Roger L. Emerson, "The Scientific Interests of Archibald Campbell, 1st Earl of Ilay and 3rd Duke of Argyll (1682–1761)," *Annals of Science*, 59 (2002), pp. 21–56.

Farington 1928
Joseph Farington, *The Farington Diary*, James Greig (ed.), 8 vols., London (Hutchinson and Company) 1928.

Fitzmaurice 1912
Lord Fitzmaurice, *Life of William, Earl of Shelburne, afterwards First Marquess of Lansdowne: With Extracts from his Papers and Correspondence*, 2 vols., London (Macmillan) 1912.

Fordham 2010
Douglas Fordham, *British Art and the Seven Years' War: Allegiance and Autonomy*, Philadelphia (University of Pennsylvania Press) 2010.

George 1959
Dorothy M. George, *English Political Caricature a Study of Opinion and Propaganda*, vol. 1, to 1793, Oxford (Oxford University Press) 1959.

Gerrard 1994
Christine Gerrard, *The Patriot Opposition to Walpole: Politics, Poetry and Myth, 1725–1742*, Oxford (Clarendon Press) 1994.

Goethe 1987
Goethe, Johann Wolfgang von, *From My Life: Poetry and Truth*, Translated by Robert R. Heitner, New York (Suhrkamp) 1987.

Haskell 1993
Francis Haskell, *History and Its Images: Art and the Interpretation of the Past*, London and New Haven (Yale University Press) 1993.

Hegel 1975
G. W. F. Hegel, *Aesthetics. Lectures on Fine Art*, Translated by T. M. Knox, Oxford (Oxford University Press) 1975.

Hilles 2015
Frederick. W. Hilles (ed.), *Letters of Sir Joshua Reynolds*, 2nd edition, Cambridge (Cambridge University Press) 2015.

Holloway 1989
James Holloway, *Patrons and Painters: Art in Scotland, 1650–1760*, Edinburgh (National Galleries of Scotland) 1989.

Hoock 2003
Holger Hoock, *The King's Artists: The Royal Academy of Arts and the Politics of British Culture, 1760–1840*, Oxford (Oxford University Press) 2003.

Humfrey 2013
Peter Humfrey, "Made in Venice," *Apollo*, 178:612 (September 2013), pp. 76–83.

Jaffe 1971
Michael Jaffe, "Rubens and Snijders: A Fruitful Partnership," *Apollo* (March 1971), pp. 184–196.

Jenkinson 1757
Charles Jenkinson, *A Discourse on the Establishment of a National and Constitutional Force in England*, London 1757.

Kettering 1999
Alison McNeil Kettering, "Gerard ter Borch's Portraits for the Deventer Elite," *Simiolus: Netherlands Quarterly for the History of Art*, 27:1/2 (1999), pp. 46–69.

Korthals Altes 2000
Everhard Korthals Altes, "The Eighteenth-Century Gentleman Dealer Willem Lormier and the International Dispersal of Seventeenth-Century Dutch Paintings," *Simiolus: Netherlands Quarterly for the History of Art*, 28:4 (2000), pp. 251–311.

Korthals Altes 2015
Everhard Korthals Altes, "International rivalry at the auction of Willem Lormier's paintings in 1763: James Lowther, 1st Earl of Lonsdale, and August III, Elector of Saxony and King of Poland," *Simiolus: Netherlands Quarterly for the History of Art*, 38:4 (2015), pp. 273–288.

Langford 1989
Paul Langford, *A Polite and Commercial People: England, 1727–1783*, Oxford (Oxford University Press) 1989.

Lazarus and Pardoe 2011
Maureen H. Lazarus and Heather S. Pardoe, "Bute's Botanical tables: dictated by Nature," *Archives of Natural History*, 36:2 (September 2011), pp. 277–298.

Lipking 1970
Lawrence Lipking, *The Ordering of the Arts in Eighteenth-Century England*, Princeton (Princeton University Press) 1970.

Lugt 1938–1987
Frits Lugt, *Répertoire des catalogues de ventes publiques intéressant l'art ou la curiosité*, 4 vols., The Hague (M. Nijhoff)1938–1987.

Luton 1799
Catalogue of Pictures at Luton Park Bedfordshire, ca. 1799, manuscript, Bute Archive, Mount Stuart.

Mahon 1847
Lord Mahon (ed.), *The Letters of Philip Dormer Stanhope, Earl of Chesterfield*, 4 vols., London (Richard Bentley) 1847.

Manners and Williams 1920
Victoria Manners and C. G. Williams, *John Zoffany, R.A., His Life and Works, 1735–1810*, London and New York (John Lane Company) 1920.

Mannings 2000
David Mannings, *Sir Joshua Reynolds: A Complete Catalogue of his Paintings*, London and New Haven (Yale University Press) 2000.

Marples 1970
Morris Marples, *Poor Fred and the Butcher: Sons of George II*, London (M. Joseph) 1970.

Marsden 2005
Jonathan Marsden (ed.), *The Wisdom of George the Third: Papers from a Symposium at the Queen's Gallery, Buckingham Palace, June 2004*, London (Royal Collection Publications) 2005.

Martyn 1766
Thomas Martyn, *The English Connoisseur: Containing an Account of Whatever is Curious in Painting, Sculpture, etc. in the Palaces and Seats of the Nobility and Gentry ...*, 2 vols., London (L. Davis and C. Reymers) 1766.

McKelvey 1973
James Lee McKelvey, *George III and Lord Bute: The Leicester House Years*, Durham, NC (Duke University Press) 1973.

Meadows 1988
Ann Meadows, "Collecting Seventeenth Century Dutch Painting in England, 1689–1760," PhD diss., University College London, 1988.

Mijers 2012
Esther Mijers, *"News from the Republick of Letters": Scottish Students, Charles Mackie and the United Provinces, 1650–1750*, Leiden and Boston (Brill) 2012.

Mount 1991
Harry Mount, "The Reception of Dutch Genre Painting in England, 1695–1829," PhD diss., University of Cambridge, 1991.

Mount 1996
Harry Mount, "The Monkey with the Magnifying Glass: Constructions of the Connoisseur in Eighteenth-Century Britain," *Oxford Art Journal*, 29:2 (1996), pp. 167–184.

Mount Stuart Trust 2001
Mount Stuart: Isle of Bute, Rothesay (Mount Stuart Trust) 2001.

Murdoch 1988
Alexander Murdoch, "Lord Bute, James Stuart Mackenzie, and the Government of Scotland," *Lord Bute, Essays in Re-interpretation*, Karl W. Schweizer (ed.), Leicester (Leicester University Press) 1988.

Murdoch 2004
Alexander Murdoch, "Campbell, Archibald, third duke of Argyll (1682–1761)," *Oxford Dictionary of National Biography*, Oxford (Oxford University Press) 2004, accessed 1 December 2016, http://www.oxforddnb.com/view/article/4477.

Nagler 1847
George Kaspar Nagler, *Neues Allgemeines Künstler-Lexicon*, vol. 17, Munich (E. A. Fleischmann) 1847.

Namier 1961
Lewis B. Namier, *England in the Age of the American Revolution*, 2nd edition, New York (St. Martin's Press) 1961.

Pares 1951
Richard Pares, "George III and the Politicians," *Transactions of the Royal Historical Society*, 5th ser., 1 (1951), pp. 127–151.

Phillips and Shane 2014
Charlotte Phillips and Nora Shane (eds.), *John Stuart, 3rd Earl of Bute (1713–92): Botanical and Horticultural Interests and Legacy*, Luton (Luton Hoo Estate) 2014.

Rembrandt Corpus 1982
Josua Bruyn et al., *Rembrandt Corpus*, vol. I, 1625–1631. The Hague (M. Nijhoff) 1982.

Roberts 1971
Keith Roberts, "Dutch Paintings at the Queen's Gallery," *The Burlington Magazine*, 113:819 (June 1971), pp. 348–351, 353–354.

Roberts 2004
Jane Roberts (ed.), *George III & Queen Charlotte: Patronage, Collecting and Court Taste*, London (Royal Collection Publications) 2004.

Roding et al. 2003
Juliette Roding, Eric Jan Sluijter, Bart Westerweel, Marijke van der Meij-Tolsma and Eric Domela Nieuwenhuis (eds.), *Dutch and Flemish Artists in Britain 1550–1800*, Leiden (Primavera Pers) 2003.

Rorschach 1985
Kimerly Rorschach, "Frederick, Prince of Wales (1707–1751) as a Patron of the Visual Arts: Princely Patriotism and Political Propaganda," PhD diss., Yale University, 1985.

Rorschach 1989–1990
Kimerly Rorschach, "Frederick, prince of Wales, 1707–1751, as collector and patron," *Walpole Society*, 55 (1989–1990), pp. 1–76.

Röthlisberger 1961
Marcel Röthlisberger, *Claude Lorrain; The Paintings*, 2 vols., London (Zwemmer) 1961.

Rowell 1996
Christopher Rowell, "A Seventeenth-century 'Cabinet' Restored: The Green Closet at Ham House," *Apollo*, 143 (April 1996), pp. 18–23.

Russell 1984
Francis Russell, "Engagements at Sea: The 3rd Earl of Bute's Marine Collection at Highcliffe," *Country Life* (26 January 1984).

Russell 1989
Francis Russell, "The Hanging and Display of Pictures, 1700–1850," *Studies in the History of Art*, 25 (1989), pp. 133–152.

Russell 1996
Francis Russell, Introduction, *Works of Art from the Bute Collection*, Christie's 3 July 1996.

Russell 2004
Francis Russell, *John, 3rd Earl of Bute, Patron & Collector*, London (Merrion Press) 2004.

Russell 2016
Susan Russell, "Dr Robert Bragge (1700–1777), gentleman dealer," *British Art Journal*, 17:2 (2016).

Schweizer 1988
Karl W. Schweizer (ed.), *Lord Bute, Essays in Re-interpretation*, Leicester (Leicester University Press) 1988.

Schweizer 1997
Karl W. Schweizer, "English Xenophobia in the Eighteenth Century: The Case Against Lord Bute," *Scottish Tradition*, 22 (1997), pp. 6–26.

Schweizer 2002
Karl W. Schweizer, "Lord Bute and the Historians," *Statesmen, Diplomats and the Press: Essays on 18th Century Britain*, Karl W. Schweizer (ed.), Lewiston, NY (Edwin Mellen Press) 2002, pp. 5–20.

Schweizer 2014
Karl W. Schweizer, "John Stuart, 3rd Earl of Bute: Image and Counter Image in Hanoverian Studies," *International Review of Scottish Studies*, 39 (2014), pp. 81–105.

Scott 1973
Barbara Scott, "The Duc de Choiseul. A Minister in the Grand Manner," *Apollo*, 97:131 (1973), pp. 42–53.

Sedgwick 1939
Romney Sedgwick (ed.), *Letters from George III to Lord Bute, 1756–1766*, London (Macmillan) 1939.

Shawe-Taylor 2014
Desmond Shawe-Taylor, "Ruling a Free Nation," *The First Georgians: Art & Monarchy, 1714–1760*, Desmond Shawe-Taylor (ed.), London (Royal Collection Trust) 2014.

Sheppard 1966
F. H. W. Sheppard (ed.), "Leicester Square, North Side, and Lisle Street Area: Leicester Estate: Leicester House and Leicester Square North Side (Nos 1–16)," *Survey of London: Vol. 34, St Anne Soho*, London (London County Council) 1966.

Simpson 1953
Frank Simpson, "Dutch Paintings in England before 1760," *The Burlington Magazine*, 95 (1953), pp. 39–42.

Smart 1952
Alastair Smart, *The Life and Art of Allan Ramsay*, London (Routledge and Kegan Paul) 1952.

Smart and Ingamells 1999
Alastair Smart and John Ingamells (eds.), *Allan Ramsay: A Complete Catalogue of his Paintings*, New Haven (Yale University Press) 1999.

Smith 1829–1842
John Smith, *A Catalogue Raisonné of the Works of the Most Eminent Dutch, Flemish and French Painters*, 9 vols., London (Smith and Son) 1829–1842.

Smith and Taylor 2009
Hannah Smith and Stephen Taylor, "Hephaestion and Alexander: Lord Hervey, Frederick, Prince of Wales, and the Royal Favourite in England in the 1730s," *English Historical Review*, 124:507 (2009), pp. 283–312.

Stearn 1962
William Stearn, "The Influence of Leyden on Botany in the Seventeenth and Eighteenth Centuries," *The British Journal for the History of Science*, 1:2 (December 1962), pp. 137–158.

Stephens 1883
Frederic George Stephens, *Catalogue of Political and Personal Satires in the British Museum, up to 1770*, 4 vols., London (British Museum) 1870–1883.

Stourton and Sebag-Montefiore 2012
James Stourton and Charles Sebag-Montefiore, *The British as Art Collectors: From the Tudors to the Present*, London (Scala) 2012.

Sunderland 2014
John Sunderland, "Dalton, Richard (c. 1715–1791)," *Oxford Dictionary of National Biography*, Oxford (Oxford University Press) 2014, accessed 29 November 2016, http://www.oxforddnb.com/view/article/7068.

Sutton and Wieseman 2004
Peter C. Sutton and Marjorie E. Wieseman, *Drawn by the Brush. Oil Sketches by Peter Paul Rubens*, Greenwich, CT (Bruce Museum of Arts) 2004.

Thomas 1987
Peter D. G. Thomas, "'Thoughts on the British Constitution' by George III in 1769," *Historical Research*, 60:143 (1987), pp. 361–363.

Thomas 2002
Peter D. G. Thomas, *George III: King and Politicians, 1760–1770*, Manchester (Manchester University Press) 2002.

Tinniswood 1989
Adrian Tinniswood, *A History of Country House Visiting: Five Centuries of Tourism and Taste*, Oxford (Basil Blackwell) 1989.

Urstad 1999
Tone Sundt Urstad, *Sir Robert Walpole's Poets: The Use of Literature as Pro-Government Propaganda, 1721–1742*, Newark, DE (University of Delaware Press) 1999.

Vertue Notebooks 1930–1935
George Vertue, "Vertue Notebooks," Notebooks I–VI, *Walpole Society*, 15, 20, 22, 24, 26, 30 (1930–1955).

Vivian 1989
Frances Vivian, *The Consul Smith Collection. Masterpieces of Italian Drawing from the Royal Library, Windsor Castle, Raphael to Canaletto*, Munich (Hirmer Verlag) 1989.

Vivian 2006
Frances Vivian, *A Life of Frederick, Prince of Wales, 1707–1751. A Connoisseur of the Arts*, Lewiston, NY (Edwin Mellen Press) 2006.

Waagen 1838
Gustav Waagen, *Works of Art and Artists in England*, London (John Murray) 1838.

Walpole 1747
Horace Walpole, *Aedes Walpolianae, or a description of the collection of pictures at Houghton-Hall in Norfolk, the seat of the Right Honourable Sir Robert Walpole*, London 1747.

Walpole 1927–1928
Horace Walpole, "Journals of Visits to Country Seats," *Walpole Society*, Paget Toynbee (ed.), 16 (1927–1928), pp. 9–80.

Walpole 1937
Horace Walpole, *Anecdotes of Painting in England*, ed. Frederick W. Hilles and Philip B. Daghlian, 5 vols., New Haven (Yale University Press) 1937.

Walpole 1937–1983
Horace Walpole, *The Yale Edition of Horace Walpole's Correspondence*, W. S. Lewis (ed.), 48 vols., New Haven and Oxford (Yale University Press) 1937–1983.

Walsh et al. 1996
David Walsh, Adrian Randall, Richard Sheldon and Andrew Charlesworth, "The Cider Tax, Popular Symbolism and Opposition in mid-Hanoverian England," *Markets, Market Culture and Popular Protest in Eighteenth-Century Britain and Ireland*, Adrian Randall and Andrew Charlesworth (eds.), Liverpool (Liverpool University Press) 1996.

Walters 1972
John Walters, *The Royal Griffin: Frederick Prince of Wales 1707–1751*, New York (Stein and Day) 1972.

Waiboer 2012
Adriaan Waiboer, *Gabriel Metsu: Life and Work – A Catalogue Raisonné*, London and New Haven (Yale University Press) 2012.

Whitley 1928
William T. Whitley, *Artists and their Friends in England, 1700–1799*, 2 vols., London and Paris (Medici Society) 1928.

Wraxall 1815
Nathaniel William Wraxall, *Historical Memoirs of My Own Time. Part the First, from 1772 to 1780. Part the Second, from 1781 to 1784*, 2nd edition, 2 vols., London (T. Cadell and W. Davies) 1815.

Wyndham 1924
Maud Wyndham (ed.), *Chronicles of the Eighteenth Century: Founded on the Correspondence of Sir Thomas Lyttelton and His Family*, 2 vols., London (Hodder and Stoughton) 1924.

Young 1937
George Young, *Poor Fred: The People's Prince*, London (Oxford University Press) 1937.

EXHIBITION CATALOGUES

Edinburgh 1949
Dutch & Flemish Paintings from the Collection of the Marquess of Bute: an Exhibition held in the National Gallery of Scotland during the Edinburgh International Festival of Music and Drama, Edinburgh (National Gallery of Scotland) 1949.

Edinburgh 1992
Julia Lloyd Williams, *Dutch Art and Scotland: A Reflection of Taste*, Edinburgh (National Gallery of Scotland) 1992.

Edinburgh 2004
Peter Humfrey, Timothy Clifford, Aidan Weston-Lewis and Michael Bury, *The Age of Titian: Venetian Renaissance Art from Scottish Collections*, Edinburgh (National Galleries of Scotland) 2004.

Edinburgh 2012
Anthony Crichton-Stuart and Christian T. Seifert, *Masterpieces from Mount Stuart: The Bute Collection*, Edinburgh (National Galleries of Scotland) 2012.

Glasgow 1884
Jean Paul Richter, *Catalogue of the Collection of Paintings Lent for Exhibition by the Marquess of Bute KT*, Glasgow (Corporation Galleries) 1884.

Hull 1981
Christopher Brown, *Scholars of Nature: The Collecting of Dutch Paintings in Britain 1610–1857*, Hull (Ferens Art Gallery) 1981.

London 1883
Jean Paul Richter, *Catalogue of the Collection of Paintings Lent for Exhibition by the Marquis of Bute KT*, London (Bethnal Green Branch Museum) 1883.

London 1964
The Orange and the Rose: Holland and Britain in the Age of Observation, London (Victoria and Albert Museum) 1964.

London and Rome 1966
Andrew Wilton and Ilaria Bignamini, *Grand Tour: Lure of Italy in the Eighteenth Century*, London and Rome (Tate Britain and the Palazzo delle Esposizioni) 1966.

London 1976
Christopher Brown et al., *Art in Seventeenth Century Holland*, London (National Gallery) 1976.

London 1977
Mary Webster, *Johan Zoffany 1733–1810*, London (National Portrait Gallery) 1977.

London 1986
Christopher Brown, *Dutch Landscape: The Early Years*, London (National Gallery) 1986.

London 1993
Jane Roberts, *A King's Purchase: King George III and the Collection of Consul Smith*, London (Queen's Gallery) 1993.

London, Edinburgh, The Hague 2015
Desmond Shawe-Taylor and Quentin Buvelot, *Masters of the Everyday: Dutch Artists in the Age of Vermeer*, London (Royal Collection Trust) 2015.

Manchester 1885
Jean Paul Richter, *Catalogue of the Collection of Paintings Lent for Exhibition by the Marquess of Bute KT*, Manchester (Queen's Park Museum and Art Gallery) 1885.

INDEX

PHOTOGRAPHIC CREDITS

For permission to reproduce works in their collections, we are very grateful to the following:
The Trustees of the British Museum: fig. 1, 14, 20, 24, 30, 31, 32, 34, 36;
© The Bute Collection at Mount Stuart: fig. 5, 6, 10, 12, 15, 16, 18, 25, 27;
photography at Mount Stuart was carried out by
Keith Hunter: fig. 2, 18; cat. 12, 13, 15, 16, 22, 23, 24, 27, 30, 33;
Bruce Pert: cat. 5, 18, 21;
John McKenzie: cat. 2, 3, 7, 31;
© Oliver Cox: fig. 22
© Fitzwilliam Museum: fig. 33;
© the Trustees of the National Gallery: fig. 35;
Royal Collection Trust, © Her Majesty Queen Elizabeth II 2016: fig. 19, 23, 26;
© Scottish National Portrait Gallery: fig. 9;
© Sir John Soane's Museum: fig. 3, 4, 7, 8, 11, 13;
Fotoarchiv, Staatliche Museen zu Berlin – Gemäldegalerie, photography Jörg P. Anders: fig. 29;
The University of Glasgow, photo Samuel Dyer: fig. 21;
© Victoria and Albert Museum: fig. 17, 28.